A Shell Guide

EAST SUSSEX

W. S. Mitchell

Out Speciality
PLAICE-COD
ROCK EEL
HAILBUT
SKATE
SOLE CHE
KIPP
SMOK

FRE
PACKS
14" OR
PLAIC
COD
BUY
NOW

A Shell Guide

EAST SUSSEX

by W. S. Mitchell

Guest house, **Saltdean**

Faber & Faber   3 Queen Square   London

First published in 1978
by Faber and Faber Limited
3 Queen Square London WC1
Printed in Great Britain by
Butler & Tanner Ltd, Frome and London
All rights reserved

© Shell U.K. Ltd 1978

To Jack Beddington,
Publicity Manager of Shell-Mex and B.P. Ltd.,*
under whose aegis the Shell
County Guides were conceived.

*Mr J. L. Beddington was the original Publicity Manager of Shell-Mex and B.P.
Ltd. whose Shell trading activities have been taken over by Shell U.K. Ltd.*

British Library Cataloguing in Publication Data

Mitchell, William
    East Sussex.—(Shell guides).
    1. East Sussex—Description and travel—Guidebooks
    I. Title II. Series
    914.22′5′04857   DA670.E2

    ISBN 0–571–10751–6

Illustrations

Front endpaper
  (*left*) Viaduct, London Road, Brighton
  Duncan McNeill
  (*right*) Balcombe Viaduct
  John Piper

Frontispiece
  Net Shops, Hastings
  Peter Burton

Title page
  Saltdean
  John Piper

Page

7 Brighton Pavilion
  Edward Piper

8 Saltdean
  John Piper

9 Bodiam
  John Piper

10 Beachy Head
  Peter Burton

11 Newhaven
  Noel Habgood

12 Seven Sisters
  Noel Habgood

13 Seven Sisters
  Peter Burton

14 Pevensey Levels
  John Piper

15 Winchelsea marshes
  Peter Burton

16 Cuckmere Haven
  Edward Piper

18 Glynde
  Edward Piper

19 High and Over
  Noel Habgood
  Poynings
  Christopher Dalton
  Rodmell
  Christopher Dalton

20 The Long Man
  Edward Piper

22 Hastings Beach
  Edward Piper

23 Rye
  John Piper

25 Iron tombs at Wadhurst and Streat
  G. L. Remnant

26 De La Warr Pavilion
  Peter Burton
  Palace Pier
  Edward Piper

27 West Pier
  Peter Burton

28 Brunswick Square
  Duncan McNeill

30 Bodiam
  John Piper
  Hurstmonceux
  Edward Piper

32 Northiam
  John Piper
  Rotherfield
  Christopher Dalton

33 Beckley
  John Piper
  Iden
  John Piper

35 Royal Crescent
  Edward Piper

36 Brightling
  John Piper

37 Bishopstone
  John Piper

38 Bishopstone
  John Piper

39 Worth
  Christopher Dalton

40 Playden
  Edward Piper

41 Chailey
  Edward Piper
  Telscombe
  G. L. Remnant
  Burwash
  Edward Piper
  Catsfield
  Edward Piper

43 Harmer Plaques
  John Piper

46 Wakehurst
  Peter Burton

47 Sheffield Park
  Peter Burton

48 Nymans
  John Piper

50 Alciston
  Christopher Dalton

53 Burnt House Farm, Alfriston
  Christopher Dalton
  The Clergy House
  Peter Burton

54 Ashburnham
  Christopher Dalton

55 Ashburnham
  John Piper

56 Barcombe
  G. L. Remnant

57 Balcombe
  Christopher Dalton

59 Battle Abbey
  Edward Piper
  Battle
  Peter Burton

60 Battle Abbey
  Peter Burton

63 Beckley
  John Piper

66 Bishopstone
  John Piper

67 West Blatchington mill
  Duncan McNeill

68/69 Bodiam
  John Piper

70 Wykehurst
  John Piper

71 Wykehurst
  John Piper

72 Brightling
  John Piper

73 Brighton station
  Edward Piper

74/75 Brighton Pavilion
Edward Piper

76 Hove
Duncan McNeill

78/79 Brighton and Hove (7)
Duncan McNeill

80 Brighton and Hove (4)
Duncan McNeill

81 Kemp Town
Edward Piper

82 St. George's, Kemp Town
Duncan McNeill
All Saint's, Hove
Peter Burton

84 St. Peter's, Brighton
Edward Piper
St. Paul's, Brighton
Duncan McNeill

85 St. Bartholomew's, Brighton
Edward Piper

87 Henry Wilson Altarpiece
Duncan McNeill

89 Camber Castle
John Piper

90 Chailey mill
Edward Piper

93 Chiddingly
Christopher Dalton

94 Clayton
Peter Burton

96 Cuckfield
Edward Piper

97 Cuckfield ceiling
Edward Piper

100 St. Saviour Eastbourne
John Piper

101 St. Saviour Eastbourne
Peter Burton

102 Etchingham
John Piper

103 De Echyngham brass
John Piper

104 Sussex University
Edward Piper

105 Sussex University
Duncan McNeill

106 Firle Place (2)
John Piper

109 Fletching
Christopher Dalton

110 Glynde (2)
Edward Piper

113 East Grinstead
Christopher Dalton

114/115 Hammerwood (2)
Peter Burton

116 Hamsey
John Piper

118 Shelley's Folly
Edward Piper

119 Hartfield
Christopher Dalton

120 Pelham Crescent, Hastings
Edward Piper

121 Hastings shops
Peter Burton

122 Hastings Net Shops
Edward Piper

123 Cade Street Chapel
John Piper

124 Bentley Wood
Edward Piper

126 West Hoathly
Christopher Dalton

127 Hooe
Christopher Dalton

128 Dacre Monument
Christopher Dalton

129 Sussex Trugs
Edward Piper

131 Icklesham mill
John Piper

134 The Ouse, Lewes (2)
Christopher Dalton

136 Lewes
Peter Burton

137 Lewes
Christopher Dalton

139 Jireh Chapel
Christopher Dalton

141 Mark Sharp's tombstone
G. L. Remnant

143 Mayfield
G. L. Remnant
Mountfield
G. L. Remnant

144 Newhaven
Kenneth Scowen
Newhaven
John Piper

146/147 Great Dixter (3)
John Piper

148 Penhurst
John Piper

150 Pevensey Castle (2)
Peter Burton

151 Pevensey Castle (3)
John Piper

152 Piddinghoe
Edward Piper

153 Playden
Christopher Dalton

158 Rotherfield
Christopher Dalton

159 Church Square, Rye
John Piper

160 Rye Town Hall
John Piper

161 Rye
John Piper

163 Rye Harbour (2)
John Piper

164 Salehurst
John Piper

165 Sedlescombe
Christopher Dalton

166 Sheffield Park
Edward Piper

167 The Bluebell Line
Edward Piper

168/169 Nymans (2)
John Piper

171 Southease
Edward Piper

172 Ticehurst
Christopher Dalton

174 Udimore
John Piper
Udimore
Christopher Dalton

176 The Hoo, Willingdon (2)
Christopher Dalton

178/179 Wilmington Priory (2)
Edward Piper

181 Winchelsea Beach
Peter Burton

182 New Gate, Winchelsea
John Piper

183 Winchelsea church
Edward Piper

6

184 Winchelsea mill
John Piper

185 Winchelsea
Edward Piper

187 Withyham
John Piper

188 Worth
Christopher Dalton

190 Rye Harbour
John Piper

Back endpaper
Brunswick Terrace, Brighton
Duncan McNeill

Note: Captions to the photographs include place names in **bold type**. These refer to entries in the gazetteer, pages 51–189

Brighton Pavilion

'Evening is kind to Sussex, for Sussex is no longer young, and she is grateful for the veil of evening as an elderly woman is glad when a shade is drawn over a lamp, and only the outline of her face remains. The outline of Sussex is still very fine. The cliffs stand out to sea, one behind another. All Eastbourne, all Bexhill, all St Leonard's, their parades and their lodging houses, their bead shops and their sweet shops and their placards . . . all are obliterated. What remains is what there was when William came over from France ten centuries ago: a line of cliffs running out to sea.'

Virginia Woolf—Essay—*Evening over Sussex*
from The Death of the Moth.

Saltdean

Foreword

In 1888 Sussex was divided administratively into two counties – West Sussex with its capital at Chichester, East Sussex at Lewes. The division between the two counties was the 800-year-old boundary between the Rapes of Lewes and Bramber. Under the Local Government Act 1972 the boundary was shifted eastwards, and East Grinstead, Haywards Heath, Burgess Hill and the surrounding villages now find themselves in West Sussex. For the purpose of this Guide I have disregarded the Act, and have included every place east of the older and more historic boundary.

No guide can be an original work, since all the places and buildings mentioned have been described before. I spent forty-five years of my life in East Sussex and started to look at Sussex churches when I was eleven. The county has therefore long been familiar; but writing a guide requires a new scrutiny and every place has been re-visited within the last two years. It is a curious and sombre reflection that in a pagan and egalitarian era the buildings of most interest are always the church and, where there is one, the great house. Days and times are not given for the opening of Houses and Gardens to the public. *Historic Houses, Castles and Gardens*, published annually, is the most reliable guide.

Among publications I have consulted are the *Victoria County History*, Pevsner and Nairn's *Sussex*, E. V. Lucas's *Highways and Byeways*, J. H. Ford's *Sussex*, E. C. Curwen's *Archaeology of Sussex*, W. H. Godfrey's *Guide to Lewes*, Anthony Dale's *About Brighton*, and an enormous number of church guides which have provided me with some curious snippets of information. The Sussex Archaeological Society has helped me greatly in answering various questions. Mr G. L. Remnant has given me valuable information about Harmer's plaques and Dr Alan Hartley about Royal Arms. To the General Editor, John Piper, I am most deeply grateful for many suggestions and for the extreme care with which he has read and improved the manuscript.

Bodiam castle

Sussex stretches along the English Channel from Rye on the east to Thorney Island on the west; it is seventy-six miles long as the crow flies, but more like 100 miles by road. East Sussex starts at Portslade-by-Sea, just west of Brighton. The coastline has been largely ruined by maritime suburbia, except for the Downs between Seaford and Eastbourne, which belong to the National Trust, and should be immune.

The coastal resorts now bring tourists and holiday-makers to Sussex; but the sea has not always been tame. Up to the 18th century it was a dangerous enemy, and by advancing

Force 10 at **Newhaven**

◁ **Beachy Head**

The Seven Sisters looking east

and receding brought destruction or decay. It destroyed Old Winchelsea and left New Winchelsea high and dry. It deserted Pevensey and left it to decline, while the Ouse by changing its course in the 16th century brought new importance to Meeching (Newhaven) and caused Seaford to dwindle into insignificance. Brighton, after being almost wiped out at the beginning of the 18th century, rose again owing to Dr Russell, and achieved Royal patronage. To the north of the county, stretching from Worth to Fairlight is the Forest Ridge, a belt of clay which starts at Worth and Balcombe as a genuine forest, continues to Ashdown Forest, mostly a high plateau with very little forest left, and then onwards to Heathfield, Brightling and Battle until it makes an unsensational entry into the sea at Fairlight. On the south are the South Downs, a range of waterless chalk hills, within a mile or two of the Channel. They begin, in East Sussex, at the Devil's Dyke and finish dramatically and magnificently at Beachy Head. The line is broken only by the pass at Pyecombe, the river valleys at Lewes and Alfriston, and the Jevington combe. The highest point in East Sussex is Ditchling Beacon, 813 ft. They used to

The Seven Sisters looking west ▷

present a markedly different appearance from the West Sussex Downs; these, especially west of the Arun, are lower and tree-clad, while the higher East Sussex Downs were green and bare owing to the incessant nibbling of the South Down sheep and rabbits. In recent years the decline in sheep farming and the drastic reduction in the rabbit population has altered the Downs; their clean, grassy slopes have a scrubby growth of hawthorn and other wild shrubs, and begin to look unshaven. Up the side of the Downs run steep lanes called bostels, often tunnelling their way through thickets festooned with Old Man's Beard. On the top

are dew-ponds, circular pans for watering sheep and cattle; they are made with straw, puddled clay and loose stones, which act as an insulator and cause the dew to collect. Dew-ponds have been ascribed to the neolithic or iron ages; but E. C. Curwen (1954) says that there is no evidence that any are older than the 18th century and some are definitely 19th. Some of the farms are right in the middle of the Downs—Balsdean, Standean, Balmer—and in deep snow almost inaccessible. Between the Forest Ridge and the South Downs is the Weald, a wide tract of heavy clay with pockets of greensand, which was in early medieval days a forest. In Saxon

Pevensey Levels from near **Hooe**

Winchelsea marshes ▷

Cuckmere Haven

and Norman times the villages were no more than clearings; in later centuries the trees provided fuel for the furnaces of the iron industry. Winter is a good time to see the Weald. The picnickers and 'furriners', as Sussex men used to call visitors from other counties, have gone, and you can walk, or better still ride, alone in woods and ways that are relics of the old agricultural England. In

the flat country round Ripe and Chalvington are several green lanes, narrow medieval bridle paths with high thorn hedges on either side, and Plashett, Laughton and Wilmington woods cover large acreages where foxes, stoats and badgers have bred for generations.

East Sussex has three rivers—the Ouse, the Cuckmere and the Rother. The Ouse and Rother were certainly in primeval and medieval times far bigger than they are today. The escarpment north of Hamsey church and the valley spanned by the Balcombe viaduct, absurdly wide for an insignificant stream, both seem to offer evidence, and barges went up as far as Sheffield Park until 1862. The Rother was navigable up to Etchingham, where the boats loaded iron ore to take down to Rye. There is no evidence to suggest that the Cuckmere was ever of much significance, and since it never had a port at its mouth, it seems reasonable to suppose that it was not.

The earliest human inhabitant of East Sussex—and of Britain—was thought for forty-one years to have been of the Pleistocene period. His skull was allegedly found by Dr Smith Woodward of the British Museum and Mr Charles Dawson, a lawyer and amateur archaeologist, between 1910 and 1912 on Piltdown Common, near Fletching; he became known as the Piltdown Man, and the pub at Piltdown was renamed after him in the 1920s. But in 1949 Dr K. P. Oakley applied the fluorine test to the bones, and after many successive tests it was announced in 1953 that the jaw was that of a young orang-utan and that none of the finds came from Piltdown. It was the biggest hoax ever planted upon the archaeological world.

There is, however, much genuine evidence of Stone Age habitation. Few palaeolithic remains have been found; but there are many neolithic earthworks, and stone implements—scrapers, simple flakes and cores—can be seen in the museums at Lewes, Brighton, Eastbourne and Hastings. These were mostly found on the southern slopes of the Downs; the art of well-boring had not yet been discovered and the settlements had to be near the sea or a river. The finds in the kitchen middens below the rocks at Hastings

The South Downs: ▷
p18 **Glynde**
p19 (*top*) Windover Hill from High and Over near **Alfriston** (*centre*) **Poynings** (*bottom*) **Rodmell**

between the castle and the sea are evidence of a largish settlement. Major finds have also been made near Eastbourne and Beachy Head.

Bronze Age relics have been found at Hove—an amber cup 3½ in. in diameter—at Beachy Head in 1807, four gold bracelets, and the base of a bronze sword blade (all in the British Museum) at Hollingbury Hill near Brighton in 1825 and an important hoard at Wilmington in 1861, where thirty-three bronze articles in an earthenware pot were found. (These are now in the Lewes Museum.)

The Iron Age, the last period before the coming of the Romans, has so far yielded up fewer antiquities than the two previous Ages, but they show a higher degree of culture. In 1863 a quantity of gold ornaments was turned up by a ploughman at Mountfield; thinking them to be old brass, he sold them for 5s 6d, and they finally reached a London dealer who melted them down. Later General Pitt-Rivers found a number of iron objects and pottery on Mount Caburn.

The East Sussex coast, so near to France, was constantly a prey to invaders. The Romans came twice—first Julius Caesar and later in A.D. 43 Aulus Plautius, who was sent by the Emperor Claudius. Caesar probably never saw Sussex, but Plautius made his headquarters at Regnum (Chichester) and the Stane Street was built from Regnum to London. In East Sussex the most important town was Anderida (Pevensey), though the walls now standing may not be earlier than the 4th century A.D. There is no evidence of any road between Regnum and Anderida

and, although one would expect to find a road from Anderida to London, there are very few traces, and those much nearer London. Fragments of Roman villas have been discovered at Clayton, Hurstpierpoint, Preston and near Eastbourne; but, apart from Pevensey, there is nothing in East Sussex as important as the Bignor villa or the great palace of Fishbourne in West Sussex.

The Long Man of Wilmington, one of the world's largest human figures, is an enigma. An 18th century drawing shows him holding a scythe and a rake, but the figure was restored and altered in 1874. E. C. Curwen (1954) thinks it unsafe to assume any great antiquity; but C. F. C. Hawkes (1965) finds good reason to think the Long Man is 7th century and possibly Romano-British.

Sussex, as its name implies, was the kingdom of the South Saxons; it was founded by Aella in A.D. 491 when he captured Anderida from the Britons and drove them back into the forest of Andredswald. It was the last Saxon kingdom to accept Christianity; King Aethelwalch (661) the first Christian king, gave St Wilfrid, Bishop of York, the Selsey peninsula after he had been driven out of his northern see. In 892 Hasting, the Danish pirate, and others renewed the warfare, which had ended in 878. The Danish pirates were finally defeated by King Alfred, who had a house at West Dean and a park at Ditchling where he kept horses.

In the 11th century trouble started between the Saxons and Normans after the marriage of Ethelred the Unready to Emma of Normandy. Her grand-nephew, William, claimed that Edward the Confessor and Harold, when in France, had promised him the succession to the English crown, and on 13 October 1066 William landed near Pevensey. The battle took place on the hill of Senlac, 7 miles north of Hastings, and lasted only 6 hours. Harold was pierced in the eye and fatally wounded; and both his brothers fell defending the standard. This is the traditional story, though a recent writer holds it to be quite inaccurate. (*The Enigma of Hastings*—E. Tetlow 1974.)

With the Normans a great period of development ensued. Castles, abbeys and other religious houses were built; the first was Battle Abbey, founded by William in fulfilment of a vow. The Cinque Ports were established, four of them in Kent, but Hastings was long the premier port. Henry II attached Rye and Winchelsea as 'Members' to Hastings, and later still further corporate members or 'limbs' were added, those in Sussex being Seaford and Pevensey. The Cinque Ports had to provide at least fifty-seven ships, each manned by twenty-four men, and their period of service at their own cost was at least fifteen days a year. In return they received a number of privileges, including exemption from the payment of subsidies and the freedom from arrest of their burgesses except in their own towns. When Edward III needed support for his forces at the siege of Calais, Sussex supplied 40 ships and 928 men from Winchelsea, Rye, Hastings and Seaford. But when Hastings, Winchelsea and Sandwich began to decline and Henry VIII founded a national Royal Navy, the great days of the Cinque Ports were over. The office of Lord Warden survives as a symbol of their former greatness.

The Conqueror wanted to keep contact with the Duchy of Normandy. He therefore devised a system whereby Sussex was divided into six Rapes; the word is thought to be derived from the Icelandic meaning rope, which was used to mark off a district. Each Rape was held by a Norman noble as tenant-in-chief of the King. Hastings was under the Count of Eu, Pevensey under the Earl of

Mortain, Lewes under the Earl de Warenne, Bramber under William de Braose, Arundel and Chichester under the Earl of Montgomery. Each Rape had a castle, a river, a market and a forest. By dividing the county among his followers he ensured that no one of them could lead a successful revolt. He also compiled the Domesday Book; out of 9,250 villages or manors in the whole country 387 were in Sussex. The lords of the manors derived their revenue not only from arable farming, but also in Sussex from the coastal fisheries, 157 water mills and 285 saltpans, of which there were 100 between Rye and Hastings.

When Henry III became subject to French influence, the barons headed by Simon de Montfort took up arms against him. Henry was defeated at the Battle of Lewes in 1264, and at the Mise of Lewes Simon de Montfort set up the first representative Parliament. During the Hundred Years' War with France the Sussex ports were constantly attacked. The French burnt Winchelsea in 1360 and 1380, Rye and Hastings in 1377, Pevensey in 1380, and Rye and Winchelsea again in 1448.

In the 14th and 15th centuries Sussex, like other counties, was ravaged by the Black Death; in one Rape alone the population

Hastings

22

Rye from near Camber

was reduced from 6,700 in 1349 to 1,500 in 1440. In 1381 Sussex together with Kent and Surrey was much involved in the Peasants' Revolt headed by Wat Tyler; in Winchelsea there was a rising of the craftsmen against the merchants. Craft guilds, the ancestors of the Trades Unions, were now springing up; in Rye there was a comprehensive union including grocers, haberdashers, apothecaries, goldsmiths and drapers. The wool trade was flourishing and England became the foremost wool-producing country in the world; the woolsack, on which the Lord Chancellor sits, is a reminder. Lewes was the chief wool port in Sussex, which was seventh in importance among the wool-producing counties.

23

In 1450 Jack Cade headed another revolt, this time in Kent, and was supported by a large Sussex contingent; the Abbot of Battle and the Prior of Lewes favoured his cause. Cade was pursued by Alexander Iden, Sheriff of Kent, who caught him in a garden at Cade Street, near Heathfield.

During all these upheavals the Church had been holding her own. In 1087 there were about 150 churches in Sussex; two hundred years later the number had increased to 267. But the Dissolution of the Monasteries in 1538 struck hard. Battle Abbey and Lewes Priory, two of the greatest religious houses in the country, came to an end, and Lewes Priory with its 40 acres of ground was so completely destroyed that its site was lost for three centuries.

The iron industry, which the 14th century tomb slab at Burwash shows already existed, now began to grow and reached its peak in the Tudor reigns. In the late 15th century its centre was Buxted, where in 1543 the first whole piece cannon was cast. In the forests of Ashdown and St Leonard's (West Sussex) furnaces and forges multiplied. Other iron centres were Hartfield, Warbleton, Fletching, Worth, Robertsbridge and Maresfield. Ashburnham and Horsted Keynes made nails, Crowhurst edge tools and East Grinstead armour. Ironmasters became prosperous and there are more than 30 iron tomb slabs, some with armorial bearings, in Wadhurst church. Smelting led to the steady destruction of wealden timber, and Acts of Parliament were passed in 1558, 1581 and 1585 to limit its consumption. Ashdown had in 1520 a circumference of 35 miles, and Worth Forest covered over 5,000 acres.

Two other lesser industries were weaving and brewing. Many Flemish weavers crossed the Channel to escape persecution. They wove silk, wool and linen, and are believed to have introduced hops into Kent and East Sussex.

Queen Elizabeth I visited Rye in 1573 and was received magnificently at Mayfield in 1579. As usual there were raids and threats of invasion; a Pelham repulsed the French at Seaford in 1545 and Sussex men stood to arms when the Armada sailed by, as they did 400 years later when Hitler's invasion was a daily threat.

During the Civil War Sussex was sharply divided. West Sussex, with the great feudal estates of Arundel, Petworth and Cowdray, was Royalist, while East Sussex after 1642 stood for Parliament, as did all the Cinque Ports. In 1651 Charles II after his long flight arrived at Brighton where he spent the night before embarking at Shoreham. After the Civil War the Roman Catholic Royalists suffered much persecution, and in 1678 Titus Oates, born at Hastings and educated at Sedlescombe, hatched the plot, in which he accused them of conspiring against the life of the King. The wars of the 17th century made heavy demands for iron and timber. In 1690 Waldron produced 100 tons of shot; but the wealden forests also had to provide oak for the navy, and charcoal for smelting was in short supply. Heathfield continued to make cannon for another 60 years until the furnace closed in 1787; but with competition from foreign ore and the discovery of coal in the Midlands and North, the Sussex iron industry gradually declined until the last furnace was put out at Ashburnham in 1825. So with the Industrial Revolution the agricultural north developed rapidly for trade and industry, while partially industrial Sussex returned once more to its agriculture and fisheries.

In 1750 Dr Russell had published his famous treatise on the Use of Sea Water in Diseases of the Glands. This led directly to

Cast Iron tombs: **Wadhurst** (*top*), and **Streat** ▷

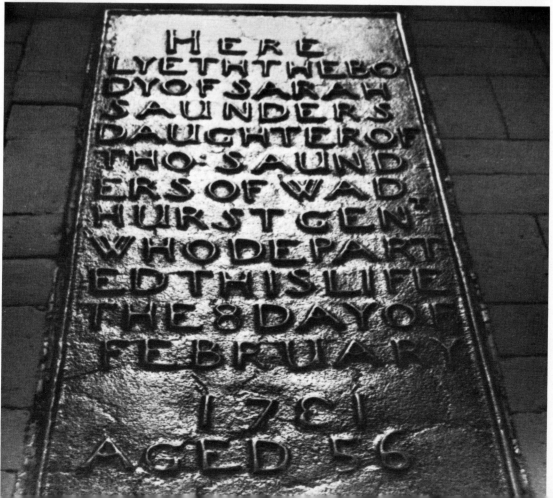

The De La Warr Pavilion,
Bexhill

West Pier, **Brighton** ▷

(*below*) Palace Pier, Brighton

a fashionable craze for sea-bathing and the resurrection of the old fishing town of Brighton. By the turn of the century Brighton, patronised by the Prince Regent, was an expanding town with elegant squares and terraces where the rank and fashion came down from London and bravely entered the sea protected by horse-drawn bathing machines. The development of Brighton was followed by that of Eastbourne, where the Duke of Devonshire owned Compton Place and much of the land, and Bexhill, largely the property of Earl De La Warr. The ancient Cinque Port and fishing town of Hastings spread westwards, and beyond Hastings to the new town of St Leonards. The layout and architecture of new Hastings and St Leonards is less distinguished and compares unfavourably with Eastbourne or Brighton.

The London, Brighton and South Coast Railway with its terminus at Victoria was opened in 1839–41 and immediately made Sussex more accessible. In succeeding years branch lines were opened—East Grinstead to Lewes, Tunbridge Wells to Lewes and Polegate—which brought the coast ever closer to London and the inland towns. The mid- and late-19th century certainly brought prosperity, though it did not add to the charm of the coastal towns.

The most distinguished medieval houses are Bodiam and Hurstmonceux, one of cool, grey stone, the other of brick, built about 69 years later in 1441, each surrounded by a moat. Both are called castles, but they are really fortified manor houses, and still remarkably complete, since neither had to withstand attack. During the 15th and 16th centuries when in other counties the great Perpendicular churches were being built and after them the exuberant palaces of noblemen, East Sussex was evidently not

particularly prosperous. The Elizabethan age is best represented by Wakehurst, though the wings have disappeared, and Danny 1582–93, an E-shaped brick house, similar to many in Suffolk. Glynde and Firle, both much altered in the 18th century, were originally Elizabethan houses; smaller examples are Brede and Friston. All these have a homely charm and are altogether lacking in ostentatious grandeur. The three best timber-framed houses of this age are Brickwall, Northiam, where the Queen stayed; Horselunges, Hellingly, and Great Ote Hall, Wivelsfield. Two Jacobean houses of distinction are Carter's Corner, Hellingly, and Streat. Of the Georgian era the best houses are Stanmer, somewhat austerely classical, 1724, and Sheffield Park, just earlier than 1779, an interesting essay in Gothick by James Wyatt. Those mentioned above are only the larger houses; but there are in East Sussex many excellent smaller manor houses from the 16th to the 18th centuries, and the streets of Lindfield, Mayfield, Burwash, Lewes, Hastings and Rye—not to mention Brighton—have a wealth of diverse architectural interest. Building materials vary; in the Weald timber and sandstone were readily available and near the Downs there were plenty of flints. Glynde Place is of flint with stone dressings, and cottages and barns in the downland area and the Ouse and Cuckmere valleys are generally flint-built.

In the Weald sandstone was used for large houses like Wakehurst, but farmhouses and cottages are usually timber-framed or brick. Like the wealden churches, houses and cottages built before the 18th century were roofed with Horsham slabs. From the mid 18th to early 19th century mathematical tiles were often used on houses, mostly in towns, as a cheap means of giving a fashionable

appearance to a timber-framed building and of avoiding the brick taxes. The tiles are hung vertically and shaped to imitate the header of a brick; they are cream or red, but smartest when black. The best examples of black tiles are Royal Crescent, Kemp Town and Patcham Place.

The London–Brighton railway line, by avoiding existing towns, gave birth to new places; Three Bridges, Haywards Heath, Burgess Hill and Hassocks are railway towns with no older core. On the branch lines old villages had new appendages round the stations as at Groombridge, Mayfield and Heathfield. The wealden ridge was much favoured for development and Crowborough with its superb views and healthy situation was especially popular. Businessmen began to prefer living in small country houses and travelling 'up and down'—the word 'com-

Hurstmonceux Castle

◁ **Bodiam** Castle

31

Kent border farms:

(*above*) **Northiam**

◁ Huggett's Furnace, **Rotherfield**

(*top*) Little Harmers, **Beckley**
(*bottom*) Oxenbridge, **Iden** ▷

mute' was unknown before the 1930s—to living in London or the suburbs.

Some large houses were built by the rich, but, as in the Elizabethan era, none of major remark. There are Horsted Place by Samuel Daukes and Pugin (1851), Balcombe Place (1856) by Clutton and Glen Andred, New Groombridge (1867) and Baldslow Place, near Hastings (1878), both by Norman Shaw. Paddockhurst, now called Worth Priory, is by Salvin (1869–72) with fanciful additions by Sir Aston Webb (1897) for the 1st Lord Cowdray. Wykehurst, Bolney, designed by E. M. Barry in 1874 for a banker's son in florid *nouveau riche* style is probably the most interesting. It has strong French influence with conical turrets, grand staircases and all the overblown splendour of its period.

The 20th century has added more in quantity than quality. The De La Warr Pavilion at Bexhill (1933) by Mendelsohn and Chermayeff, Bentley Wood, Halland (1934) by Chermayeff, and Sussex University (1960 onwards) by Basil Spence are all notable, if not yet entirely lovable; perhaps they will be in time.

The chief landowning families in East Sussex were the Ashburnhams, the Gages, the Nevills, the Pelhams, and the Sackvilles. The Nevills—Barons, Earls and Marquesses of Abergavenny—were the most powerful family in the realm towards the end of the Middle Ages, and owned lands in many counties. There was an old family place at Eridge where Queen Elizabeth I stayed; but it did not become their chief residence until about 1790. As an indigenous East Sussex family the Ashburnhams were the oldest, having held lands in the county before the Conquest. The family received a Barony and later an Earldom; but was singularly unprolific and the senior line is now extinct. The Pelhams, Earls of Chichester, received

at Poitiers their crest, the buckle, which is found on many churches; they lived first at Laughton, then at Halland and Stanmer, and provided two Prime Ministers, Henry Pelham and the Duke of Newcastle. The family suffered two untimely deaths—in the late 1920s and again in the Second World War. Stanmer was sold, and the Pelhams, who once owned a vast acreage in East Sussex, now have no house in the county. The Sackvilles lived at Buckhurst, Withyham; only a fragment of Old Buckhurst remains, but its successor is still the home of Lord De La Warr, their direct descendant. Thomas Sackville, created 1st Earl of Dorset in 1567 was also made a peer of the realm as Baron Buckhurst of Buckhurst. A year earlier in 1566 he had been granted by Queen Elizabeth I the reversion of the manor of Knole, Sevenoaks—formerly the Archbishop's Palace. The 5th and last Duke of Dorset had no heir; his estates went to his sister, Lady Elizabeth Sackville, who married the 5th Earl De La Warr (West). Since Buckhurst is the original home of the Sackvilles, the Earls and Dukes of Dorset are buried at Withyham and not at Sevenoaks. The Gages still live at Firle Place, the beautiful house under the Downs, where they have lived for over 400 years. Whatever the other distinctions of Lord Gage's ancestors, it was Sir William Gage who passed the name into the language by introducing about 1725 a new green plum, known thereafter as the Greengage.

The Normans were great church builders and very few East Sussex churches are not of Norman origin, though frequently the only evidence is the thickness of the walls, a round-headed window or a blocked north door. Several are pre-Conquest, Bishopstone with its staged tower and sundial, and Worth, with an untouched Saxon ground

Mathematical tiles, Royal Crescent, **Brighton** ▷

plan. In the 18th century churches here as elsewhere fell into a state of appalling disrepair, possibly worse in Sussex where many were 200 years older. Churchwardens often patched them up in a makeshift and unsuitable way, and in some cases, such as the chancel at Pevensey, they were even put to secular use. In the mid-19th century a restoration frenzy started, Georgian fittings were thrown out, windows rebuilt, chancel arches heightened and wall paintings, where they were found, destroyed e.g. Lindfield, Plumpton and Westmeston. The most savage restorations seem to have been between 1860 and 1870; but without them many churches would undoubtedly today be in ruins. Later restorers, realising that their predecessors had gone rather too far, used a gentler hand.

The materials used are of course all local, and the differences in soil and subsoil—chalk on and around the Downs, clay and occasional greensand in the wealden belt—produced a variety. The small downland churches are usually of rough flints, stone being used only for the quoins, windows and

Brick path, **Brightling** churchyard   Brick, flint and shore pebbles; **Bishopstone** beach tide mill ▷

Saxon details, **Bishopstone**

38

Saxon details, **Worth**

Spires: *p40* **Playden** ▷
p41 (*top*) **Chailey Telscombe**
(*bottom*) **Burwash, Catsfield**

arches. Alfriston in contrast is built of knapped flints and is a very good example. Near the sea cobbles, i.e. sea-shore pebbles, were sometimes used; the only church built entirely of cobbles, except for quoins and arches, is Pevensey. There was a green sandstone quarry surprisingly at Eastbourne and this was used in some churches in the neighbourhood. Occasionally hard chalk was used e.g. Litlington and Wilmington, but this was regarded as a cheap and not very satisfactory material. Caen stone is found in a few places, e.g. Wilmington and Ditchling, but only where there was a monastic connection, since the monks were the only people who could afford to ship it across the Channel. Further inland there were ample supplies of sandstone or ironstone and the churches are nearly all built of it. Clay provided the raw material for brick and tile making, and there were a great many brickworks. Bricks were used for the Dacre chapel at Hurstmonceux and entirely for the Tudor churches at Twineham and East Guldeford. The roofs were often covered with Horsham slabs; Cuckfield is a good example. These large thin stones are immensely heavy, though very durable, and where roof timbers have in recent years had to be renewed, they have sometimes been replaced with tiles. Horsham slabs weather beautifully and their tendency to attract moss and lichen gives the roofs a wonderful texture. The use of Horsham slabs only occurs in the central part of Sussex and they are not found east of Heathfield and Hailsham. Another Sussex feature is the shingled spire; among other good examples are Playden, Rotherfield and Cuckfield. Shingles are thin slates of oak and used to be cleft, not sawn; the wealden forest provided plenty of oak. When first put on they are a sort of corn yellow, but they soon weather to a silvery grey. Recently when re-

shingling has been done, it has been found impossible, or anyhow prohibitively expensive, to obtain oak shingles and Canadian cedar has been used instead. It remains to be seen whether cedar shingles will ever acquire the wonderful silver patina of oak. Three churches in East Sussex have stone spires—Northiam, Dallington and Chiddingly. They must have been much more expensive than timber-framed shingled spires, and there is no known reason why these three churches should have had them.

Another unexplained mystery is the three round towers in the Ouse valley—St Michael's, Lewes, Southease and Piddinghoe. One theory that there were no large stones for quoins is obviously absurd, since all the other churches around and of the same date have square towers. Another suggestion is that they were used as beacons, which seems equally unsatisfactory. The fact is that they are the only three in Sussex and some of the very few outside East Anglia. Many churchyards have large and very ancient yews, some perhaps as old as the church itself. The planting of yews was purely practical. In the Middle Ages yew wood was used for making bows; but yews could not be planted in pastures or hedgerows, because their leaves and berries are poisonous to cattle. The churchyard was a safe enclosure where cattle did not enter.

In the churchyard at Heathfield and in sixteen other churchyards in that neighbourhood may be noticed headstones, in which are set small oval, delicately designed, terracotta plaques. These are the work of Jonathan Harmer (1762–1849), the son of a stonemason at Heathfield. He sailed for New York in 1796 to join his brother John, but returned to Heathfield in 1800 and took over the family business from his father, who died during his homeward voyage. He specialised

Harmer plaques at **Salehurst** (*top*) and **Framfield** ▷

odied

AGED 28 years

in bas-reliefs for tombstones. The clays vary in colour from cream and buff to bright red; the red is thought to have come from a local claypit, probably in Heathfield Park, the paler clays from elsewhere, possibly Fulham. Harmer plaques are in seven main types; baskets of fruit and flowers, urns with ram's head handles, figure groups representing Charity, Masonic designs with figures of Faith and Hope, vases of a tureen shape, cherubs and paterae or rosettes of various designs. At Wartling is the only cast-iron example of Harmer's work and at East Grinstead the only stone specimen. The two wall tablets inside Cade Street Independent Chapel are of special interest. Each has an elaborate urn with swags; one is inscribed 'Harmer fecit 1832', the other 'Harmer 1878', which must indicate that it was taken from stock, since it was twenty-nine years after his death. There are other good examples of Harmer's work in the Museum at Barbican House, Lewes.

In 1837, the year of Queen Victoria's accession, education in England had reached a critical point. The ancient foundations of Eton and Winchester catered for the aristocracy and landowning gentry. For the rest there was a large number of grammar schools, some equally ancient; but the education they offered was rigidly confined to Latin and Greek, and occasionally Hebrew. For the middle classes, rising in number and importance, there was nothing; the upper middle classes despised the grammar schools because of their comprehensiveness, the lower middle classes because their education was useless. This situation was remedied by the Grammar Schools Act of 1840; but in the meantime a number of 'proprietary' schools had been founded by committees of people interested in secondary education. One of these, founded after the Act, was Brighton College (1845). But far more important than any committee was the curate of New Shoreham, the Revd Nathaniel Woodard. He came of a good Essex family and was the ninth of twelve children; but owing to his father's poverty he himself had no education. At the age of 20 he felt called to the Ministry and his lively social conscience made him aware of the educational vacuum. His theory was that money spent on educating the 'poor' was wasted until the middle classes, the employers, were themselves educated. Although some of his ideas sound odd today, they must be seen in the context of a rigidly class-conscious society. His conception was to cover the country with a network of schools for the middle classes. Within eighteen months of his arrival at Shoreham Woodard published his pamphlet *A Plea for the Middle Classes*, and in 1847 he founded the Shoreham Grammar School, the future Lancing College. To this he added a second, or 'middle' school, which moved to its permanent home at Hurstpierpoint in 1853. The vacant premises in Shoreham were then used for a 'lower' school which was transferred to Ardingly in 1870. Lancing was an 'upper' school, intended for the upper middle classes, who were expected accordingly to pay higher fees. Lancing would draw the money; but Woodard's real interest was in the middle and lower schools. The middle school was to be for the professional classes, the lower for tradesmen and artisans, who at that time (*vide* Jane Austen) did not mix. Woodard was an indefatigable fund raiser and could have taught much to the present-day public relations consultants; his favourite method was 'a nice luncheon', at one of which in Manchester he raised £20,000, no mean sum in those days. There are now seventeen schools administered by the Woodard Foundation; but Lancing,

Hurstpierpoint and Ardingly, the latter two in East Sussex, were the pioneers. Roedean—the first girls' public school—was built in 1898–99 high on the cliffs beyond Kemp Town. It was founded in Brighton in 1885 by the Misses Lawrence, but the great Jacobean building by Sir J. W. Simpson, containing boarding-houses, school rooms and staff quarters under one roof, gave it new status. Roedean has recently shown its pioneering spirit again by appointing a headmaster.

Sussex University, the second university established after the Second World War, is built over the eastern part of Stanmer Park, a superb site which gives it the edge over many others. It is mainly by Sir Basil Spence. The first building, Falmer House with a gatehouse and an enclosed courtyard surrounded by a shallow moat, was opened in 1962. Other notable buildings are the circular concrete meeting house with stained-glass slots and the arts centre with curved brick walls. The layout is exciting and makes good use of the undulating ground and the already existing trees. They do much to soften the stark and truncated appearance of some buildings, which closely resemble Knightsbridge Barracks, also by Spence some years later.

'We have discovered the point of perfection. We have given the true model of gardening to the world.'

Horace Walpole, 1785
Essay on Modern Gardening.

The varied soils of East Sussex—acid clays in the wealden belt, alkaline chalk in the downland areas—coupled with a benign climate, fanned by the Channel breezes, make it a natural magnet for gardeners. In some coastal places sub-tropical plants can thrive; the author's grandmother had in her

Gardens:
p46 Wakehurst
p47 Sheffield Park

garden at Rye in the 1920s two mimosa trees nearly 30 ft high standing against the house, which bloomed prolifically every spring. Chalk, although a poor soil, is not as difficult as is often thought. This was proved by Sir Frederick Stern, who made a beautiful garden in a chalkpit at Highdown near Worthing and grew many plants, which were said to be calcifuge (see his book, *A Chalk Garden*). The wealden clay is a rich soil, especially good for rhododendrons and azaleas, though it needs good drainage to produce the best results. It is hard to work, and no gardener who knows only the light soils of Essex and parts of Surrey understands the meaning of hard labour. The luckiest gardeners in East Sussex are those who live on greensand.

William Robinson, 1838–1935, one of the greatest names in English gardening, lived at Gravetye, West Hoathly; it is now an hotel and country club, but much of Robinson's layout and planting survives. Robinson was an Irishman, an eccentric and dictatorial man of fiery temper and fixed ideas. Perhaps because, rather than in spite, of this he was a pioneer in the revolution of the English garden. In the mid-19th century gardening and garden design were going through the same stifled, artificial period as dress and fashions, furnishing and architecture. What William Morris did for other arts, Robinson did for gardens. Cottagers had kept the flag flying, but the gardens of the wealthy had degenerated into a sterile formality. But before the end of the century Robinson brought a gardening revolution about by introducing the herbaceous border, and created greater change in the English garden than any of his contemporaries. Carpet bed-

ding was anathema to him; he wrote 'to make a flower bed imitate a bad carpet and by throwing aside all grace of form and loveliness of bloom is a dismal mistake'. The *English Flower Garden*, first published in 1883, ran into five editions and was reprinted in 1897; it has often been reprinted since and brought up to date where necessary. Robinson hated Latin names and was prone to invent English names for plants without them. In Chapter I he makes some pungent comments on what he considers gross and common errors among gardeners; he directed them to the more natural and informal ways of garden-making, and his views are never ambiguous.

Sharing the honours with Robinson was Gertrude Jekyll—a gentler but also a formidable character. She lived at Munstead Wood near Godalming, Surrey, and was a close friend for many years of Lutyens, who consulted her about the garden of any building he undertook, including New Delhi. She designed beds at Nymans, where some of her roses still survive. At Great Dixter, where Lutyens designed the additions, the gardens were laid out by him and Nathaniel Lloyd, and Miss Jekyll did not have a direct hand in them, though Lutyens was fully imbued with her ideas. A charming garden of a different kind because it is on chalk is at Charleston, West Dean, laid out by the late Sir Oswald Birley. Sheffield Park, laid out by Brown and Repton, and planted by Arthur Soames, is the most distinguished shrub and tree garden in East Sussex.

East Sussex is not one of the great sporting counties; but there are three packs of foxhounds: the Southdown, which hunts the country from the London–Brighton road to the Cuckmere valley; the Eridge with its kennels at Eridge Green; and the East Sussex and Romney Marsh, which covers the country from the Cuckmere valley and over into Kent. The Southdown country includes the Downs, which enables it to go on hunting later than many packs. Much of the downland has recently been ploughed up and the fields enclosed with wire, but there are still some splendid gallops in uncultivated combes. The Brighton and Storrington Foot Beagles cover a wide area in mid-Sussex.

There are racecourses at Hampden Park, Plumpton and Brighton; Lewes Racecourse is now closed.

Stoolball, a game somewhat similar to rounders, was played in the south of England from the 16th to the 18th century. Since then it has largely been confined to Sussex—and especially East Sussex, where between the wars Major W. W. Grantham, K.C. of Barcombe, was very active in promoting stoolball for the benefit of men who had lost a limb in the First World War. There is a large number of stoolball clubs.

The London to Brighton run, generally known as the Old Crocks' Race, was started in 1927 by the *Daily Sketch*. It begins in Hyde Park and finishes in Madeira Drive, Brighton; it is usually on the first Sunday in November and cars entered have to be pre-1905.

◁ Borders planted by Gertrude Jekyll at Nymans (*see* **Slaugham**)

49

Note. *Places are listed under substantives, e.g. Dean, West and Groombridge, New. Numbers in brackets refer to the map to be found at the end of the book. Places transferred in 1972 to West Sussex are marked *.*

Alciston [8] lies at the end of a lane and just below the northern slope of the Downs. Originally a Saxon farming village, it has changed little since medieval days, and still has its manor house, Court Farm, (an old priest's house, the remains of a 14c dovecote and a tithe barn. The small aisleless church was originally Norman, as one round-headed window in the N wall of the chancel shows. It was altered in the 13c when the Early English windows in the chancel were inserted. Further Perp windows were inserted in the nave in the 15c. The chancel has no arch and its roof was renewed in 1898; but the nave has a fine roof of stilted trusses with heavy tie-beams, moulded king-posts and wall plates. There is a plain old oak pulpit, but new pews have recently been installed in the nave and stained a peculiarly hideous orange colour. At the time of Domesday Alciston was one of the manors belonging to Battle Abbey, part of whose grange is incorporated in Court Farm. At the Dissolution it was given to Sir John Gage in return for a knight's fee, the provision of armed horsemen for the King's service. It still belongs to the Gages.

Aldrington [7] is an ancient parish now submerged in Portslade-by-Sea. The village seems to have been at the former mouth of the Adur, now at Shoreham, but coastal erosion swept it away. The church was already ruinous in 1638 and

became increasingly so until it was rebuilt in 1878. The tower and S aisle are 13c and there are six contemporary windows in the S wall.

Alfriston [8] is a miniature market town and the capital of the Cuckmere valley with a distinguished and beautiful church known as the Cathedral of the Downs. At the N end of the long high street is a little square with a large chestnut tree and the battered stump of a market cross, which has been knocked down by lorries more than once and devotedly repaired. Further down the street are two splendid half-timbered inns—the Star (1500), and the George. The Star is the more famous because of its well-known association with smugglers, who no doubt found the lonely Cuckmere Haven an easy place to land contraband, and Alfriston a willing recipient. The Star has some external carvings of St George and the Dragon and a gaily coloured figurehead; it also has a large modern extension at the back and a car park, which have been so tactfully built that they are invisible from the high street. Hardly any houses in the street are later than the 18c and many are very much earlier. Altogether Alfriston is a singularly attractive place which should be, and is being, preserved, although the narrow street is no place for juggernauts. The church, built about 1360, stands slightly aloof from the street across a large green and near the river on

a site known as the Tye. There is a legend about the supernatural removal of the stones from another site when it was being built. It has a circular churchyard (cf. Hellingly) which is probably of pre-historic origin. It is built in the form of a Greek cross and has a central tower with a graceful shingled spire. The materials used are well-knapped flints, which can be seen at various houses, e.g. Offham House; but the little churches in the Cuckmere valley and downland are built of rough, undressed flints. The flintwork at Alfriston is one of the best examples in the country, the flints having been carefully selected, skilfully knapped and placed so that they fit perfectly like many Norfolk churches. The inside is spacious and well-planned; it is thought that Poynings church, also in the form of a Greek cross and built around the same time, may have been influenced by Alfriston. The central tower is supported by lofty arches with octagonal, fluted piers. The well-proportioned E window is modern, and is marred by an unsightly reredos; but the side windows and those in the N transept have their original Dec tracery. There is some medieval glass in the N window of the transept showing a figure of St Alphage, Archbishop of Canterbury; beside it is a modern but successful figure of St Andrew. The windows in the S transept are by C. E. Kempe and his assistant W. E. Tower (*see* Lindfield). In the chancel are three round-headed sedilia with richly decorated canopies, and beside them a similarly canopied piscina. There are two other piscinae in the transepts, showing that they were used as chapels. On the N wall is an Easter sepulchre and above it two carved figures, one with the face of a woman, the other of a dog-like animal with its head between its hind legs. On the easternmost beam in the chancel roof are the hooks and staples from which before the Reformation the Lenten veil was hung from the first Sunday in Lent until the Wednesday in Holy Week; there are very few churches where these survive. There is a large George I Royal Arms 1725. Near the church is the 14c Clergy House, timber-framed and thatched; it was the first building bought by the National Trust in 1896, and was restored for it by Alfred Powell.

Ardingly* [4] (pronounced -lye) is on high ground on the wealden ridge, nearly 400 ft above sea level. The church is half a mile W of the village, which used to be called Hapstead Green. It is a solid-looking sandstone building, mostly 14c with a Perp tower. Inside are medieval roofs: plain collar-beam in the chancel and more elaborate in the nave with king-posts and curved braces. The chancel has early 18c altar rails with barley-sugar balusters and a five-bay screen of very delicate Perp work. On the N wall is the recumbent effigy of a priest in mass vestments 1330 with an elaborate canopy and shafts on either side. Also a table tomb to Richard Wakeherst and his wife with canopied brass effigies. On the floor of the chancel are more brasses: Richard Culpeper and his wife (1504) and Nicholas and Elizabeth Culpeper, the Wakeherst heiress, (1510); the brasses to Nicholas and his wife still have their coloured armorial shields, and all four brasses are finely executed and in good condition. In the tower is

a medieval oak staircase. Ardingly College, a public school belonging to the Woodard Foundation, lies about a mile to the S (see Introduction). It is built of red brick, was designed by Slater and Carpenter and opened in 1870.

Wakehurst Place was built in 1590 by Sir Edward Culpeper, presumably on the site of an older house of the Wakehersts. It is a fine house of local sandstone with Horsham slabbed roofs. The original house had a courtyard plan, but this was changed when a large part of the side wings was demolished in 1845. It was bought a few years ago by the Royal Horticultural Society, and the gardens are used as an extension to Kew.

Arlington [8] is on the upper reaches of the Cuckmere, which is hardly more than a ditch and has probably been made even smaller by the recent building of a reservoir. There is an inn and a few cottages of no great note, but the church is of great archaeological and architectural interest. The earliest written records, the church-warden's accounts (1455–1479), show that the church possessed thirty cows, which were let out to farmers who paid for them in beeswax (2 lbs per cow p.a.) to supply lights for the shrines of SS Pancras, Michael, Katherine, Margaret and Nicholas. Of the Saxon church long and short work at the corners and one small window above the porch remain; but there is evidence that it stood on the site of even earlier buildings, since two strata of burnt stones, clay and flint have been discovered. Roman bricks at the head of the Saxon window and various fragments of tiles and pottery suggest that Arlington was on a Roman road from Lewes to Canterbury. The church today has nave, chancel and N aisle with a low tower and a shingled spire, springing, unusually, from below the apex of the roof. The inside has features of all periods; there are two round-

headed windows in the N chapel and an EE arch with dog-tooth moulding leading from the chapel to the N aisle. In the 14c the chancel was built, and to this period belong the fine Dec E windows in it and the chapel, the nave arcade and the arch over the tomb in the chancel; the traces of wall paintings also date from this time. The nave and chapel have trussed and raftered roofs. In the chapel behind a glazed recess is a large jar, found in pieces under the floor and identified by the British Museum as a 13c food storage jar; it is not, as earlier guides say, a British urn, but is none the less interesting. There is a Queen Anne pulpit with some modern carved panels inserted, and a George III Royal Arms. The chancel screen was carved at Mayfield from old wood out of the tower as a memorial to the Revd Thomas Bunston (Vicar 1889–1918) who restored the church after finding it, according to the Bishop, 'in a state of dirt, decay and ruin worse than that of any parish church in Sussex'.

Ashburnham [5] has a great park and several hamlets among woods, which once provided fuel for smelting and resounded to the clank of iron, as the names of Ashburnham Forge and Furnace still testify. The last surviving labourer died in 1883 and remembered the extinguishing of the fire in 1825, the casting of firebacks being the last work. Ashburnham Place was for 800 years the seat of the Ashburnhams, a very ancient family, who were of eminence before the Conquest. John Ashburnham, groom of the bedchamber to Charles I, built a house in 1665 in classical Wren style, which was enlarged and reconstructed in the 18c. It had two alterations in the 19c, being first adorned with mock Tudor turrets, and later refaced and enlarged again in early Victorian red brick. The park was laid out by Capability Brown; it is in undulating

Alfriston; Burnt House Farm (*top*) and The Clergy House ▷

Ashburnham chancel

wealden country with great stretches of grass broken up by clumps of trees and lakes fed by the Ashburn stream. The house stands high and overlooks the lakes; but it is bleak and undistinguished among such ravishing scenery. John Ashburnham was given the shirt and silk drawers worn by Charles I on the scaffold, as well as his watch and the sheet, bearing the monogram CR, that was thrown over his body. From 1743 to 1830 the royal relics were kept in the church for the convenience of people who wished to touch them as a guard against scrofula, the King's Evil. But after a theft they were removed to the house where they remain. Various documents, including a collection of letters from the King, are now on loan to the County Record Office in Lewes. John's descendant, another

John, was raised to the peerage in 1780 as Earl of Ashburnham; but the family was latterly not prolific. The last of the line, Lady Catherine Ashburnham, the daughter of the 5th and penultimate Earl, succeeded to the estate on the death of her uncle. She was a Roman Catholic postulant, but was given special permission to leave her order and return to manage her ancestral estates. She died in 1953, after which many of the treasures had to be sold and part of the house was demolished. It is now the Ashburnham Christian Trust, founded by the Revd John Bickersteth, the present owner, great-grandson of the 4th Earl.

The church stands behind the house and close to the 18c stables. The embattled tower is 15c with a later window inserted and below it a door with Pelham buckle label-

stops; but the rest of the church was built by John Ashburnham 1665–67, and is a rare example of late Gothic against the classical trend of the time. The chancel arch may also be 15c and rebuilt from the previous church. The inside is rather like a college chapel; the nave has complete 17c furnishings, including box-pews, cut down in 1893, and an organ gallery supported by columns and approached by a staircase with balusters, a moulded handrail and carved newel finials. On the S wall in a carved gilt frame adorned with doves and cherubs are the Commandments, flanked by paintings of Moses and Aaron; this is dated 1676 and used to be the reredos until the late 19c. The chancel has an Elizabethan altar table with bulbous legs enclosed by 17c Communion rails; it stands 3 ft 6 in

Ashburnham monument by Bushnell ▷

Barcombe

above the nave and was raised at the rebuilding in order to accommodate the Ashburnham vaults, which contain the coffins of 44 members of the family. There are 17c wrought-iron screens in the chancel arch and between the chancel and the chapels. All the mullions except those in the E window are of oak. N of the chancel is the Ashburnham chapel containing monuments to John and William Ashburnham, who rebuilt the church. John's monument is of black and white marble; he lies between his two wives and beneath are his four sons and four daughters. On the W wall is a large white monument by John Bushnell to William Ashburnham kneeling before his dying wife, Jane, Countess of Marlborough, a remarkable Renaissance group, which contrasts with the late medieval tradition of John's monument. There are various helms, gauntlets, swords and spurs.

Balcombe* [1] is just S of the great forest, known variously as Balcombe, Tilgate and Worth Forest, under which Balcombe tunnel burrows. The centre of the village has a few timber-framed and tile-hung cottages, and the Half Moon Inn has a Horsham-slabbed roof. The church has a 15c tower with a dwarf octagonal spire; but contains nothing of interest since the rebuilding of the nave and chancel in 1850 and an enlargement in 1872. Balcombe Viaduct built in 1839–41 carries the Brighton line over the Ouse valley, and has an impressive span of 37 brick arches; it is seen well from the Haywards Heath road and even better from underneath.

Barcombe [4] A scattered place in wooded country with the main village at Barcombe Cross. The church is a mile away, on a low knoll with charming views eastwards across the Ouse. Flint-built with a low W tower and shingled spire rising from below the apex of

Balcombe; White House garden by Lutyens and Jekyll   57

the roof (cf. Arlington, Mountfield), it was heavily restored in 1879–80. Its origin is Norman—N wall—but no feature remains. The S arcade is EE and most of the windows rebuilt Perp. On the N side is some stained glass with the Grantham arms (1657) brought here from Goltho, Lincs, in 1889 by Mr Justice Grantham of Barcombe Place. Other windows have glass by Kempe. In the chancel is a little cartouche to John Raynes (1687) with putti holding up his coat of arms, and in the S aisle a large and handsome monument to Susannah Medley (1730) with Juno-esque caryatids supporting the canopy. Also a hatchment. The 14c font has panels with slightly recessed ogee arches and quatrefoils on alternate sides. At the back of the nave is a plain oak pulpit—disused, but much nicer than its dreary successor and a bookcase (1682).

Barcombe used to have two railway stations, one on the Lewes–East Grinstead line, and another, Barcombe Mills, on the Lewes–Tunbridge Wells line. A hundred years ago there were three mills on the Ouse; two are long since defunct, but the third and largest stood by the old road where it crosses the river. There was until 1939 a group of handsome white weatherboarded buildings, but in its latter days the mill became a button factory and was burnt to the ground. Nothing remains but water lapping round the disused sluices. The Ouse is tidal as far as here and occasionally sea trout are taken.

Battle [6] Anyone who has been to Santa Maria de Guadaloupe in Spain and stayed within its walls can easily imagine the relationship between the great Benedictine Abbey of Battle and the small town that grew up beneath its shadow. When William, Duke of Normandy, looked down upon Harold's forces from Telham Hill, he vowed that, if he was victorious, he would found a monastery to the

Glory of God. William, a Benedictine monk from Marmoutier, heard his vow and urged him after the battle to fulfil his promise. He and four other monks from Marmoutier were given the task of building it. The King undertook to provide stone from Caen, but there were transport difficulties and a quarry was found close to the abbey. He never saw his abbey completed, since the church was not consecrated until 1095. The Abbot was by the King's intention a very powerful personage in the S of England. He was absolute ruler within 1¼ miles of the abbey, no bishop or royal officer could interfere with him and danegeld and other dues were not levied. He had residences in London and Winchester, and, most remarkable privilege of all, was permitted, when passing through the King's forests, to kill and take two beasts with his dogs. The abbey owned property in Kent, Surrey, Essex, Berks, Oxon and Devon, and when the church was consecrated it was given nine churches and 12 chapels in East Anglia. The Abbot must have been a thorn in the flesh of the Bishop of Chichester. When Stigand tried to make Abbot Gausbert from Marmoutier come to Chichester to be consecrated, the King ordered the ceremony to take place in Battle Abbey church. In 1175 during the reign of Henry II when Odo, a prior of Canterbury, became abbot, the Bishop again tried unsuccessfully to intervene. The Abbot was consecrated by the Archbishop at the College of South Malling, a peculiar of the Archbishop. In 1338 an embattled wall was erected round the precincts. William the Conqueror intended the abbey to have at least 60 monks and to increase the number to 140; but in 1393 there were only 33. The King bequeathed to the abbey his royal embroidered cloak. By 1535 things had deteriorated and Richard Layton after his visitation declared to Cromwell, 'the black

sort of devilish monks I am sorry to know, are past amendment' and describes the Abbot as 'the arrantest churl'. Sir John Gage reported to Cromwell that the furniture and vestments were very poor, and Layton again writes to Wriothesley, 'so beggary a house I never see, nor so filthy stuff. I will not give 20s for all the hangings in this house.' John Hamond, the last abbot, was elected in 1529; nine years later he surrendered with the prior and 15 monks.

The magnificent gatehouse faces the market place and still dominates the town. It was built in about 1338 when the Abbot obtained permission to crenellate the abbey, and has a square tower with octagonal angle turrets. It is richly adorned with Dec panels on the N and S. On the W side is the porter's lodge and on the E a range of buildings traditionally built by Sir Anthony Browne, owner of the abbey after the Dissolution; in both wings are remains of earlier Norman work. Inside was the outer court, surrounded by stables, workshops and farm buildings. Opposite was the abbot's house, converted for his own use by Sir Anthony Browne in the 16c and made into a neo-Gothic mansion by Henry Clutton in 1857. It was burnt in 1932 and again restored; the supposed curse laid by the monks on all lay owners that they would die by fire or water has more than once come tragically true. The house has for some years been a school and is not shown; but within it much of the original abbot's house remains. On the E side is an arcade, a relic of one side of the cloister, though only the four southern bays are EE; the rest have been restored in 15c style. The next most important survival is the dormitory; this was on the first floor, which is roofless, but beneath it is a pillared and vaulted undercroft divided into four parts. The first has three naves and slender round piers, the second is a tunnel-vaulted

Battle; Abbey Gatehouse (*top*) and High Street detail with tilehanging ▷

passage, perhaps to the infirmary, the third a smaller room like the first and the fourth a beautiful and higher room with two naves and taller piers owing to the fall in the ground. The first was the monks' common room and the last the novices'; it appears to be the grandest room, but perhaps its greater height made it colder.

To the N of the dormitory was the church. It was deliberately destroyed at the Dissolution and very few stones remain above ground; but the 14c undercroft of three chapels of the polygonal apse has been excavated. The other surviving building at the S end of the outer court is the guest house. The first floor contained the rooms, which were subsequently altered by Sir Anthony Browne into a great house for Princess Elizabeth. All Browne's building, except for the two octagonal towers, was destroyed in the 18 and 19c. But below is a range of eight tunnel-vaulted cellars 13c; each is connected by a square-headed doorway at alternate ends.

The foundation of the abbey, the work connected with it and the management of its great estates caused a small town to arise. An early entry in the Chronicles of Battle Abbey mentions 115 houses and gives the names of the tenants. The town today is a compact and substantial place, mainly 18c in appearance with many tile-hung houses. A medieval survivor is The Pilgrim's Rest, a close-studded 15c hall house. Opposite the Abbey Gateway is a particularly pretty house—now half bank and half house-agent—with bow-fronted windows and elegant Gothic glazing bars. The George Hotel is late 18c; No. 17 High Street is a Queen Anne brick house of three storeys with a carved frieze, and No. 27 an earlier Carolean house 1688 of ashlar with a brick string-course. In Mount Street running eastwards off High Street is a largish 17c timber-framed house, Lewin's Croft. The

southern extension of High Street is called Upper Lake and the same sort of Georgian houses continue. Behind the church is the Deanery, a handsome brick house of 1669 with battlements and mullions.

The large church, standing just outside the abbey walls, was built originally in 1115, because the presence of laity in the abbey church was an infringement of the Benedictine rule. The Dean of the Abbey conducted the services and the incumbent is still called the Dean of Battle. Of the first church the only relic is the square Norman font with round-headed arches in relief on each side; the elegant Perp font cover has been ostentatiously painted in scarlet and gold. The church was enlarged in the late 13c and given aisles, divided from the nave by five-bay arcades; the piers are alternately round and octagonal and have capitals of large stylised leaf designs, except for the W bay. The clerestory has single lancet windows. Extensions were made to the E end in the 14c but the church was given its present appearance in the 15c, when the Norman tower S of the chancel was pulled down and the embattled Perp tower built at the W end. St Katherine's chapel was built on the site of the Norman tower. Butterfield restored the church in 1869 and regrettably removed the tie-beams and king-posts from the roof, heightened the chancel arch and rebuilt the E window. Sir Anthony Browne and his wife, the first lay owners of the Abbey, lie on a large tombchest of 1548 on the S of the sanctuary, she beneath a canopy. Rich and riotous Renaissance decoration with wreaths, shell-tops and cherubs, all made even richer by recent repainting in contemporary colours. Two Deans of Battle are commemorated by brasses: Robert Clere 1450, a 22 in figure in the chancel, and John Wythines 1615, a larger brass with the Dean wearing a flat Tudor cap. Another brass in the N chapel is to Sir John Lowe 1426, surveyor

to the manors of the Abbey, with a Latin inscription. Two other smaller brasses to William Arnold 1435, a 13 in demi-figure in armour, and to Thomas and Elizabeth Allfraye.

Bayham Abbey [2] In 1207 Sir Robert de Turnham began to build an abbey at Bayham. To it came the canons of the small Premonstratensian house at Otham (*see* Polegate); to swell their numbers he added the monks from Brockley near Deptford. Jordan, the Abbot of Otham, became the first Abbot of Bayham. A quarrel, which was to drag on for 180 years, broke out between Bayham and Michelham Priory over the advowson of the church at Hailsham, the former canons of Otham claiming that, since Hailsham was a chapelry of Hellingly, which they owned, the advowson was rightly theirs. It ended in victory for Michelham; but the Priory was nearly ruined in the process. St Richard of Chichester stayed at Bayham in 1242, and Edward II in 1324. Bayham and St Radegund's, near Canterbury, were the only daughters of the Abbey of Prémonstré colonised direct from the mother house. In 1472 there were an abbot, seven canons and one novice; six years later the visitor found the buildings in utter ruin, the number of canons insufficient and three of them apostate. But ten years later and again in 1497 the visitor reported on the Abbot's excellent management in reducing debts and increasing the stock of the community, though the canons were rebuked for wearing fashionable boots and shoes like laymen; in 1500 nothing was found amiss. In 1524 when Wolsey was at the height of his power Bayham was one of the houses appointed to be suppressed. But the monks were evidently popular, since the threat was much resented in the neighbourhood and a large force assembled, led by Canon Thomas Towers, whom they reinstated as abbot. For a short time the abbey was held by force, but finally resistance flickered out and it was dissolved in 1525.

The ruins stand peacefully in a romantic valley watered by the little river Teise, a tributary of the Medway. After Battle, they are the most complete monastic ruins in Sussex. On the N is the gatehouse with a very pretty Dec arch altered by Repton, but more important is the 13c church with a long narrow nave 170 ft by 24 ft and a polygonal apse to the chancel, in the centre of which grows a fine beech tree, its gnarled roots gripping the stones like ancient fingers. The transepts also survive, the S fairly ruinous, but the N with two chapels retaining their vaulting. The only other buildings are the Chapter House with three lancets resting on bell-necked capitals and the cloisters. The abbey is well cared for by the Dept. of the Environment and further excavations are in progress. The ground has risen quite a bit; so the entire foundations of the abbey may at length be revealed. The modern 1870-Tudor house of Bayham Abbey looks well standing high on the hill opposite—in Kent.

Beachy Head [8]. Seen from the Channel, Beachy Head with the Seven Sisters to the W of it is as exciting as the white cliffs of Dover. Here the South Downs end abruptly just as the North Downs do in Kent. The whole stretch between Eastbourne and Seaford is preserved, and immune from the possible horror of another Peacehaven. On top of Beachy Head is the Belle Tout lighthouse, built in 1831 and disused as such; the new lighthouse stands in the sea at the foot of the Head.

Beckley [6]. The long village street has an interesting variety of cottages and houses. Several are timber-framed 16c, others are weatherboarded or tile-hung, one is faced with black mathematical tiles, and opposite the church is Church House, a red-brick, early 18c house with handsome Doric pilasters. The church dates from the 11c and the tower has herringbone work and narrow Norman slit windows. The broach spire and aisles were added in the 13c; there are three-bay arcades on each side, differing in detail. The chancel arch is unusually wide, the chancel itself a 14c addition, with Dec tracery in the E window, and an ogee-headed piscina. The font is an 18c marble bowl. There is a churchwarden's chest made out of a tree trunk and bound with iron; the tower screen was made out of 1686 Communion rails. And so to the 19c, when in 1885 the church was restored. Two dormers with fussy and elaborate woodwork were inserted in the roof on each side and the nave roof was largely rebuilt, though it has its medieval tie-beams. Over the chancel arch timber was set into the plaster including a foliated rood cross; but the old quarry-tiled floors were allowed to remain.

Beddingham [7] (accent on -ham) is a very small farming village just above the level of the Brooks E of Lewes. It is mentioned in a Saxon charter of 801, and was attached to Wilmington Priory until its dissolution in 1414. The church was originally Norman, but the sturdy embattled tower of chequered stone and flint with a low tiled cap was built about 1557. Hardly a trace of the Norman church remains, as it was enlarged just after 1200; the nave arcades are EE, differing in detail on the N and S. Soon after the aisles were built, ogee cinquefoil clerestory windows were inserted in the nave walls (cf. West Firle). In one arch of the S arcade are some 13c red scrolls and a restored figure. The W end of the church has its old tiled floor. Near Beddingham are two important prehistoric sites: Mount Caburn, an isolated piece of the Downs, has an Iron Age hillfort built about 1100 B.C., and Itford Hill to the SW has a Bronze Age settlement of eleven small embanked enclosures.

Berwick [8] (pronounced Burwick) is one of a string of small villages below the Downs between Lewes and Eastbourne. The church is built on high ground, which may have been the site of pre-Christian barrows. Its shingled spire pierces through the clump of trees surrounding it, but on closer approach it is quite difficult to find. It was originally built about 1130, but has been much restored. In 1837 the Revd E. Boys Ellman, curate from 1837 to 1843 and rector from 1846 to 1906, described the deplorable state of the church as he found it. The tower was struck by lightning in 1774, the spire destroyed and four bells were lying in the floor. The N aisle was derelict and bricked up, the E end had been shortened by 14 ft and had a makeshift thatched roof. Three graves were in the aisle. But Mr Ellman was a Tractarian, and had not sat under Pusey and Newman for nothing. As rector, he rebuilt the tower, spire and N aisle, extended the E end to its original foundations, and restored the beautiful 14c Easter sepulchre, which was in pieces in the churchyard. He also had the church re-roofed and a screen made from the timbers of the old chancel. The church was re-opened at a Thanksgiving Service on 4 August 1857 at which the Bishop of Chichester was present. An earlier rector, the Revd George Hall is commemorated by a stone in the vestry floor where he 'together with his son George both origenal and transcript are reposed in the hope of a joyfvl resvrrection the first vnborn Janvary the 15th 1668'. 'Origenal and transcript' means father and son, and 'vnborn' means died. The only other ancient feature of interest is the unusual 11c font built into the base of the pillar on the N side of the nave. Until the Second World War Berwick church was

whitewashed and rather bleak inside; but when the bombs fell and many stained-glass windows in Sussex churches were destroyed, Bishop Bell of Chichester felt that loss could be turned into gain by asking artists to adorn walls rather than windows. He suggested that Duncan Grant and Vanessa Bell, who both lived at Firle, should be asked to paint at Berwick. The Glory over the chancel arch by Grant shows a soldier, a sailor and an airman, and includes Bishop Bell and the Rector of Berwick. The outer screen and the 'Victory of Calvary' on the W wall are also by Grant. The paintings in the nave, the Annunciation and the Nativity, are by Vanessa Bell; all the paintings within the screen are by her son, Quentin Bell. The liveliness and colour of these wall paintings are an echo of the Middle Ages, when churches were filled with colour in wall and window, though the artists were no doubt often far less talented.

Bexhill [9] The seaside town was developed in 1880 by Lord De La Warr, who is the chief landowner. Although tolerably well laid out, it is lacking in distinction and style, and is a dreary and rather genteel resort. The De La Warr Pavilion, a large lump of a building, designed by Mendelsohn and Chermayeff in 1933–6, squats upon the sea front. The old village is up the hill behind, a mile from the coast and the dangers of the sea and raiders. Not much is left, but High Street and Church Street are unexpectedly pretty and have a number of white weatherboarded cottages; one of three storeys is an antique shop and has a projecting clock, a jubilee memorial of 1887. There is one Georgian house with pilasters and a pediment, and opposite the church are some ruins of the medieval manor house with a buttress and a trefoil-headed window. The church has a low embattled tower surmounted by a

cap and looks over-restored from the outside; but inside it is rewarding. The tower has Norman arches N and S, and the two western bays of the nave arcades are late 12c with round piers and round-headed arches; the piers have simple Norman capitals, scallops on the N, stylised leaves on the S. The next two bays on the N are EE and a Perp, on the S 19c, rebuilt by Butterfield in 1878, who restored the church, enlarging the chancel and S aisle. The N chapel was founded about 1450 as the Batesford chantry by Dame Joan Brenchley in memory of her parents. The Archbishop of Canterbury executed the deed and the document is still preserved. In it he ordains that 'no monk, Welshman, Irishman or Scotsman or anyone born in Wales, Ireland, Scotland, or elsewhere than in England may hereafter be made chaplain of the said chantry....' No Race Relations Act in those days. The oldest thing in the church—evidence of its Saxon origin—is the Bexhill Stone, a finely carved 8c slab thought now to have been a reliquary lid, mounted in a case under the tower. It was found under the floor in 1878; it has early Christian symbols in low relief. In the N aisle is a window containing some 15c glass with whole figures. The glass was acquired by Horace Walpole about 1750 from the rector, Sir William Ashburnham, to adorn his villa at Strawberry Hill. After his death it was bought by Sir Thomas Cullum of Hardwick House, Bury St Edmunds, and bequeathed to Bexhill church by his descendant in 1921. Walpole thought the central figures were Henry III and Queen Eleanor, but they are more likely to be Christ and the Virgin Mary. Also in the N aisle is a little barrel organ (*see also* Brightling and Piddinghoe). In 1893 the chancel ceiling was decorated and the walls painted—typical of the period and pleasing. Much more recently in 1951 the late Alan Sorrell was commissioned to paint the large

mural over the arch into the N chapel; the theme is St Richard of Chichester and his work has strongly Florentine influence. The elaborate carved oak screens in the nave and S chapel, heavily cusped and latticed, were given in 1892 and are good late Victorian work. Above the rood screen are a rood, Virgin Mary and St John by Martin Travers 1948.

Bishopstone [7] The villas creep up the lane off the Seaford–Newhaven road, but stop short ½ mile from the small farming village, and should certainly not be allowed to advance further. The age of the place is immediately apparent from its distinguished church, and its name records an early connection with the bishops of Chichester. The bishop often stayed here until the 17c, and in 1324 entertained Edward II for two days. The church's most striking external features are the Saxon porch, really a side chapel with a sundial on its gable bearing the name EADRIC, and the tower of four stages, built about 200 years later. The sundial shows a style hole and 13 lines, five with cross bars longer than the others; these mark the four Saxon tides of the day, each tide being divided into three parts, equivalent to 6 a.m. to 6 p.m. in Roman time. The nave walls are Saxon; they are less than 2 ft 6 in thick and have large stone quoins forming the western angles. The nave and porch may be 9c, and are certainly not later than 10c. The tower, built by the Normans early in the 12c, is of well-constructed flintwork, now visible but formerly covered with fine plaster. It has a round window on the W face, twin bell-openings (like Newhaven) with a central shaft, and a corbel table adorned with heads and monsters, above which is a Sussex cap. They also built the porch entrance, probably to replace a W door, which has a double chevroned archway and two shafts, each with differently carved capitals. The Normans also enlarged the Saxon church by building or rebuilding the chancel and adding the N aisle. Towards the end of the 12c the sanctuary was added in Transitional-Norman style, on a slightly lower level than the rest of the church. It was intended to be vaulted, though the present vaulting dates only from 1849; at the same time the windows were restored, but the chevroned string-course on the S wall and the triple shafts and wall arches are in the main original. Between sanctuary and chancel the pointed Transitional arch has rich dog-tooth mouldings and triple shaft responds with scalloped cushion capitals. The nave appears 13c, since the chancel arch and the arcades of the N aisle are all EE. The chancel arch has three orders like the earlier sanctuary arch; the stiff-leaf capitals have two well-carved stops above them. Lancets were inserted in the S wall of the nave and choir; some Norman windows remained until the restoration of 1849. But the N wall still has its little round-headed windows; those at the E and W end of the aisle are modern. In the porch on the E wall is a canopied 14c niche with crockets and floral decoration. Below it is a 13c grave slab with a floral cross and the fragment of a pier with interlacing ornament. On the S wall of the tower is a well-carved 12c coffin lid. It is adorned with three rope-moulded circles; the lowest has the head of a Calvary, the middle the Agnus Dei and the uppermost a tall pitcher from which two doves are drinking—a common symbol in Early Christian art.

Blackham [2] *see* Withyham

Blatchington, East [8] A few flint cottages and walls are all that survive of the village; the rest is a residential suburb of Seaford. That the church stands on an ancient site was proved in 1860 when two coarse pottery funeral urns of Roman or ancient British origin were found under the tower. The thick walls at the E end seem to indicate a Norman nave and the round-headed priest's door survives as evidence. The walls are of flint with stone quoins, but the flints have among them some chestnut-coloured stones, which may be sarsens—brought here from the N in the glacial period; there are many also in the walls of Seaford church. The tower has a low shingled spire. Inside, restoration has done its worst. There are lancet windows in the chancel and 13c piscina and sedilia; but everything is smothered in whitewash including the stonework of the piscina and sedilia and the window surrounds. It should be removed and left only on the plaster. The parish register of 1586 records a very curious Puritan Christian name—'Syn-deny' (deny sin) given to a girl.

Blatchington, West [7] once a lonely downland hamlet consisting only of Court Farm and its outbuildings, a windmill and the church, is now being swallowed up by the northern spread of Hove. Court Farm, though now looking quite modern, is built around the core of a late 15c manor house. The church was practically disused by 1550, and during successive centuries fell entirely into ruin until it was rebuilt in 1890. The nave walls and two round-headed windows in the W wall are 12c and the S doorway 15c, otherwise no ancient features remain. The church has recently had a N aisle added to it. More interesting than Court Farm or the church is the windmill, built in 1724. It is unique in Sussex in being a barn and smock mill combined, with the mill standing on the roof of the barn; but the farmyard in which it used to be has gone, and it now stands on a trim island of mown grass surrounded by villas.

Bodiam [6] 'Four grey walls, and four grey towers, Overlook a space of flowers...' Bodiam is not Camelot, and the courtyard has mown grass; but Tennyson might well have had it in mind, when describing the bower of the Lady of Shalott. Peaceful and romantic, Bodiam Castle rises from the still waters of its moat; yet it is a reminder of days when the Sussex coast was constantly being raided by the French and it was easy for a marauder to penetrate into Sussex up the tidal Rother, a much larger river then than now. Bodiam had long had maritime and strategic importance, proved by the excavations of a Roman river port on the S bank of the Rother, which was probably used for the export of iron ore. In Norman times it belonged to the Wardeux family and passed later to Sir Edward Dalyngrigge, a member of a family long established near East Grinstead, by his marriage to the Wardeux heiress. Sir Edward fought in the French wars during Edward III's reign and was familiar with French architecture. In 1385 during the Hundred Years' War, with Rye and Winchelsea sacked and burnt, the Rother was highly vulnerable and Sir Edward was given a royal licence by Richard II 'to strengthen and crenellate his manor house of Bodyham and to make thereof a castle in defence of the adjacent country-side'. The ancient manor house was on the hill NE of the church; but Sir Edward preferred to build a new castle close to the river. It cannot have been completed before 1387, when England had regained control of the Channel; it never therefore withstood attack from foreign invaders. Earlier castles had an isolated keep; but in the 14c they were built around a rectangular courtyard guarded by a gate tower. The great gatehouse on the landward side has two massive rectangular towers pierced with machicolations through which boiling oil could be

poured on invaders. Under the high arch is a row of three shields with the arms of the families who held Bodiam, Dalyngrigge in the centre. The entrance was guarded by no less than three portcullises; the ribbed vaulting in the inner part is still intact. In the courtyard the construction of the house is easily seen; though the roof and floors have long since disappeared, 33 fireplaces are still visible, as well as 10 stone spiral staircases and 28 garderobes or latrines, each with its own drain shaft to the moat. The plan is simple and well-arranged. On either side of the gatehouse are the steward's offices and garrison; to the left, or E, are the chapel, the Lady's Bower and the Great

Chamber, which was the Lord's audience chamber and receiving room. Next, on the S side is the Great Hall with screens leading to the buttery and kitchen. Next to the kitchen in the SW drum tower is the well, and on the W side are the servants' hall and servants' kitchen—a very compact plan, which could hardly be bettered today. On the first floor were the bedrooms. The postern tower on the S side had a drawbridge leading to the harbour, from which food supplies could be brought straight to the buttery.

Bodiam Castle has been singularly lucky in its preservation. In 1644 it was probably taken by Parliamentary forces and the castle was dismantled. It was left ruinous

until 'Mad Jack' Fuller of Brightling bought it in 1829 to save it from demolition. In 1864 it was sold to George Cubitt (Lord Ashcombe) who did some repairs, and then in 1916 Lord Curzon bought it, carried out extensive repairs and excavations, and bequeathed it to the National Trust, in whose care it remains. In 1970 the moat was dredged and drained, and the original bottom found; the springs feeding it run so strongly that it was refilled in less than six months.

The village is very small. Near Bodiam Bridge are hop-fields belonging to Guinness, and a little station on the now disused Kent and East Sussex Light Railway. Over the hill behind the castle and less than a mile from the Kent Ditch is the church. It has a stout Perp tower with an angle turret and an EE chancel; but it was very drastically restored in about 1850 by R. C. Carpenter.

Bolney* [4] is a small village in wooded country just off the Brighton road. It was threatened with becoming another new town, but has now been reprieved (1974). The church has a nave and chancel of about 1100, but the massive tower with four stone pinnacles and copper weather vanes is Tudor and was added in 1536 at the expense of John Bolney. His arms and those of St Leger are carved on each side of the doorway, and there is an inscription 'This steple is 66 ft high'. The peal of eight bells was until 1724 the only one of this number in the county. The tall, narrow round-headed S door has a scratch sundial on a jamb stone; it is so similar to the blocked N door at Wivelsfield that it is thought to have been built by the same mason. Until 1840 there was a round-headed chancel arch with chevron moulding; restorations in 1853 and 1901 removed other ancient features, including another round-headed doorway

Bishopstone

West Blatchington mill ▷

and the oak roof. There are some 17c brasses to the Bolney, Pellett and Culpeper families, and a Queen Anne Royal Arms. There are some examples of 15c and 16c farmhouses in the parish, but none of particular importance.

North of the village and high up in the woods is Wykehurst, a French-style chateau with conical turrets and elaborate detail, built for Henry Huth by E. M. Barry 1872–4. (*See* Introduction).

Brede [6] is pleasantly set on a southern hillside, sloping down to the small river which bears its name. The large and dignified church appears to be 14c and 15c, but like most neighbouring churches it has a Norman origin. The first church had a nave, chancel, narrow S aisle and, probably, a SW tower, suggested by a Norman impost in the S arcade. The S aisle was enlarged in the 13c and the N aisle added in the 14c. Finally in the 15c the Perp tower with battlements and an angle turret was built, replacing the earlier tower, the chancel was rebuilt and Perp windows added in the aisles. The church was then much as it is today, the only subsequent addition in about 1537 being the Oxenbridge chapel. There is a round-headed arch between it and the chancel, and the eastern pier has carved upon it a coat of arms with supporters—a decidedly post-medieval adornment. The E window of the chancel has unusual flamboyant tracery, more French than English, and was most likely altered when the Oxenbridge chapel was built. Sir Goddard Oxenbridge (1537), thought to be the builder of the chapel, lies finely carved in Caen stone on a tomb chest adorned with shields. An earlier Robert Oxenbregg also has a tomb chest with two brasses to him and his wife; Robert only has

Bodiam Castle

one leg and two feet, but his wife is undamaged. Brede has been a High Anglican church for many years, and has been enriched with a number of modern furnishings, including a font cover, a rood and various small statues. The best works are the Virgin and Child by Clare Sheridan, carved out of an oak from Brede Place, and the Stations of the Cross by W. T. Monnington. Two windows have some medieval glass, figures of Edward the Confessor and other saints over the S porch and some later heraldic glass in the Oxenbridge chapel. Brede Place (not open to the public) was the home of the Oxenbridges and can be seen across the fields from the valley below. It is a stone 15c house with later alterations in brick and has a chapel containing three stalls with misericords and linenfold panelling.

Brightling [5] On the crest of Brightling Down, 620 ft above sea level and the highest point on the southern Forest Ridge, is a 65 ft-high pillar, known as Brightling Needle, and near it an Observatory, from which there are splendid views over the Weald. Both were built by 'Mad Jack' Fuller, M.P. for many years and a member of a well-known family of ironmasters. He was an amiable eccentric, and was once sent to the Tower for abusing the Speaker. He was also a patron of the arts and saved Bodiam Castle from demolition by buying it. At Brightling Park, where he lived, he built a temple designed by Smirke, who also designed the Observatory. The house itself is 1699; it was much enlarged by Mad Jack, but his additions have now been demolished. In the centre of the very small village two yew trees stand sentry on either side of a flight of stone steps leading to the brick churchyard path. The first eye-catcher is the extraordinary stone pyramid, which Fuller had built for

himself 24 years before his death in 1834; he is buried within it, supposedly seated and holding a bottle of claret. The stone is now mellowed and grasses spring from the crevices; but it must have looked a monstrosity when it was brand new. There is one tomb with a Harmer terracotta plaque—a typical bowl of fruit. The church has a low embattled and heavily buttressed tower dating from the late 12c; the only sign of an earlier building is a round-headed doorway in the S wall of the nave. Inside, the church is unusually attractive owing to the mixture of styles and the different heights of the arches. The N arcade of the nave is 14c; but the arches of the chapel are lower and 13c, while the E windows of the chapel and chancel are again 14c with Dec tracery. During a recent restoration a number of wall paintings were revealed; some

are 17c texts, but over the arch into the chapel are some earlier medieval fragments. The pulpit is Gothick, and the W gallery church 18c, resting on Doric columns. On it is Brightling's much treasured barrel organ, given by Mad Jack about 1820. It has two barrels, each with twelve tunes of hymns, carols and canticles. It has six stops and a variety of pipes and is considered the best and largest barrel organ in the country; it is still occasionally used. When Fuller gave it, he presented the choirmen with white smocks, buckskin breeches and yellow stockings, and the girls with red cloaks—all very disturbing for the devout. In the N chapel, somewhat hidden by the new organ, are four 17c and 18c cartouches to the Collins family of Socknersh, an early 17c timber-framed house to the NE of the village. There are two small brasses—to a man and his wife, late

Wykehurst, **Bolney**, entrance front

◁ Wykehurst, **Bolney**, south front

15c, and to Thomas Pye (1592) as a child. Mad Jack Fuller is commemorated in the nave by a white tablet with a bust by Henry Rouw.

Brighton [7] is above all else an exciting place. The four reasons for its attraction are its old town—a maze of fascinating lanes—its fantastic palace, the Pavilion—that strange, pseudo-Oriental extravaganza by the normally sedate Nash—the fine series of squares, crescents and terraces of Regency houses, and especially, since they were the cause of Brighton's fame, the marvellously exhilarating air and the sea. Brighton still has, and probably always will have, a feeling of Regency raffishness, and 'a weekend at Brighton' has totally different undertones from a weekend at Hastings, Eastbourne or Bournemouth.

Brighton is also a very ancient place; it is recorded in Domesday Book and the name means Beorhthelm's tun. It was called Brighthelmstone until the early 19c, when the modern abbreviated spelling was adopted, and although it was quite a large fishing village, it was of far less importance than Lewes; the address in the 18c was 'Brighthelmstone near Lewes'. The only dramatic event in its history was the arrival in 1651 of the fugitive Charles II; he spent the night with his friends Lord Wilmot and Col. Gunter at an inn called The George, and set sail the next day in Nicholas Tattersell's boat the *Surprise* from Shoreham. Later in the 17c the sea ravaged Brighthelmstone, and in 1700 the population had sunk to under 1,500, less than half the population in 1580. Then came two great storms which caused unbelievable havoc and reduced the people to such poverty that most of the houses were exempt from rates.

'Mad Jack' Fuller's house, and mausoleum, **Brightling**

Brighton station ▷

Brighton; The Pavilion

The storm of 1703 'stript a great many houses, turned up the lead off the church, overthrew two windmills and laid them flat on the ground, the town in general looking as if it had been bombarded'. Besides being a victim of the sea, Brighthelmstone was difficult of access. The old coach road from London came through Henfield and then over the Downs by Saddlescombe and the Devil's Dyke, a very steep pull for horses; from Lewes the road went up over Newmarket Hill. Only in the late 18c was the road through Falmer built and not until 1810 was the new road from London through Bolney opened. So the beginning of the 18c found Brighthelmstone a forlorn place. But the sea, which had destroyed, brought it a new and unexpected prosperity owing to the fashionable craze for sea-bathing started by Dr Richard Russell of Lewes, who published in 1750 *A Dissertation concerning the Use of Sea Water in Diseases of the Glands*. In 1754 he built himself a house, Russell House, on the site of the Royal Albion Hotel, with gardens leading down to the sea; he died there in 1759, but he had established the fortunes of Brighton on an undreamt-of scale and two other doctors continued his practices. By 1780 a guide book was lyricising 'the salubrity of the air, the excellent quality of the water, the pleasing healthful and convenient situation of the town, its moderate distance from the metropolis, the unrivalled beauty of the circumjacent country and many other advantages both of nature and art contribute to give Brighthelmstone a superiority to the other watering places'. Dr Russell prescribed seawater as beneficial not only for immersion but for drinking; he also had a curious theory that bathing was unwise unless the bather's temperature was as low as that of the water. Fanny Burney describes how at 6 a.m. on a November morning in 1782 she plunged into the ocean

by 'the pale blink of the moon'.

In 1750, the *annus mirabilis* in its history, Brighton consisted of the old town, laid out in a rectangle down to the sea, and, standing apart from it to the NW in a high, commanding position, the parish church of St Nicholas. The site may have been chosen as a landmark for sailors, or perhaps it was a site of pagan sanctity as there are a number of barrows and possibly cromlechs there.

The old town is bounded by East, North and West Streets, and on the S by the sea. There was originally a South Street, but this was destroyed in the great storms of 1703 and 1705, and for a long time after there was no direct connection along the front between East and West Streets. King's Road was opened by George IV in 1822. Within this rectangle is a network of narrow streets, now called the Lanes, and well-known for its antique shops. Although the houses in the Lanes are not older than the 18 and 19c, they represent in design and proportion a medieval town, when streets were pedestrian alleys and the upper floors of houses projected until they nearly met. The narrowness of the Lanes is well illustrated by an incident in the 18c when a well-known athlete was challenged by an old and very fat man to race him with a start of only 10 yards, provided that the challenger could choose the site. He chose Black Lion Lane, a mere slit, and since his vast bulk nearly touched either side of the Lane, his opponent was never able to pass him.

In Black Lion Lane are two houses now called Sea Nest and The Nook, which may be earlier than 18c. The jettied first floor, now hung with slates, probably indicates a 16c origin. The end house is faced with cobbles as are many others in the Lanes. Black Lion Lane emerges into Ship Street, named after the Old Ship Hotel on the front, the oldest licensed house

in Brighton, although the present building is 19c; behind it are the old Assembly Rooms built in 1767. No. 69 Ship Street is one of the few houses faced with knapped flints instead of cobbles, and No. 7 is a good example of an 18c double bow-fronted house; Nos. 7, 9, 62 and 63 all have good doorways. Off Ship Street is a passage named Ship Street Gardens, which opens out into a court containing a large fig tree. In Middle Street the houses are somewhat smaller; Nos. 18 and 19 were probably fishermen's cottages. At the corner of Union Street and Meeting House Lane is the Elim Four Square Tabernacle built by Amon Wilds in 1825 in a semicircular plan; it stands on the site of the earliest nonconformist chapel in Brighton erected in 1683. Between Market Street and East Street is the Town Hall, built in 1830 by Thomas Cooper; grand and ponderous, it was originally designed as a Greek cross, but the S wing was never built. North of Market Street is Brighton Place, a little piazza with some bow-fronted shops, and off it is Brighton Square, a recent insertion, tactful in elevation and style. West of the Town Hall is Prince Albert Street, one of the best-preserved streets in the old town. Adjoining No. 10 is The Cricketers' Arms, originally called The Last and Fish Cart (a Last equals 10,000 fish); it was built in the late 18c, and is unusual in that the premises extend over the whole floor-space of the yard. It is of all buildings in Brighton the most reminiscent of the great coaching days.

To the NW, high on the hill, is the old parish church of St Nicholas, well away from the inroads of the sea and the only building of the medieval town outside the original rectangle. There was a church at the time of Domesday, not necessarily on this site, but the only relic of this date is the magnificent stone font with panels representing the Baptism of Christ, the

p80 Adelaide Crescent, Hove
Brunswick Terrace, Hove
Regency Square, Brighton
Brunswick Terrace, Brighton

p81 Lewes Crescent
Kemp Town

Last Supper and scenes from the life of St Nicholas. The church itself is 14c and has a squat embattled tower with a small flèche; but apart from that only the chancel arch and nave arcades have survived the drastic restoration and enlargement by R. C. Carpenter in 1853. The elaborate crocketed rood screen is late 15c and seems East Anglian in character; the carved and painted rood-loft, rood and candlesticks were added in 1890. The stained glass is by Charles Eamer Kempe (he added the final *e* himself), a cousin of Thomas Read Kemp, who was also responsible for the mural paintings above the chancel and tower arches with excellent foliage designs by Somers Clarke. Banished to the NW corner is the sumptuous Wellington memorial font cover in the form of an Eleanor cross, designed by R. C. Carpenter; the Duke attended a private school in Brighton. There is a wall tablet to Thomas Read Kemp, builder of Kemp Town, and in the floor a tablet to an infant son of the Thrales, who had a house here; Dr Johnson's association with the church is commemorated in the N aisle. In the churchyard are, among memorials, one to Capt Tattersell in whose boat Charles II escaped to France, and another to

Opposite page
Hove: (*top*) The Drive, Second Avenue
(*bottom*) Western Road by Wilds, Third Avenue

This page (*top*) The Drive, Hove by H. B. Measures
(*centre*) All Saints Vicarage, Hove by J. L. Pearson
(*bottom*) New Road, **Brighton**

79

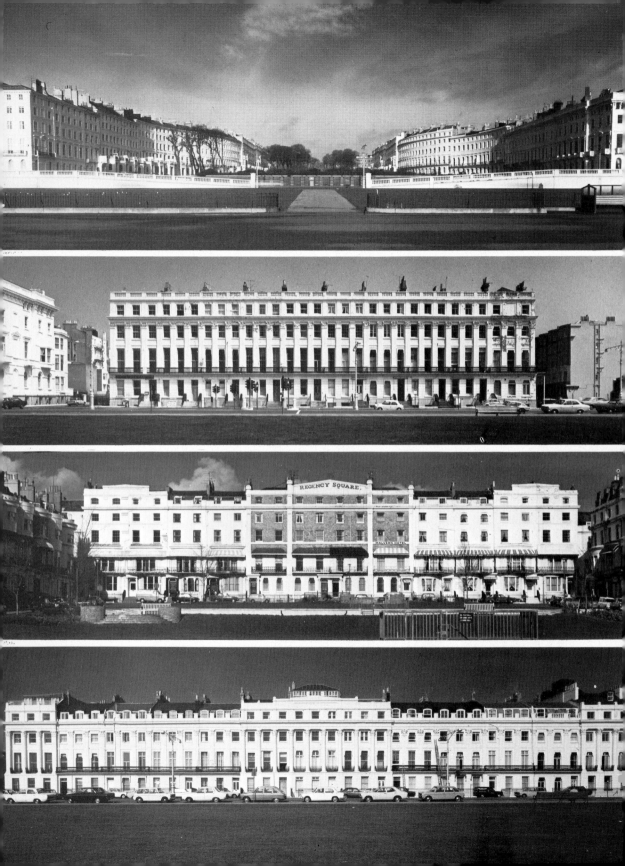

Martha Gunn, a famous character who was one of the original 'dippers' (bathing women), became a favourite of George IV and lived to be 89. At the bottom of the churchyard is a large tomb, adorned with a shell ornament, to Amon Wilds, one of three architects responsible for the finest Regency squares in Brighton and Hove. It was probably designed by his son, Amon Henry Wilds, also an architect, who frequently used shell ornamentation on his houses.

A little E of the old town is the Old Steine (pron. Steen); the name is of Nordic origin and may derive from a sacrificial monolith in the remote past. The Steine was an open common through which flowed the Wellesbourne, a small chalk stream rising at Patcham and entering the sea through the Pool or Valley. The Steine was enclosed in 1793 and the stream encased in a brick underground channel. At the end is the Palace Pier (1898–9), rather gorgeous with a dome and pagodaed roofs, reflecting the style of the Pavilion. Around the Steine were built the elegant houses of Regency Brighton. Most important of these is Marlborough House (No. 54) built originally for the 4th Duke of Marlborough; he sold it in 1786 to William Gerald Hamilton, M.P., who employed Robert Adam to build the present house. The inside has fine Adam chimneypieces and ceiling; the house is now used as Education Offices. Next to it is Steine House, long the home of Mrs Fitzherbert, and built for her in 1804 by William Porden. She always stayed here when the Prince of Wales came to Brighton; she never slept at the Pavilion. Some years ago her marriage certificate to the Prince was discovered, proving beyond doubt what had hitherto been conjecture.

But the most famous and arresting building in Brighton is, of course, Prinny's Pleasure Dome, the Royal Pavilion. The first house built on the site for George IV,

when Prince of Wales, was designed by Henry Holland in 1786. It was a simple classical building with a curved projection in the centre, fronted by six Ionic columns. It was called the Marine Pavilion, a name which has survived all its transformations. In 1801 the house was enlarged and given its first Chinese interior; about the same time the Prince commissioned William Porden to build the Stables and Riding House, now the Dome and the Corn Exchange. Porden's use of a Hindu style for the stables gave the Prince the idea of orientalising the outside of the house itself. Several architects submitted designs, including Repton, who laid out the grounds at Sezincote, the prototype for the Pavilion. But Nash's design was chosen, and between 1815 and 1820 he gave the house its Hindu exterior, while the inside was refurbished with elaborate Chinese decoration. It was not admired at the time. William Cobbett described it as 'a parcel of "cradle spits" of various dimensions sticking up out of the mouths of so many enormous squat decanters', and Sydney Smith declared that 'the dome of St Paul's must have come down to Brighton and pupped'. Basically the Pavilion is still Henry Holland's house; the bow-fronted central saloon has a trellised oriental veranda, replacing Holland's Ionic portico. The great dome above it contains five rooms, originally bedrooms for the court entourage. The gaiety and gorgeousness of Nash's internal decor has to be seen to be believed. It is remarkable that the Pavilion survived the Victorian age, associated as it was with a dissolute and far from exemplary monarch. However, survive it did, tolerated as an oddity; it became dirty and ill-kempt, and much of the original furniture disappeared. It was not until the 1930s that Brighton realised that the Pavilion was not only a remarkable building, but a potential money-spinner. It has been

p84 (*left*) St Peter's, Brighton ▷ by Sir Charles Barry
(*right*) St Paul's **Brighton** by R. C. Carpenter

p85 St Bartholomew's Brighton by Edmund Scott

tastefully and carefully restored; the beautiful wallpaper of bamboo on a pink ground was so heavily coated with varnish that it was a dingy brown. When its original colour was discovered, new wallpaper of the exact design was made. Some pieces of furniture, known from marks to have been made for the Pavilion, were discovered in antique shops and bought back. Rex Whistler celebrated its renaissance by painting a large allegorical picture of George IV in the almost-nude awaking the spirit of Brighton, which the Corporation had the wisdom and humour to place in the Pavilion.

By 1800 Brighton had become a considerable place and the old church of St Nicholas was no longer adequate. In the course of 70 years 11 new churches of architectural importance were built. The first was the Unitarian Church in New Road near the Theatre Royal, which has a fine Doric portico, designed by Amon Henry Wilds in 1820. St Peter's (1824–8) which became the parish church in 1873, stands on an island site just N of Valley Gardens. Designed by Sir Charles Barry, the tower and nave are of Portland stone, which gleams in the sunlight; it is a highly successful design and is one of the finest churches in England built during the early stages of the Gothic revival. The chancel was added in 1896–1902 by Somers Clarke and most unfortunately is not in Portland stone. There are two other churches of 1824: St Margaret's, built as a chapel-of-ease for Regency Square by a jack-of-all-trades, Barnard Gregory, and called after his wife, Margaret, and St George's, Kemp Town, by

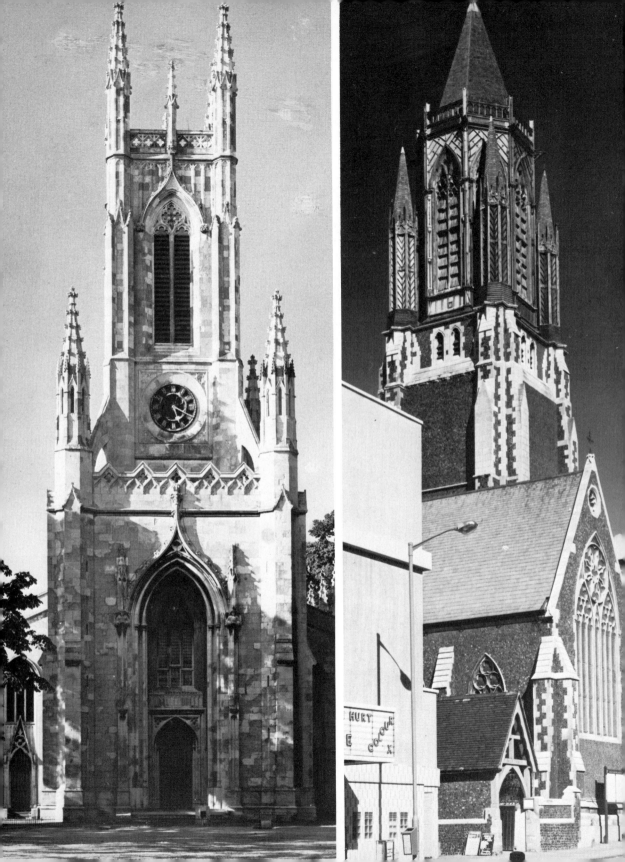

Charles Augustus Busby; both churches have contemporary galleries. The Roman Catholic church of St John the Baptist, Bristol Road, (1835), on the site of an earlier church, contains Mrs Fitzherbert's tomb designed by Carew; it shows her kneeling, with three wedding-rings on her left hand, the last being her marriage to the Prince of Wales. St Paul's, West Street, designed by R. C. Carpenter in 1846–8 has a wooden lantern surmounting the spire, which is one of the chief landmarks in Brighton; it has stained glass by Pugin and an altar-piece painted by Burne-Jones. In 1850 when the Pavilion was sold by the Crown to Brighton Corporation, the Church authorities claimed the Royal Chapel and bought it for £3,000. It was built in 1766 by John Crunden as the ballroom for the Castle Hotel; when George IV bought and demolished the hotel in 1822, he converted the ballroom into a chapel for the Pavilion. In 1850 it was taken down and re-erected as St Stephen's Church in Montpelier Place. It is no longer a parish church but is used by the Deaf and Dumb Institute. Not far from it in Montpelier Villas is the Gothic revival church of St Michael and All Angels; the first church, which is now the S aisle, was designed by G. F. Bodley (1860), but the larger northern section by William Burges was built in 1895 after his death. The two do not harmonise with each other; but the church has some good stained glass by Dante Gabriel Rossetti and William Morris. St Bartholomew's, Ann Street, (1874) by Edmund Scott, badly sited just W of the London Road, is a remarkable and impressive building. It is incomplete, since it was intended to have an apsidal chancel with two bays and transepts; but its great height and majestic brick arcades with a dazzling gilded reredos by H. Wilson give it a cathedral-like splendour. The Chapel Royal in North Street was rebuilt by Sir Arthur Blomfield in 1877–82 on the site of the previous chapel built in 1793–5. The Prince of Wales refused to attend services there after hearing a too outspoken remark from the pulpit; it was then that he converted the Castle Hotel ballroom and transferred his worship to it.

The development E of the Old Steine, originally called the East Cliff, but now all known as Kemp Town, began about 1800. New Steine was built about 1810 and has doorways arranged in pairs with the unusual design of a joint tympanum of blocked fanlight over each pair. Charlotte Street has some good bow-fronted houses, and Royal Crescent built between 1799 and 1807 by a West Indian speculator, J. B. Otto, has houses faced with black mathematical tiles (see Patcham Place) which give a particularly smart appearance and are a feature of seaside architecture. Beyond it, Marine Square by Attree 1824 and Portland Place 1830, the last work of Charles Augustus Busby, remain as they were and this is the best-preserved part of Brighton's sea front. At the extreme E end are the squares and terraces built for Thomas Read Kemp, one of the joint lords of the manor of Brighton, whose tomb in St Nicholas's churchyard has already been mentioned. He chose Amon Wilds and John Busby for his architects, and they planned the magnificent area of Sussex Square, Lewes Crescent, Arundel Terrace and Chichester Terrace. This was the original Kemp Town and there were then no buildings between it and Royal Crescent. The design was almost certainly inspired by Nash's Regent's Park. The chief builder employed was Thomas Cubitt, who built Belgravia; but the interiors of the houses were completed by each owner to his own taste and many of them were not finished until 20 or 30 years after the completion of the façades. The garden enclosure was laid out for Kemp by a local botanist, Henry Phillips; this was connected by a tunnel with a series of private slopes and esplanades built by the proprietors at their own expense. These have now been taken over by the Corporation, and are the only part of the sea front which has remained as originally designed in 1830. The Marina, now in course of construction, may alter the whole character of Kemp Town.

The extension W of the old town is equally dramatic in a different way, the sea front being dominated by the Grand and Metropole Hotels. There are also two good squares; Regency Square, designed probably by Amon Wilds, has houses with hooded bow windows, and Bedford Square has an untouched group in the NE corner, though many houses have been spoilt by alteration. Beyond Bedford Square the statue of King Edward VII marks the boundary between Brighton and Hove.

The West Pier (1863–6) is earlier and plainer than the Palace Pier; it was threatened with demolition but has recently (1977) been reprieved.

Brighton is exhilarating, elegant and gay, and fully deserves the title first given to it by Horace Smith, poet and novelist, who lived in Hanover Crescent from 1826 to 1840, 'Queen of Watering Places'.

Hove [7] although for long a separate borough, is so much a continuation of Brighton that it must be considered with it; there is no perceptible division between the two towns. Hove was once a fishing village, though smaller than Brighthelmstone; but nothing of it remains except the name of Hove Street and the old parish church of St Andrew, which stands unhappily beside a gasometer. It fell into ruin in the 18c and was rebuilt by George Basevi in 1836; there are two Transitional–Norman arcades and original oak tie-beams in the roof. There are two more recent

Altarpiece by Henry Wilson, St. Bartholomew's, **Brighton**

churches, St Andrew's, Waterloo Street, 1827 by Sir Charles Barry, extended in 1882 by his son, and All Saints' by J. L. Pearson, built in 1889–91, which then became the parish church. The style is EE Dec and it is a stately and extremely successful building, though it really needs a tower. Most of the streets and avenues of Hove were built from 1850 and are lacking in distinction. But Brunswick Square and Brunswick Terrace, designed by Wilds and Busby in 1826, are together the most complete and beautiful architectural unit after Kemp Town. The Terrace in particular is a fine piece of scenic architecture in the Carlton House Terrace manner. Adjoining Brunswick Terrace is a modern block of flats, Embassy Court, within Brighton, by Wells Coates, a pioneer of modern architecture. It is, however, an egregious example of bad manners and bad planning.

Broomhill [Inset] the last parish in Sussex, is beyond Camber. It had a church, marked on Thomas Stonham's map of 1599; but it has long since disappeared, and the place today is represented only by Broomhill Farm—apart from a continuation of Camber's shacks and shanties.

Bulverhythe [9] A melodious name for an ancient port between St Leonard's and Bexhill; in medieval times it was a non-corporate member of the Cinque Ports, the only one which can be located. Until 1935 there was only marshland with no building but the Bull Inn, 18c or earlier, which is now modernised almost out of recognition and surrounded by maritime suburbia. Behind it are the fragmentary ruins of St Mary's chapel, which ceased to be a place of worship in 1372.

Burgess Hill* [4] like Haywards Heath and Hassocks, is a railway town. It has a red-brick church of St John built by T. Talbot Bury in 1863 and was formerly called St John's Common. The name of Burgeshill is mentioned in 1524 and in 1605 Thomas Alderton, gentleman, forfeited 1½ yardlands called Burgeshill for the murder of his wife. It doesn't sound a heavy punishment.

Burwash [5] The long and well-kept street—brick paths, mown grass plots and pollarded limes—has some striking houses, evidence of prosperity in the 17c. The best is Rampyndene (1699), a large, square, brick and tile-hung house, built by John Butler, a timber merchant. The N front is very well-proportioned and has an elaborate entrance with brackets carrying a hood with a plasterwork design of a cherub, doves and flowers; there is plasterwork inside and a fine staircase. The White House is early 18c with an ashlar front and wood cornice; its doorway is flanked by Roman Doric pilasters supporting a cornice and hood with acanthus brackets. Other houses worth noticing are Sones Cottage, 15c, Burghurst, 18c brick, and the Mount House, 16c and 17c. The Davenport Pharmacy is a nice early Victorian house with black columns flanking the entrance, and Old Rectory Court is a sensitive piece of recent in-filling—brick with white weatherboarding. The church at the E end of the street has a 12c tower with a broach shingled spire, and nave arcades of the 12c and 13c. The chancel and aisles were rebuilt in 1856, but in such faithful imitation that it is barely noticeable; the nave roof has tie-beams and king-posts. On the wall in the S chapel is a 14c iron tomb slab with a floriated cross to John Colins, the earliest in the country, also a small brass (1440) to a standing civilian. There are two black marble tomb slabs, 1686 and 1716, with coats of arms, both to Anthony Cruttenden, father and son. Against the W wall is a cartouche to John Cason (1675) with a gaily coloured coat of arms. The 15c font has the Pelham buckle. Two tombs in the churchyard have Harmer terracotta plaques—the usual basket of fruit and flowers. Batemans, south of the village, built in 1634 by John Brittan, an ironmaster, was the home of Rudyard Kipling. It is built of coursed ashlar and has some fine brick chimney stacks; it now belongs to the National Trust. Holmshurst (1610) is another house, built of brick with stone dressings.

The old spelling of the place was Burghersh, the courtesy title of Lord Westmoreland's eldest son.

Burwash Common [5] straggles along the ridge between Heathfield and Burwash. The church is by Slater and Carpenter 1867. Solid, sensible and successful, it is EE and has nave, two aisles and an apsidal chancel. The aisles have eight lancets on the N, six on the S and the clear glass admits plenty of light. The three-bay arcades, N and S, have round granite piers contrasting with the sandstone of the pointed arches. The chancel has a rib-vaulted roof and the nave a waggon roof.

Buxted [5] is on two hills—mostly Victorian villas round the station to the E; in the valley the Georgian White Hart, a former mill and a few older cottages, and on the western hill Buxted Park. By the entrance is Hogge House, once the home of Ralph Hogge, who made the first iron cannons; the rebus of a hog on the N wall is dated 1581. Some way down the drive through a lime avenue is the church, dedicated unusually to St Margaret, Queen of Scotland, (1045–93). The living was given by Caedwalla (see South Malling) to the Archbishop of Canterbury, who is still the patron. The battlemented porch has gargoyles and as label-stops rather weather-worn angels holding shields. The tower is 13c and has a short

Camber Castle

shingled spire. The nave has four-bay EE arcades, the S earlier than the N; the 17c clerestory has rectangular windows with glazing bars. There is a barrel roof with tiebeams, and five hatchments over the tower arch. The chancel is early 14c; but over the barrel roof is an elegant plaster ceiling, 17c with a design of hops and stylised marguerites. It is said to have been given by the rector in gratitude for an exceptionally good crop of hops on the glebe. The altar rails are also Laudian, 17c. The chancel is stone-floored and the rector's desk has fleur-de-lys poppy-heads. Other features: a Jacobean pulpit with a

marguerite motif, and two brass candelabra in the sanctuary and N transept. There are two small brasses to priests: on the floor, Britellus Avenel, late 14c and under glass, Deonicius Slon (1485)—each a demi-figure; also a tablet (1796) to George Medley by Regnart. The high, but short, vestment chest (1260) has well-carved details and is one of the earliest surviving. Buxted Park was an early Georgian house, but was burnt in 1940. The last private owner, Mr Basil Ionides, imported a number of Georgian features from London houses and elsewhere; it is therefore somewhat of a hotch-potch.

Cade Street [5] *see* **Heathfield**

Camber [Inset] The trippers and holidaymakers who pour through Rye in the summer months are mostly bound for Camber Sands, a range of sand dunes stretching eastwards from the Rother estuary. At low tide the sea goes out for half a mile and at all times Camber is a paddler's paradise. The place itself, apart from Camber Farm, is a haphazard collection of bungalows, shacks and shanties built mostly in the last 50 years. The Camber was the name given from early times to the estuary running past Old Winchelsea to Rye. Camber Castle is on

the W of the Rother, out on the levels between Rye Harbour and Winchelsea; it can only be reached on foot. It was one of five polygonal blockhouses built by Henry VIII in 1538 for the defence of the SE coast and was celebrated by Paul Nash in several beautiful water-colours. It seems badly sited for defence, but the sea was presumably nearer then than now. The others are all in Kent: Sandown, Deal, Walmer and Sandgate. The plan is an octagon with a semi-circular bastion at each angle, and a central tower, which may be 20 years earlier than the rest. It has a string-course halfway up decorated with carved animal heads, shields, fleurs-de-lys and Tudor roses. Round the tower is an unusual vaulted passage with four radiating arms.

Catsfield [6] In the centre of the village is what appears to be a Victorian EE church with a stone spire; but this is in fact the Methodist church, built by Blackman in 1912, and is not Victorian at all. The parish church lies S of the village perched on a bank beside the lane. Rough herring-bone work in the S wall shows its Norman origin, and it has a solid W tower (1200) with a short shingled broach spire. The inside suffered much from the restoration of 1849, when Carpenter added the N aisle, wrecked the EE chancel and widened and ruined the chancel arch. The 14c windows in the S wall of the nave have four panels of Victorian glass commemorating the Revd Burrell Hayley, rector for 37 years. The nave roof has moulded tie-beams and king-posts. Above the tower arch is a monument to John Fuller by Nollekens 1810. Against the wall of the N aisle, but completely obscured by the organ, is a trefoiled recess containing a gravestone with a floriated cross in relief, which may be that of a monk from Battle Abbey. In the churchyard is a tomb with a terracotta plaque by Harmer. Catsfield Manor, next to

the church, is a square, brick 18c house, tile-hung on one side.

Chailey [4] is a large parish with three villages: North Common, Chailey and South Common: North Common, high, breezy and gorse-clad, has a modern village with a church built in 1876 in EE style by J. Oldrid Scott. It has a curious saddle-backed tower between the nave and chancel, and though the outside is somewhat ponderous and unattractive, the inside is well-proportioned and the golden sandstone of the arcades, lancets and two tower arches is extremely pleasing. Two well-known landmarks are the windmill, restored but no longer working, and the chapel spire of the Heritage Craft Schools for Crippled Children. The chapel was built in 1913, and designed by Sir Ninian Comper. The architecture is restrained, but the decoration inside has a richness and splendour typical of Comper's work. The fine panelled ceiling is painted in blue and gold with heraldic bosses and carved angels on the cornices, and the reredos, added later, is in burnished gold and various colours. The rood-loft and screen are Perp. The chapel is full of stained-glass windows, all connected with people who helped to build the Heritage; the Nunc Dimittis window is by Comper.

South Common is a straggling and rather more attractive village, but the common has long been enclosed. Chailey, or Chailey Green as it is sometimes called, consists of a group of brick-and-tile cottages gathered round a green with a large cedar. Behind it is the 13c church with a tower and pyramidal shingled spire. The nave was modernised during the enlargement in 1878; but the chancel is EE. It has three recessed lancets on either side with slender shafts and foliated capitals, and a triple lancet E window. There is a Victorian Royal Arms.

Chailey Moat, formerly the rectory, originates from the 16c, but is externally 18c brickwork; the moat is said to have been dug by a rector. Wapsbourne is a 17c house in timber-framing and brick with some clusters of brick chimneys.

Chalvington [8] Lord Sackville held the manor here in 1346. The small church of nave and chancel, late 13c is approached by a brick path and stands just above the Glynde Levels with a fine view southwards to Firle Beacon. It has a little wooden turret with a short shingled spire springing from the roof, and is built of flint with stone quoins. The Dec E window was added later and was the gift of Thomas Diliwyt, rector from 1388 to 1409, as shown in the fragments of old glass. The nave has paired windows on each side; the SE window has human heads as stops on the outside. The NE window has late 13c glass in the head; it shows the demi-figure of an archbishop with a nimbus and his right hand raised in blessing. The inscription is S.TH/OM/AS, and it is thought to be of St Thomas à Becket. The chancel roof has a tie-beam with a long thin king-post (cf. Ripe) and the nave has tie- and collar-beams with arched braces. There is a hatchment at the W end.

Chiddingly [5] (pronounced -lye). The church stands on a slight eminence and has a fine view southwards to the Downs and on a clear day to the Long Man of Wilmington. Its outstanding external feature is the stone spire 130 ft high, springing from a Perp tower with polygonal pinnacles at the corners; it is one of the only three in Sussex (*see* Dallington and Northiam). The W door has Pelham buckles as label-stops and defaced shields in the spandrels. The chancel was rebuilt in 1864, when remains of Norman masonry were found; but the rest of the church is EE with later additions. It is built of local sandstone. The nave has two 14c arcades of three bays. On the S side is a transept containing a massive monument to the Jefferay family 1612; one above the other lie Sir John Jefferay, Baron of the Exchequer to Elizabeth I, propped on his elbow, and his wife, recumbent, with a daughter kneeling beneath. But Sir John and his wife are overshadowed by the much larger standing figures of their daughter, Lady Montague, and her husband, Sir Edward Montague; he wears crinkled robes, she a vast farthingale. At the foot of the monument are three large carved shields bearing the arms of Jefferay and Montague, which must have surmounted it. According to tradition this damage was done as an act of anti-papist feeling, because it was believed there was a connection with Judge Jeffreys, notorious for the Bloody Assize. On the E wall of the transept are the Royal Arms of George IV. On the S wall of the aisle is a much smaller monument to William Jefferay and his wife (1611), who kneel facing each other, flanked by their sons and daughters. On the floor of the centre aisle there is a black letter brass inscription to an earlier Jefferay (1512) and on the N wall of the chancel a tablet to Margaret Jefferay (1618) with the macabre device of a skull in an urn and the inscription 'Margarita fui'. On the S wall of the chancel is an architectural tablet to John Bromfield (1735), whose hatchment hangs above it. The nave is furnished with deal box-pews and has an 18c pulpit with sounding board. The E window in the N aisle has some glass 1877 showing SS John Baptist and Evangelist attributed to Powell.

All that remains of Chiddingly Place, the Tudor mansion of the Jefferays, lies ¼ mile to the W. It is now a small, square farmhouse and has two transomed windows on the N front with depressed arched lights and some unusual classical ornamentation; at right angles to the house and formerly no doubt a wing, is a handsome brick barn with some blocked windows and fireplaces. Drawings by Grimm made in 1780, show much more, but record the curious architectural mixture that still survives.

Stonehill House, 1½ miles NE, is a well-restored 15c timber-framed house; the oversailing upper floor and the curved braces supporting the eaves are a typical wealden arrangement. Peke's House, 1¼ miles SE, has an Elizabethan stone porch with caryatids. Inside there is a room with wall paintings of 1572.

Chiltington, East [4] is just N of the Downs on the same sandstone ridge as Streat. It is a scattered place with no real village. The church is remote, charmingly situated with a southward view towards Blackcap. It is of 12c origin, built of sandstone and rubble, and has the usual capped tower added about 1200; the two surviving Norman features are a small window in the S wall of the nave and a blocked-up N door. The nave roof has three very roughly hewn tie-beams with curved braces and there is one in the chancel. The simple pulpit has 1719 carved on the front panel. The chancel was added in the 14c and over the arch are 18c Commandment Boards. In the churchyard is an ancient yew, possibly as old as the church and certainly much older than any of the gravestones, since until 1909 it was a chapel-of-ease to Westmeston and all burials took place there. Chapel Farm, close by the church, is 16c and the relic of a far larger house that stood on the site. An account of an early, 19c service is given in Marcus Woodward's *Mistress of Stanton's Farm*, the farm just to the S. The choir sat in the gallery, the squire and family in a wide, cushioned pew with a stove, and wine and biscuits available on a table. After an hour-long sermon they repaired to Stanton's Farm for refreshments. Exhausted, no doubt.

Clayton* [4] Two windmills on the Downs above the village, known locally as Jack and Jill, are well-known landmarks; one is a tower mill, the other a smock mill, but neither works any more. Clayton also gives its name to a long tunnel on the Brighton railway line. The village at the foot of the Downs is very small, only a few cottages and the church, a small, hump-backed building of 11c origin with a western bell-cote, roofs of tiles and Horsham slabs and walls of a rough, uneven texture. Inside there is a Saxon or early Norman chancel arch with bold half-round moulding and massive chamfered imposts. The nave too is Norman with a round-headed N door; its roof has three bays of 15c framing, the trusses having plain heavy tie-beams and king-posts with curved braces. In the chancel is a brass showing a priest in mass vestments holding a chalice and wafer, and inscribed (in 16c spelling) 'Of your charity pray for the soul of Richard Idon, parson of Clayton and Pyecombe ... 1523'. The church was restored in 1893, but by a great stroke of luck the walls, unlike Plumpton and Westmeston, were apparently untouched. Two years later Kempe discovered the remarkable series of wall paintings. Professor Talbot Rice (*Oxford History of English Art*) dates them about 1080; Dr Audrey Baker also considers them earlier than 12c. The monks of Lewes Priory were incumbents of the parish from early in the 12c, but Sir Nikolaus Pevsner considers they are not Cluniac in style. Above the chancel arch is Christ in judgement flanked by worshipping saints and below on either side another richly vested figure of Christ and a kneeling figure, probably St Peter, receiving the keys of heaven and hell. On the S wall are angels, a large red cross with several saints, four priests and

The Jefferay monument, **Chiddingly** ▷

a number of other persons. On the N wall is a hexagonal enclosure with nimbed figures of the Holy Trinity, E of it a large angel and W of it St Peter. West of him again is another angel facing three priests and then a procession of figures and an angel blowing a trumpet. The paintings have recently been restored. The church has been reseated with very decent and simple oak pews. Hammond's Place, near Burgess Hill and visible from the road, is a 16c house, originally timber-framed, but later faced with red brick. It has stone mullioned windows and a Horsham slabbed roof.

Cliffe *see* **Lewes**

Coleman's Hatch [1] is a rather scattered place with a well-placed church by Sir A. Blomfield built in 1913. It is in EE style and has a crocketed stone spire and a five-sided baptistery projecting from the W end. Inside it is dignified and spacious—altogether a success.

Crowborough [2] is in a glorious position on the highlands of Ashdown Forest; but it is a place of no charm or interest. The oldest building seems to be the church of All Saints, built in 1744 but calamitously enlarged in 1881; only the 18c tower remains untouched. The vicarage built at the same time is a fine ashlar-faced Georgian house. Writing in 1903 E. V. Lucas saw a placard advertising the neighbourhood as 'Scotland in Sussex'. He goes on 'Crowborough has shops that would not disgrace Croydon and an hotel where a Lord Mayor might feel at home. Houses in their own grounds are commoner here than cottages, and near the summit the pegs of surveyors and the nameboards of avenues yet to be built testify to the charms which our Saxon Caledonia has already exerted.' There may not be as many pegs and name-boards today; but the description holds good—only more so.

Crowhurst [9] A small village in a sheltered valley N of Bexhill. The church has an early 15c tower with a Perp W window; the W door has the Pelham buckle as label-stops. But the rest of the church was pulled down in 1856 and rebuilt in late 13c style—adequate, but uninspired. In the churchyard is the largest yew in Sussex—37½ ft in circumference. S of the church are the ruins of the old manor house built about 1360 by John, Earl of Richmond; the E gable with remains of a large window still stands. Hye House, a little to the S, is a brick Georgian house 1744. There is a viaduct on the now disused Crowhurst to Bexhill branch line.

Cuckfield* [4] (pronounced Cookfield) The village sign near Whiteman's Green shows a cuckoo; but cuckoo may be a French word and the likely but more prosaic meaning is a field of couch grass (*OED of Place Names*). Cuckfield used to be a market town; the original charter to hold a weekly market was granted by Henry III, and a new charter, displayed in the church tower, was given by Charles II in order to raise money. The market was held until 1868, when it was transferred to Haywards Heath station. During the last 40 years the place has become suburbanised on the N and E where it approaches, but is not yet joined on to, Haywards Heath. But the south-western approach up the hill, with Cuckfield Park on the left, is unspoilt and the street begins suddenly with the tapering spire of the church to the right. Noticeable houses are the King's Head, a pillared Georgian coaching inn, the grocery stores—a substantial house with a Horsham-slabbed roof—and the old vicarage, another Georgian house standing slightly back. Further up on the right used to be the Talbot Hotel, another coaching inn; the brick upper storey is unchanged, but the ground floor is a terrace of shops. Further up still is

Marshalls, an upstanding house with 17c brick chimneys and an ashlar Georgian front. Viewed from the N it is still a very pretty street, and there are clearly 18c shops. In its Georgian heyday Cuckfield had a regular coach service; in 1780 the 'Brighthelmston and Cuckfield Machine' left London at 5 a.m. on three days a week, and the fare to Cuckfield was 10s 6d. In 1804 Cuckfield provided 50 pairs of horses for private posting and by 1828 50 coaches a day were passing through; many travellers spent the night at the King's Head or the Talbot. The Talbot had assemblies every other week and petty sessions were held in the ballroom. When it was proposed to bring the London–Brighton line through Cuckfield, the local landowners held a protest meeting at the Talbot, as a result of which the line made a detour through the heath now called Haywards Heath. At the S end of the high street is the large church with a panoramic view of the Downs. Richard de la Wych, Bishop of Chichester, encouraged the building of a stone church in the late 13c and the battlemented W tower and three of the S arcades belong to this date; from the tower rises a tall shingled spire, one of the best in Sussex and the roofs, N and S, have fine sweeps of Horsham slabs. The rest of the church is mainly 14c, including the N arcade, one bay on the S and the aisle windows. In the 15c the waggon roofs with tie-beams resting on traceried spandrels were put in; the clerestory windows were blocked up, but were rediscovered in 1925, though no longer admitting light. At the intersection of the ribs on the roof are bosses of the Nevill family, and the areas between were elaborately painted by Kempe in 1886. At the restoration the box-pews, Commandment Boards and Royal Arms were thrown out. The Boards were found blocking up the louvres of the tower a few years ago and the George III Royal Arms re-

Cuckfield

a Sergison. An avenue of limes leads up to the house, one of which was supposed to drop a branch whenever a Sergison heir was about to die. The local legend is that a Sergison set his hounds upon a witch, who uttered a curse as she died. In front of the house is a charming late 16c brick gatehouse with angle turrets. The E front is also brick but was covered in stucco in the 19c, when the S range was added. The N range has fine twisted chimney stacks. Ockenden Manor belongs to the Burrells of West Grinstead (West Sussex) and was built by Walter Burrell, another ironmaster, in 1658; it is partly timber-framed and partly stone, and is now an hotel. Borde Hill, in a valley to the NE, takes its name from the Borde family, and was built in the 16c. About 70 years ago it was bought by Col. Stephenson Clarke, who added to it and made a distinguished garden, in which he collected many rare plants and shrubs; the gardens are often open to the public.

Cuckmere Haven [8] (pronounced Cookmere) is the only river-mouth in Sussex which has never had a harbour town. The Cuckmere after a serpentine course below Alfriston, which is best seen from the Eastbourne road, enters the sea surreptitiously through banks of shingle. Perhaps on this account or because of its tortuosity it could never have had a port, and in any case the Cuckmere is a very small river. Exceat Bridge and Exceat Farm preserve the name of a long extinct Saxon village. Exceat, or Essetes, was a more important place than West Dean in the 12c and had fishing rights off the coast. The foundations of Exceat church were discovered in 1913 by the son of the rector of West Dean, and a block of Portland stone on the E side of Cuckmere Haven marks the site; it ceased to exist as a building over 500 years ago and in 1460 there were only two houses

moved from the village hall; both are now back in the church. The fine rood screen is by Bodley and the pulpit by Kempe, who also designed windows in the N aisle. High up in the chancel is a helm and banner staves of the Hendleys. In the Lady Chapel is a wall monument to Henry Bowyer 1589 with kneeling figures. There are also two memorials of 1628—to Guy Carleton, a slate plate with allegorical devices attributed to Epiphanius Evesham, and to Ninian Burrell, a small young man kneeling. In the sanctuary the white figure of Truth gazes into a mirror and sits on a grey sarcophagus; it commemorates Charles Sergison 1732 and

is by Thomas Adye. The Flaxman tablet to Sir William Burrell is unspecial; better are two later tablets to Mary Sergison 1804 by Westmacott and to Percy Burrell 1810 by John Bacon Junr. N of the church is the old grammar school, a two-storey stone building of 1632 with mullioned and transomed windows and a Horsham-slabbed roof. Cuckfield Park was built by Henry Bowyer, an ironmaster, in 1574; it passed through his daughter to his grandson, Walter Hendley, whose daughter sold it to Charles Sergison in 1691. The estate remained with the Sergisons until recent years, the last owner being the present Lord Brookeborough, whose mother was

in Exceat. Perhaps a combination of the Black Death and exposure to the French raids destroyed it.

Dallington [5] is a small village on the wealden ridge. In the iron-smelting days Dallington Forest produced fuel for the furnaces; but it exists no more. The cottages are mostly brick-and-tile, 18c, but next to the church is an earlier timber-framed cottage, a good example. The church is interesting chiefly for its short stone spire, springing from a battlemented 15c tower; the only other stone spires are at Northiam and Chiddingly. The rest of the church was rebuilt in 1864; the N arcade has big, coarse leaf capitals. In the chancel is an oil painting, *The Adoration of the Holy Family*, attributed to Andrea del Sarto. There is a Perp W window and an octagonal font with shield motifs.

Danehill [4] a misleading name, since it has nothing to do with the Danes. A small village, standing high with a handsome and well-placed sandstone church in Dec style by Bodley and Garner, built in 1892 to replace a chapel. The S door is approached by an avenue of pleached limes, and, without and within, the church has an atmosphere of solid prosperity. The embattled tower has a Sussex cap and the roofs are covered with Horsham slabs. Inside, there is a gaily painted ribbed and bossed ceiling, a reredos by Comper and a fine rood screen with a small organ perched centrally upon it. All the windows are by Kempe.

Dean, East [8] Although there is a suburban outcrop along the main Eastbourne road, East Dean remains a charming village of flint-built cottages grouped around a green. The churchyard is entered by a tapsell gate as at Friston. The earliest part of the church is the tower, which is late Saxon and in three stages; its walls are 3 ft thick. The nave is 11c, but square-headed

Perp windows were inserted in the 15c; it has a 15c oak roof with tie-beams and moulded king-posts. The chancel is very noticeably askew with the nave. On each side are twin blocked-up windows; those on the S are round-headed 12c. The chancel arch was rebuilt in 1887, when the church was restored. The basket-work font is mostly a skilful 1870 reproduction, but a fragment of the medieval font, similar to one at St Anne's, Lewes, is included in it. The church has recently been extended westwards to accommodate a growing congregation; the extension has been built in flints and has been so tastefully done that it is externally hardly noticeable. There is a handsome pulpit with sounding board dated 1623.

The road S from East Dean leads to Birling Gap, the only point of access to the sea between Cuckmere Haven and Beachy Head.

Dean, West [8] lies at the end of a long wooded combe near Cuckmere Haven. It is thought by many authorities to be the 'Dene' where King Alfred met the Saxon historian Asser. Alfred certainly had a royal residence here and he could hardly have chosen a more enchanting place, one which has changed little in a thousand years. The small aisleless church has a gabled tower, unique in Sussex, with a shingled 'bonnet' rather than cap. The fine Norman arch under the tower and two small windows in the nave and chancel are 11c. The other windows are 14c. On the N wall of the chancel are two tomb canopies, one more elaborate than the other; these are almost certainly those of Sir John Heringod, lord of the manor, and his wife, Isabella. Sir John would have welcomed Edward I when on 25 June 1305 he rode over to West Dean from Lewes. Against the S wall is a handsome alabaster tomb with kneeling figures of William Thomas (d. 1639) and his wife, Anne. Another smaller 17c monument is to his daughter Susanna

Tirrey; on either side is a cherub, one holding a spade, the other what appears to be a whip. William Thomas was a wealthy man from Lewes, who bought the manor of West Dean in 1611. In the nave are two modern busts of unusual distinction, one of the first Lord Waverley by Epstein and the other of Sir Oswald Birley by Clare Sheridan. The old rectory next to the church used to be the oldest inhabited rectory in the country; it is still inhabited, but not by the rector. The house dates from 1220 and is built of flint and brick with walls 2 ft 6 in thick; they still contain the old oak shutters, which closed the lancet windows before the clergy could afford glass. Opposite the rectory are the ruins of the manor house, which may stand on the site of Alfred the Great's palace. There is a flint-built dovecote. Charleston Manor, in a neighbouring combe, is an ancient house mostly 16c and 18c, but incorporating the relic of a 12c hall house with a two-light window, a rare example of Norman domestic architecture; it was formerly known as Alured's chapel. Charleston was for many years a farmhouse, but was bought and carefully restored by W. H. Godfrey for Sir Oswald Birley, whose widow still lives there. The gardens, designed by Godfrey, are beautifully laid out; on the N side of the lawn is a long barn with a steeply pitched tiled roof, on the S rising terraces of low yew hedges. Around are flint walls covered with clematis, climbing roses, magnolias and other well-chosen shrubs. There is a flint dove-cote with a conical tiled roof, which, unlike most, is inhabited by white doves.

Denton [7] is almost opposite Newhaven. The small manor house, two flint cottages near the church and The Flying Fish Inn are all that survive of the village, which has become engulfed by suburbia. The small aisleless church is of flint and has a weatherboarded bell turret roofed with Victorian tiles. Inside, the oldest feature is the Norman tub-shaped font with a basketwork design, similar to that at St Anne's Lewes and the refashioned font at East Dean. The church is mostly Early English but the E window with Dec tracery, the sedile and the ogee-headed piscina were inserted in the 14c; the E window has glass by Kempe (1897). There is no chancel arch. The nave roof has tie-beams, king-posts and rafters, revealed after a ceiling was removed at the restoration. In the garden of the old vicarage, W of the church, are the ruins of the Priest's House (1280).

Dicker [8] The Dicker, once known as Dyker Waste, has two villages—Upper and Lower. Upper Dicker is round a cross-roads, dominated by a large house formerly owned by Horatio Bottomley, who built many of the cottages. The small church of flints and Caen stone by W. J. Donathorne (1843) is set at an angle to the road—very emphatically Norman. The flints came from Alfriston and were brought by barge up the Cuckmere to Sessingham bridge; the blocks of stone were sawn and carved on the site. The octagonal Carolean font is dated 1663.

Ditchling [4] A trifle arty-crafty, and perhaps conscious of the fact that Frank Brangwyn and Eric Gill lived here, it is nevertheless an attractive village. Four streets of close-packed, warm-coloured houses converge at a cross-roads. Most houses are 18c, but some are earlier and timber-framed. Opposite the church is a brick and timber-framed 16c house called Wing's Place. It was known for many years as Anne of Cleves's house; but there seems to be no authority for the name. It has a strange, irregular plan; two windows in the eastern half project on brackets, and the first storey is reached by a long flight of external steps at the side by a built-out chim-

ney. Ditchling Beacon, 813 ft, 1½ miles S of the village, is the highest point in East Sussex. There is a circular neolithic entrenchment at the top, which was later occupied by the Romans. From it there is a magnificent view northwards over the Weald; it shows it to be still densely wooded, and it needs little imagination to see the impenetrable wealden forest, pierced only by miry lanes, that covered the central part of Sussex in Saxon and Norman times. To the N of the village is Ditchling Common, a wide gorse-covered expanse, on which the rare wild columbine used to grow. In the northern corner of the common is Jacob's Post, the relic of a gibbet, on which a highwayman, Jacob Harris, was suspended after being hanged at Horsham in 1734 for robbing and murdering three travellers.

Ditchling church stands near the centre of the village on rising ground close to a duck pond and opposite Court House Farm. It is a handsome, flint-built cruciform building, mainly 13c, but with a plain 12c Transitional nave, and windows of the 14c and 15c. The tower, transepts and chancel are all EE, as is the Abergavenny chapel. Both the chancel and the chapel show fine craftsmanship in their detail and may have been built by monks from the Cluniac Priory of Lewes, to which Ditchling church belonged. Materials used are Caen stone and local chalk; the monks were probably the only people who could afford to import stone from France, but the liberal use of chalk is thought to have been due to a failure of supply of Caen stone owing to lack of money or high demand. The four great pillars and arches of the crossing have foliated capitals, and the chancel and Abergavenny chapel have windows flanked by slender supporting shafts and arches with exceptionally well carved capitals; the arch terminals of the E window have busts of a king and queen. The

Abergavenny chapel has an early 14c E window with very good reticulated tracery; it also contains a monument to Henry Poole (1580) who married a Nevill, the family name of the Abergavennys. The chapel was formerly used as a vestry, but was restored as a memorial to the fallen in the Second World War. The carved oak screens were designed by J. L. Denman and much of the carving was done by local craftsmen. A major restoration took place in 1863, in that fatal decade for churches; traces of mural paintings were destroyed and the box-pews removed. But much remains, and the church is substantially as it was in the 15c.

Eastbourne [8] Each watering-place in East Sussex has its own particular character. Eastbourne is the most aristocratic, and its parades along the sea front can vie with Nice as an example of Victorian and Edwardian opulence and grandeur. It was already a fashionable watering-place in 1813, but it was not until 1851 that the chief land-owner and lord of the manor, the Duke of Devonshire, began to develop it. To the west King Edward's Parade, flanked by a high hedge of Spanish brooms on one side and low cedars on the seaward side, continues into Grand Parade with the Grand, Burlington, Claremont and Queen's Hotels, all dazzling white, pillared Victorian, though harking back to Georgian style. On the sea front is the Wish Tower, really a Martello tower built by the Royal Engineers between 1805 and 1810 as a bulwark against Napoleon's invasion. Further east is the pier with all the gaiety of glass and domes and Victorian ironwork. Leading off the front are Devonshire Place, a wide, handsome boulevard with a seated statue of the Duke of Devonshire, and Cavendish Place, a narrower street with pretty bow-fronted houses and wrought-iron balconies.

St Saviour, **Eastbourne** by G. E. Street

Away from the front the Town Hall 1884–6 has a jaunty Renaissance-type tower with a dome, and the railway station (1861) is an interesting essay in yellow brick with plenty of spirited Victorian quirks. The church of St Saviour's in South Street 1867–8 was designed by Street and has a tall broach spire. Inside, the nave has stone clustered piers and walls of red brick—not a visually restful material—and the proportions are fine; the clerestory has large 'Decorated' windows. The chancel is a rib-vaulted apse, richly adorned with a reredos,

arched recesses and sedilia with a great deal of gold and colour.

About a mile inland is the old town. Gathered close together are the large church of St Mary, the timber-framed Lamb Inn and behind the church the 16c Old Parsonage of rubble and flint with transomed windows. The Towner Art Gallery is 18c brick, and opposite is a timber-framed 16c house. Two other old houses are The Goffs and Gildredge Manor House and there are several cobbled walls about. The church, beside and a little below the level of the main

road, has a 14c tower of the local green sandstone, embattled, with a tiled cap, but the rest of the church is of flint and rubble interspersed with sandstones. The most interesting external feature is the low sacristy projecting from the E end, unique in East Sussex. The inside is grand and spacious. The nave arcades have five bays—four EE and one Dec, added when the tower and clerestory were built. The roof has tie-beams and king-posts. The high round-headed chancel arch has late Norman mouldings like the chancel arcades. The sanctuary has a central recess behind the altar with a cusped ogee arch as have the Easter sepulchre, aumbry, piscina and triple sedilia. All these as well as the parclose screens and the screens in the N and S chapels are 14c. In the first pillar of the S chapel is a little circular recess, now used as an oratory. In the chancel is a handsome George III Royal Arms with a stylish carved wooden frame, and three hatchments to the Cavendish family. The E window of the S chapel has in it the last glass designed by Douglas Strachan, who did the windows at Winchelsea. The monument to Katherine Gildredge 1625 has weeping angels, armorial shields and a slate tablet with wording. A later tablet in the S aisle to Henry Lushington 1763 has an ogee Gothic arch over a bust with a canopy of draperies, swags and an armorial shield. Before you leave this dignified church, notice the small triangular-headed stoup recess just inside the door. The Norman cross in the churchyard with an interlacing pattern on the shaft and a wheel-head was imported from St Erth in Cornwall. Compton Place is up the hill a little W of the old town. Built in 1726–31 by Colen Campbell for Spencer Compton, Earl of Wilmington, the Prime Minister who followed Walpole, it replaced an earlier Tudor or Jacobean house. It was remodelled in 1800, given a stucco coat-

St Saviour, **Eastbourne**

ing, a Tuscan four-columned porch and various other features. It then belonged, as it still does, to the Cavendishes, Dukes of Devonshire. The late Duke still used it; but it is now the Ladies' College of English. Externally it is a charming two-storey unpretentious house in a small park with chestnuts and elms. It is not normally open to the public; but the inside is well worth seeing if it is. There are sumptuous fireplaces and a fine staircase; but best of all is the state bedroom with an elaborately decorated contemporary ceiling by Charles Stanley. There is a bust of the architect Colen Campbell. Beyond Compton Place is the part of Eastbourne known as Meads—an area of well-spaced detached houses with gardens of lilacs and laburnums, about the same date as, and curiously reminiscent of, North Oxford.

De Echyngham brass, **Etchingham**

Eridge [2] The small village of Eridge Green calls for no comment. Eridge Park is the seat of the Nevills, Earls and Marquesses of Abergavenny, one of the leading Sussex families (*see* Introduction). They have owned Eridge since at least 1300 and there was a shooting lodge where Queen Elizabeth I stayed in 1573. The house was enlarged in the 18c and re-modelled into a vast Gothick castle by the 2nd Earl in 1810. He re-named it Eridge Castle and made

it his chief residence instead of Kid-brooke Park, near East Grinstead, which his grandfather built about 1724. It survived until 1938 when the late Lord Abergavenny demolished it and built a large modern house on the site; this has been reduced to one third of its size by the present Lord Abergavenny, and is now known by its original name of Eridge Park.

Etchingham [6] (accent on -ham) The village is strung out along the

A265 in a pleasant but undistinguished way until, at the eastern end and just short of the station, the road passes the great, gray church, arresting in its stately dignity. It once had a moat round it, and is one of the finest examples of Dec work in Sussex. It was built by Sir William de Echyngham about 1360, and should be compared with Poynings, built 10 years later, when Dec had begun to change to Perp. With its massive tower crowned by a pyramidal roof and a 14c weather vane, its clerestoried nave and high-pitched roofs, it looks—and was—collegiate, so superior is its architecture to that of the average village church. It must look today very much as it did when built, since no structural alterations have been made, except for a modern vestry, and many of the contemporary fittings remain. The chancel has triple sedilia with cinquefoil-headed canopies, and the original stalls, nine a side, which are in an unusually perfect condition. All of them have misericords, mostly carved with leaves; the easternmost on each side has a fox preaching to geese. The stalls stand on their original stone platform. A low screen divides the chancel from the tower space, and below it are some decorated 14c floor tiles. The flamboyant E window is similar to one at Lindfield, and the two-light windows of the chancel show great variety in their flowing tracery. The S aisle has a bulbous-legged Jacobean Communion table, and both aisles have three-light E windows with bands of quatrefoil above the lights and two-light W windows with flat segmental heads. The small W window has three lights with curious tracery; the font is an octagonal bowl with a shaft of clustered columns. In the E and W windows, the clerestory and in the aisles are numerous remains of 14c heraldic glass; the E window has—sandwiched between some rather gaudy glass by Clayton 1857—the shields of Edward III, the Black Prince, John Duke of Lancaster and the Duke of Brittany. Others have the shields of Echyngham and other local families. There are two fine brasses in the chancel to the de Echynghams—one to the founder, Sir William, (1387), headless, another, canopied, to Sir William with his wife and son (1444); against the S wall is an altar tomb to Thomas (1482) with a brass inscription only. In the S aisle are two small brasses to Elizabeth Echyngham and her sister—also a banner and helm. Two 19c monuments are

Sussex University (**Falmer**) by Sir Basil Spence

an interesting contrast in styles—one to John Snepp (1823) Grecian, the other to Henry Corbould (1844) Gothic revival; they are similar in having profile medallions at the foot. There is a small Royal Arms (1710). Among good houses in the parish are Seacocks Heath, said to have been built by smugglers, and Haremere Hall of ashlar and brick 17c. More modest houses are Kitchingham Farm, 16c, of plastered timber-framing on a stone plinth, Court Lodge, 1615, timber-framed, but refaced, and Shoyswell Old Manor, mostly 17c, timber-framed on an ashlar plinth. Etchingham was in the prosperous iron country; in the 14c the Rother took iron ore down to Rye.

Ewhurst [6] A most attractive village on a high ridge just S of Bodiam. Brick and weatherboarded cottages, a group of oasthouses, now converted into a private house, and the Preacher's House, timber-framed with a tile-hung upper storey. In the centre is a well-shaven green with the church on one side and a row of recently built weatherboarded cottages in the East Sussex tradition. The church has a peculiar curved spire, caused by a change in the pitch half-way up; the previous spire was struck by lightning in 1792, and may not have been the same shape. The earliest parts—the tower, the inner arch of the W door and the round-headed S arcade—are 12c Transitional. In the 13c the N aisle was added; the arcade has pointed arches and octagonal piers. The western pier has a curious fat face of a man, embraced within his folded arms and holding his ears—perhaps the mason's record of his pleasure that the work was finished. The font is a 13c bowl of Sussex marble. The tower arch is off-centre with the nave; beside it on the wall is a small brass to William Crysford (1520), 10 in high. The inscription has gone, but details were recorded. The churchyard is very

well kept and full of roses. In 1666 after the Great Fire of London Ewhurst contributed 'seven shillings and eightpence for the relief of the poor of St Bartholomew Exchange and St Bene't Fink of London for their losses sustained by the fire'—generous for a small remote place whose inhabitants had probably never been to London.

Fairlight [9] stands 533 ft above sea level at the end of the southern Forest Ridge, which breaks off into the sea in sandstone cliffs. The humble 13c church was pulled down in 1845, and a new and grander successor, designed by T. Little, was built. Its high,

embattled tower is a landmark for many miles. Fairlight Glen, much advertised in Hastings as a beauty spot, has a thick belt of trees stretching nearly to the water's edge and is the only place in Sussex where trees can be seen growing luxuriantly beneath the cliff and close to the sea. Fairlight Place is a stone-built house of about 1550, but a good deal altered.

Fairwarp [5] A small and unremarkable village on the southern slope of Ashdown Forest. The handsome sandstone church was built in 1881, designed by Rhode Hawkins; it was enlarged and enriched by the Eckstein family in

Sussex University

1930. The E end is a polygonal apse with no windows; the floor is of travertine marble. The church-yard has various monuments to the Ecksteins 1930, 1932 and 1950, all by Sir William Reid Dick.

Falmer [7] is on the Lewes-Brighton road and is a downland chalk village of very little interest. The 12c church was pulled down in 1815 and a new church in flint and brick built on its site. This in turn was completely altered in the 1860s, the brick dressing covered with Roman cement and pseudo-Norman features added. The mere from which Falmer takes its name is quite near the church. For Sussex University *see* Introduction.

Firle, West [8] is always referred to locally as Firle. There is no East Firle, though there was once, an alternative name for Heighton St Clere, a vanished village recorded in the name Heighton Street, the lane on the E side of Firle Park. Eleanor St Clere married John Gage of Cirencester in the early 15c, bringing her estates with her; these were augmented by the marriage of their son, William, in 1472 to Agnes Bolney, co-heiress of the manor of Firle, where the Gages have lived ever since. The village of flint-built cottages is securely hidden behind the great park and just below the Downs, a peaceful and feudal little place; its inn—the Ram—the Gage crest, proclaims its ownership. The church is at the end of the street and close to the back entrance to the park. The oldest feature is the Norman N door; the embattled tower, nave and chancel are early 13c, and the aisle arcades and clerestory, similar to Beddingham, 14c. The Gage chapel built between 1556 and 1595 is late Perp. There are many monuments and brasses. The best brass, above the vestry door, is to Bartholomew Bolney 1476 and his wife Eleanor—he in armour, she in a long gown with fur collar and cuffs. Then, on

the N side, a brass probably to George Gage 1569, a bearded figure in armour, on the S Thomas (d. 1590) and his wife with two kneeling daughters, and lastly a shrouded figure of Mary Lady Howard, who died at Firle in 1638. In the Gage chapel are three altar tombs all of the same pattern made in 1595 by Gerard Johnson (Janssen); the drawings are among the archives at Firle Place. The most distinguished is to Sir John Gage 1556 and his wife Philippa. They lie in alabaster side by side, he in armour, wearing the Order of the Garter with a ram at his feet, she in a long gown with the Guldeford crest, a flaming tree trunk, at her feet. Sir John remained friendly with Henry VIII, although he stayed loyal to Rome. The other two tombs have brasses—Sir Edward (d. 1569) and his wife, and John and his two wives. Johnson's drawings of John Gage and his wives have the criticisms of the client as well as the sculptor's comments in the margin.

Firle Place, at the end of a long drive through a park with ancient and well-spaced elms, stands just beneath the hanging woods of the Downs and harmonises so fitly with its surroundings that it seems to be implanted in the Sussex earth. The outside is nearly all 18c; but here are no Italian airs and graces, the only concession to Palladio being the arched entrance to the large courtyard, and the Venetian window over it beneath a modest pediment. The core of the house is Tudor and must have been built by Sir John Gage (1479–1556) whose tomb is in the church; Tudor features that remain are a gable at the back of the house, a fireplace and some wall paintings in the dining-room, and a doorway in the hall. The great hall between the courts is certainly part of Sir John's house and still has the original hammer-beam roof above the plaster ceiling. It is not known whether Sir John built on a new site

or enlarged an existing house. It seems that the house changed little between the 16c and 18c; but extensive alterations were made by the 1st Viscount who succeeded his cousin at Firle in 1744, and built the front to contain a gallery for his large collection of pictures. The material used was local stone, which acquires a wonderfully mellow colouring and texture, in contrast to the Portland stone used for the entrance archway and the Venetian window above it. Two charming and somewhat old-fashioned features are the hipped roofs and eaves cornices. The masons were probably Arthur or John Morris of Lewes, one or other of whom did work at Stanmer, Ashburnham and Glynde Place. Inside, the re-modelling of the great hall was done by local builders; but the staircase hall and downstairs drawing-room were done by a London man, possibly Kent, but more likely one of his successors. The pictures were considerably augmented when the late Lady Gage, first wife of the present Lord Gage, inherited through her mother, Lady Desborough, a large part of the Cowper collection. This collection was started at Panshanger by the 2nd Earl Cowper and greatly increased by the splendid Italian pictures bought by the 3rd Earl, who spent 30 years in Florence. There is also a distinguished collection of Louis Quinze and Seize furniture.

Fletching [4] is not nearly so well-known as Piltdown, of temporary but spurious fame, (*see* Introduction) or Sheffield Park (*see* separately), both of which are within the parish. The village street has four timber-framed cottages, one 15c, the others 17c, and two old inns, but is rather dominated by a row of modern half-timbered houses put up by the Sheffield Park estate. The castellated Gothic gateway into the park stands at the angle of the street. The church, in

◁ **Firle** Place; from the north (top) and from the east

the centre of the village, has an early Norman tower with twin bell-openings divided by a baluster, and a graceful shingled broach spire about 1340. The porch and nave are roofed with Horsham slabs. When the spire was built, the nave walls were heightened and Dec clerestory windows inserted; the roof has 15c tie-beams and king-posts, revealed when the ceiling was removed in 1880. The aisles and transepts are 13c and the nave has two EE arcades with round piers. The transepts have three lancets filled with 14c glass, dug up in the churchyard. The S transept has a Dec window, the N transept a squint and a piscina with a hood-mould forming a bracket with a flat top for an effigy. The long and un-usually wide chancel—4 ft wider than the nave—was much restored by J. Oldrid Scott in 1880; the E window, which closely follows the original, has intersecting tracery and three cusped circles at the head. The glass is by Kempe and rather good; two other Kempe win-dows are in the S wall and in the S transept. In the nave are ac-coutrements of the Nevills, Earls of Abergavenny, former lords of the manor—two helms with swords, gauntlets and spurs, each group surmounted by a crest. There are four hatchments, three of them to the Sheffield family, and a Stuart Royal Arms. The pulpit is Jaco-bean with carved panels, and there is a 16c monument and two brasses. The tomb has recumbent alabaster figures of Richard Leche (d. 1596) and his wife, Charitye. After his death she married the 2nd Earl of Nottingham, who was as unkind to her as Richard Leche had been kind; in consequence 'shee of her own accorde caused this monument to be made and herself livinge, to be pictured lying by him as you see'. The small brass to Peter Denot (1450), who took part in Jack Cade's Rebellion, has simply an in-scription and a pair of gloves, show-ing that he was a glover. The large,

and very fine brass (1380) is to a Dalyngrygge and his wife, the family who built Bodiam Castle; he wears full armour and she a long kirtle and the two figures are under a double canopy divided by a shaft. At the NE corner of the church is the Sheffield mausoleum; all that can be seen is a wall covered by rather dull wall tablets. The only one of interest is that of Edward Gibbon, the historian, who was a friend of the 1st Lord Sheffield and often stayed at Sheffield Park.

Flimwell [3] is centred round a cross-roads and almost in Kent with the church a little to the E. It is by Decimus Burton 1839 EE and built of ashlar; but the shingled spire was added in 1873 and the chancel in 1879. The nave is lit by pairs of lancets and has a hammer-beam roof, and the chancel arch is of wood with a carved rood screen and a modern rood. The pulpit is inset with carved 17c panels. The altar has paintings of tile and mosaic on either side. Burton is not at his happiest here and the impres-sion is rather cold and uninviting.

Folkington [8] (pronounced Fow-ington) must be one of the most shyly secluded villages in Sussex; it lies at the foot of the Downs behind the great park of Folkington Manor. The church is on the edge of a downland hanger. Built of rough flints and stone, its origin is about 1250, and four windows in the chancel are of this date; it measures only 67 ft by 24 ft. The N door is early 14c and further addi-tions were made in the 15c, when two Perp windows were inserted in the nave and the little bell-cote steeple built to house the bell, which still exists. The nave has its 15c roof with king-posts and rafters, and the seating includes on either side three large oak box-pews. There is no chancel arch dividing nave from chancel. There are two 17c wall monuments in the sanc-tuary, to the Thomas family. Folk-

ington Place was a large 18c brick house with a formal garden; a print of it as it was can be seen in the Star Inn at Alfriston. Only a fragment now remains and the large formal garden has disappeared. Folk-ington Manor is a somewhat pre-tentious house of 1837; its best feature is the knapped-flint facing.

Forest Row [1] A trim village on the East Grinstead–Lewes road with a church (1836) at the junc-tion of two roads in the centre. It was built as a chapel-of-ease to East Grinstead, and no doubt Forest Row became more consequential when it achieved the status of a par-ish in 1894. The church, built of sandstone and with a slim tower and shingled spire is well enough from the outside, but the inside is disappointing. The elaborate roof with pendants, E window of triple lancets under an arch and the three tall stepped arches at the W end seem to strain after effect, which would have been better gained by a chancel arch. The church is some-what barn-like, and not a great suc-cess.

A little to the N is Brambletye, the pathetic relic of a fine Jacobean house built by Sir Henry Compton in 1631; it was left to ruin when the owner fled to Spain. All that remains is three sections of the front, one still surmounted by a stone cupola and finial, and the arch of the gatehouse. The porch and one or two mullioned and transomed windows survive; but the ruins are in a sad state of decay, surrounded by rusty iron railings, the courtyard a wilderness of docks.

Kidbrooke Park, now Michael Hall Rudolf Steiner School, was built in about 1724 for Lord Aber-gavenny after a fire at Eridge. An engraving of 1809 shows a central block with a pediment, the en-trance beneath it and two wings; it also gives the architect as Robert Milne, though he cannot have designed the original house. It now looks lop-sided, since the S wing has been removed and a heavy Victorian porch built on the right of the centre block. The pediment has the Abergavenny arms. Inside, many of the rooms have delicate Adam-style plaster ceilings, which have recently been carefully redecorated. The long room, probably early 19c, has a plain ceiling, but has elegant painted pilasters and other decoration in Pompeian style. Beside the house are charming 18c stables with lunette windows and a cupola. The grounds were laid out by Repton.

Ashdown House, now a preparatory school, is superbly sited with a southward view and is no less excellent itself. It was built in 1795 by Benjamin Latrobe before he emigrated to America. The house is of gray ashlar, square and classical, but relieved by a semi-circular portico with four Ionic columns. On

either side the windows are set in blank arches. A most elegant and sophisticated house, and less austere than Hammerwood, built two years before. Inside there is a staircase with a thin wrought-iron railing. There is a brick summer-house adjoining in the Lutyens manner.

Framfield [5] A small village with some nice tiled and timber-framed cottages, flanking the short road to the church, which has Horsham slabbed roofs. The usual brick path has an avenue of clipped tub-shaped yews, and the churchyard has one terracotta Harmer plaque. After a fire in 1509 the nave was rebuilt and the EE arcades heightened and given a clerestory. The chancel and tower were not repaired; the chancel became increasingly ruinous, until it was rebuilt by the vicar in 1842. The

tower had collapsed in 1667, and the church was without one until 1892. In the S chapel is a monument to Edward Gage 1595 and his wife with two brass kneeling figures. Others are to Frances Warnet (1622), framed in alabaster, and Robert Durrant (1799), an urn and obelisk. A later memorial to Sarah Woodward (1823) by Westmacott is a fairly conventional tablet with Grecian decoration. The Hempstead chapel, the earliest part of the church (1288) and now blocked by the organ, takes its name from Hempstead Farm, now a 15c timber-framed house with its original hall. Framfield Place is 18c (privately owned and not shown).

Frant [2] is grouped around a spacious green. The church designed by John Montier stands a little back and was built in 1819–22 on the site

Fletching; church and church farm

Glynde; church and stables

of the old church. A stone over the S door records the event; one of the churchwardens was a Nevill. It is built of ashlar and has a low W tower with pinnacles at the four corners. The nave has wide depressed arches springing from iron piers. The W gallery also has elegant iron supports and an elaborate wrought-iron screen along the front. In proportion and detail it is successful, and interesting as the only country church in East Sussex built at this time. Several monuments from the old building were reinstated. On the S wall of the chancel is a white marble memorial to Henry Weller 1720 with swags and cherubs, sur-

mounted by a coat of arms. On the N wall is a hatchment, and on the S two monuments by E. Physick to John By (1836) and Esther By (1837). Each has a sarcophagus in relief and a woman mourning over it. In the N and S aisles is some 15c stained glass with whole figures.

Friston [8] is on top of the hill between the Cuckmere valley and East Dean. The church stands alone—there is no village—beside a pond where the Great Spearwort, a ranunculus rare in the S of England, grows. The churchyard is entered by a tapsell gate (see Pyecombe and East Dean). The only features of the original early Nor-

man or Saxon church are a blocked-up doorway in the S wall and a small, blocked, slightly splayed window above it. Evidently the church was extended westwards at an early date, because the plain Norman doorway in use is only a foot or so from the blocked door. The nave has a fine timber roof with tie-beams, king-posts and wall plates of oak. On the S wall mounted on an oak base are two brasses to Thomas Selwyn (d. 1539) and his wife, Margery. There is a plain Queen Anne pulpit, and the small, circular, shallow font of Sussex marble is of Puritan parentage. The chancel was built about 1300 and has a low segmental chancel arch. Over the altar is an arched recess, which may have been used for the reserved sacrament, and on either side is a projecting stone slab to support an image. There is also an arched recess on either side of the sanctuary. The Selwyn transept was built on to the N side in about 1860 to give extra seating and to provide a place for the Selwyn monuments, which had hitherto been in the chancel. The alabaster tomb shows Thomas Selwyn (d. 1613) and his wife at prayer, their six daughters kneeling below and three dead infants—? sons—beneath the prayer desk. Opposite is a later monument, a large marble slab with armorial bearings to Edward Selwyn and his son and heir, William Thomas, 'the last of the ancient family'. Friston Place, the old home of the Selwyns, is an E-shaped Tudor manor house, lying in a deep combe about half a mile N of the church. There has been a good deal of recent afforestation round Friston, and aesthetically far too many conifers have been planted.

Glynde [7] A small flint village on a spur of Mount Caburn, E of Lewes. Glynde Reach is a tidal branch of the Ouse, and Glynde Level the stretch of solitary marshland to the E of the village. Like Firle, but less obviously so, Glynde is a feudal village with a great house, Glynde Place, that has been in private ownership for over 500 years. Unlike Firle, where the Gages have always had a male heir, Glynde has belonged to four families, though it has only once been sold, and then within the family. In the 15c it belonged to the Waleys; but when Joan Waleys married Nicholas Morley of Hertfordshire he bought Glynde from the Waleys heir, who preferred to live in Devonshire. William Morley, his great-grandson, built the present house in 1569. The last Morley died at the age of 26 and his widow married his cousin and heir

John Trevor. Richard Trevor, Bishop of Durham, made many changes in the house and rebuilt the church. After the death of his nephew in 1824, the house again passed to a cousin, General Henry Brand, son of Baroness Dacre, whose mother was a Morley; it still belongs to the Brands. The house is an Elizabethan manor of flint and Caen stone with a symmetrical E front; it has a central projection, bow windows and a gable at each end. The house originally faced W and it was Bishop Trevor who altered the entrance about 1750, and built the impressive cupolaed stables entered between two massive gate piers, each with a Trevor wyvern. Inside, the four walls are found to enclose a Tudor courtyard of mown grass, roses and climbing plants. The rooms show the Bishop's influence; the Georgian hall, replacing three small Tudor rooms, has four wooden columns simulating marble. Above the hall is the gallery, panelled throughout and containing a number of family portraits; two are surrounded with richly carved frames dated 1709, possibly by a pupil of Grinling Gibbons. The marble and granite fireplace was commissioned by the Bishop from John Morris of Lewes. The most interesting picture at Glynde is the Rubens cartoon for the ceiling of the Banqueting House at Whitehall. Close to the stables and grouping well with them, is the church built for Bishop Trevor in 1763 on the site of the old church and designed by Sir Thomas Robinson. Hussey writes in 1852 'the church is in very bad taste, the style called Grecian', and again the author of a guide in the 1920s finds it 'uninteresting, chiefly because it is quite out of the picture'. Medieval bias in both cases. It is, in fact, an elegant little rectangular box, built of knapped flints, and contains a coved rococo ceiling and the original woodwork of William Langridge, box-pews, pulpit and W gallery. It is spoilt by a clumsy

pseudo-17c Victorian screen—quite out of proportion. Three windows have panels of 16c and 17c Flemish glass, but most of them are memorials to Brands—by Kempe, but not very good. There is one Harmer terracotta plaque in the churchyard.

Glyndebourne is half in Glynde, half in Ringmer. *See* Ringmer.

Grinstead, East [1] though peripherally suburban, is still at heart an old market town. It was once an Assize Town and returned two Members of Parliament for 500 years, until 1832; it still returns one. The High Street is almost always packed with cars, and only on a Sunday morning can it be seen as an unusually interesting and beautiful street. The S side has a stepped brick pavement and a number of timber-framed houses, now shops, with Horsham-slabbed roofs, gables and brick chimney stacks. The Dorset Arms and Dorset House, 18c brick, are also on the S. The N side is less interesting, but has a number of 18c and some earlier, houses. The street is divided at the eastern end, but widens at the west, suggesting that there was either an open market in the centre, or a row of houses dividing it in two. The church, standing behind some timber-framed houses and weatherboarded cottages on the N side, is striking and unusual. The tower of the medieval church was struck by lightning in 1683. It was rebuilt, evidently not very well, in the following year, for in 1785 it fell, damaging the entire church. East Grinstead was an important place, and in 1787 an Act of Parliament was passed for its rebuilding; which was begun in 1789, and finished in 1813. The result is a distinguished late Gothick church by James Wyatt. Inside, the nave arcades have slightly depressed arches with concave-sided piers and capitals; above them is a clerestory with wheel windows. The chancel is cramped, and not in proportion with the nave. A number of memorials survive from the older church—two cast-iron floor slabs to Anne Barclay (1570) and Francis Haselden (1616), a wall tablet to Lord Abergavenny (1744), with coat of arms, coloured crest and coronet above, three small brasses with figures of men (1505 and 1520), mounted on the S wall of the nave. At the W end, set into the wall, are an earl's coronet in stone, another stone inscribed M.P., possibly Matthew Prior (1664–1721) poet and diplomat, also M.P. for East Grinstead, and a roughly hewn cross, which may be a finial from the older church. There are four hatchments, and a small Victorian Royal Arms on the organ. In the churchyard is a tombstone to William and Lucy Durrant, which seems to be the only example in stone of the work of Jonathan Harmer of Heathfield. The most distinguished building in East Grinstead is the Sackville College at the eastern end. It was built in 1619 by the 2nd Earl of Dorset (see Withyham) for five brothers and six sisters, and is a low two-storeyed, gabled, stone building round a court, reminiscent of a Cambridge college. The chapel has some stained glass from Munich (about 1853) and the hall a hammer-beam roof. Dr J. M. Neale, who wrote many hymns, was Warden here for 20 years. The College is open to the public from May till September 2 p.m. to 5 p.m. not on Saturdays.

Groombridge, New [2] is a dull extension of Groombridge (which is across the Medway and in Kent) that has grown up round the station. But it has two noteworthy buildings, both by Norman Shaw. St Thomas' church 1883 stands high and is hedged in by villas. It is Perp and has a tile-hung bell turret with louvres and a shingled cap. The outside is more pleasing than the inside; the heavily timbered roof is oppressive, and the narrow

nave, with large expanses of blank wall could have done with another window on each side. The glass is by Kempe. Earlier in 1867 Shaw had designed Glen Andred, a large brick house ¾ mile SW. It has an adventurous jumble of asymmetrical gables—some tile-hung, others plastered—the centre gable bearing the date. There are Elizabethan mullioned and transomed windows and tall brick chimney stacks. The name, after Andredsweald, with romantically medieval associations, seems well-chosen.

Guestling [6] The church stands just off the Rye–Hastings road, alone by a farm. The early 12c tower heavily repointed, has twin bell-openings and a number of round-headed Norman windows. The rest of the church is mainly 14c, but suffered from a fire in 1890, four years after the restoration. Nearly all the interior stonework is modern. In the chancel is a 17c monument to John and Elizabeth Cheyney, who kneel facing each other, and in the N aisle some fragmentary 16c glass with the Ashburnham arms. Broomham, rather E of the church, was a 16c house, altered in the 18c, but was so drastically re-modelled in 1927 that it now looks rather absurd. The Ashburnhams, a cadet branch of the Ashburnham Park family, lived here from the 15c until 1935; three of them were rectors of Guestling. A 'Guestling' was a sort of Parliament instituted by the Cinque Ports to arrange matters among themselves, and negotiate with other seaport towns such as Yarmouth. Whether the court of Guestling had anything to do with the village is not known.

Guldeford, East [Inset] (pronounced Gilford). A straight road heading eastwards from Rye across the marsh comes in a mile to the last village in Sussex, no more than a few farms and cottages and a humble, barn-like church. Approached across a meadow and

surrounded by dykes and sheep, it was built of brick in 1505 by Sir Richard Guldeford, whose family lived at Benenden, Kent; they took their name originally from Guildford, Surrey. The church is a rectangular box with twin roofs and a small bell-cote in the valley between, and is supported by massive brick buttresses. Inside is a simple hall with a plaster ceiling divided into five bays, but with no division between nave and chancel. It escaped attention in the mid-19th century, but was carefully restored in 1973–4 and has much charm. The windows are all Gothic with flowing tracery probably early 19c, and above the E window extending round on either side is a frieze of large, multi-coloured seraphim with musical instruments, wreaths and censers; the date is uncertain, but from photographic records it seems to be early 20c. Four stone corbels built into the N, E and S walls have angels on the undersides bearing shields; on the N wall is an armorial stone plaque to the builder of the church with the Guldeford arms. The font is a square 12c bowl with rosettes and flat arches, and must have come from elsewhere. The church is furnished with a deal two-decker pulpit and box-pews, and has brick and tile floors—all early 19c. On the W wall are Commandment Boards and a George IV Royal Arms. The only house of any note is The Mount, 15c and 16c, timber-framed and underbuilt with brick and stone.

Hadlow Down [5] has a church by William Moseley 1856, but mostly a rebuilding by G. Fellowes Prynne in 1913. The outside is attractive— all of sandstone with a battlemented W tower and a slender crocketed shingled spire. Over the junction of the nave and chancel is a little bell-cote. Inside it is disappointing: the wide nave is rather barn-like and would have been better with arcades.

East Grinstead; Sackville College

Hailsham [8] is an old, but not specially distinctive market town. There are one or two timber-framed houses, but most are 18c. The Manor House has a Georgian front. It is at present derelict, but has recently been bought for conversion into offices. The church has a Perp tower of chequerboard flint and stone with pinnacles at each corner; it has a W window under an arch terminating in heads of a King and Queen. The nave arcades and chancel arch are EE. The bells were first cast at Bell Bank in the town, and the tenor bell used to toll the curfew until 1950. In the churchyard is a table tomb with Harmer terracotta plaques at each end.

Halland [5] *see* **East Hoathly**

Hammerwood [2] There is no village—only the church 1879–80 by E. P. Loftus Brock standing close to the main road with a panoramic southward view. It is rather grand for a non-existent place. The tower has low battlements with gargoyles at each corner and a stone spire. Windows are all Dec with elaborate tracery. There is a monument to Anthony Partridge 1943 by Eric Kennington.

Down a lane W of the church is a remarkable trio of houses. Bower Farmhouse, 15c and 16c, is timber-framed—some of it close-studded—and has Horsham-slabbed roofs and an attractively irregular plan.

Hammerwood, close by, is of brick by Norman Shaw (1872). One wing, a former chapel, has a Perp E window; there are tall Tudor chimney stacks, dormer windows and a tile-hung upper storey. Much further down the lane is Hammerwood House by Benjamin Latrobe (1793). It is now forlorn and empty, the gravel sweep moss-covered and the gardens unkempt. But the house of honey-coloured ashlar is urbane and austere with a *porte-cochère* at the front and on the S giant pilasters and low-angle pavilions with pediments. The pure classical tradition makes an interesting contrast with the homely romanticism of Shaw's house, built 80 years later.

◁ **Hammerwood**, by Norman Shaw   △ **Hammerwood** House, by Benjamin Latrobe

Hamsey [4] A large parish, which includes the village of Offham at the foot of the Downs and part of Cooksbridge near the railway station. The original village—the ham of the de Says—has long since disappeared, but was situated near the church, standing on an isolated hill, round which the Ouse in its original course makes a wide loop. The church is approached by a lane, which crosses the new cut of the Ouse made in 1790 and then goes through a farmyard; but before that the road went straight up to the church, leaving the farm on the right. Near the church have been discovered the foundations of the medieval manor house of Hamsey Place; not a trace now remains, but its name survives in Hamsey-place Farm, the mellow 16c farmhouse, tile-hung and Horsham-slabbed, at the foot of the hill. It has some fine outbuildings, including a heavily buttressed barn—sadly no longer thatched—and a former dovecote with oak-barred windows and a roof of Horsham stone. Hamsey church entirely escaped attention in the 19c; it was reduced to the status of a mortuary chapel and the chancel blocked up with a huge mausoleum to the Shiffner family, which has since been removed. It has a fortress-like Perp tower with gargoyles; but inside a rude Norman chancel arch, a squint and two-round-headed windows reveal its early origin. Beneath the squint is a small rectangular aumbry and on the S wall of the nave is an EE piscina, in addition to the Dec piscina in the chancel; both of these features are highly unusual. On the nave walls are four hatchments to the Bridgers and Shiffners and the Royal Arms of George III, and the S wall has traces of 15c paintings. Nave and chancel have their old oak roofs with tie-beams, braces and king-posts, and there are a few medieval oak pews—with very narrow and uncomfortable seats. Against the N wall of the chancel is an elaborate canopied Tudor tomb, formerly called the de Say tomb but now known to be that of Edward Markwick (d. 1538). In the 1920s the parishioners became conscious of their nearly forgotten church; much money was raised, and a thorough and sensitive restoration carried out. Tufts of pellitory spring from the outer walls, and within, the uneven texture of the plaster, the simple furnishings and the colours of the arms and hatchments make Hamsey the perfect example of a medieval church. A little to the N is a ford over the Ouse, which the Romans used.

Offham (pronounced Oafham) is a main-road village on a spur of the Downs. The flint and sandstone church stands boldly and is worthy of its position; it was built in 1859, when Hamsey church was closed for worship, and is a highly successful design by Ewan Christian. It is Early Dec in style, and the tower and shingled spire conform to Sussex tradition. There are three windows by Capronnier and one by Kempe and Tower. Opposite the church is the drive to Coombe Place, lying in the midst of the Downs as its name implies. It was built in the 17c and altered in the 18c by Richard Bridger, who bought the estate in 1657. The 18c front has a half-H plan and walls of knapped flints with stone quoins. It remained with the Bridgers until 1787, when Mary Bridger, heiress of Sir John Bridger and friend of the Prince Regent, married George, afterwards Sir George, Shiffner, whose family owned it for nearly 200 years. Two other houses are worth noticing. Offham House, standing close to but above the Lewes road, is built of well-knapped flints with dressings of plastered brick. It looks Georgian, but a square sundial on the pediment is dated 1676. If this is the date of the house, it is very advanced in style, being designed for sash windows.

Shelley's Folly, north of Cooksbridge Station, stands high on a ridge. It was built about 1700 of brick in Flemish bond with vitrified headers, but has mullioned and transomed windows.

Handcross* [1] *see* **Slaugham**

Hangleton [7] Until 30 years ago simply a lonely church on the Downs and a manor house. But recently the northward spread of Brighton and Hove has encroached, and open farmland has become a rash of villas. The church stands near the site of the vanished village, and has a low, embattled, 13c tower with a tiled cap. The walls are of rough flints and the nave is Norman, but the S wall has some pre-Conquest herring-bone flintwork. Inside, the nave has brick flooring; the roofs are trussed and raftered with no vertical supports—gabled in the chancel, waggon in the nave. On the N wall are fragmentary wall paintings with a red leaf design in the splays of a Norman window. In the chancel is a 16c tomb of a man and wife, their five sons and six daughters; the small kneeling figures are all in low relief.

The Manor House was built in the 15c; but little of the original remains after two alterations in the 16c. Inside is a screen with five bays and fluted Corinthian pilasters carved with the Ten Commandments. The staircase has an unusual design and a solid newel-post. The cottages to the N were originally the gatehouse and were probably joined to the house by a courtyard. The Manor is now an hotel. Near by is a circular 17c flint dovecote with its original potence and over 500 nesting boxes.

Hartfield [2] A pleasant, open village of tiled and weatherboarded cottages not far from the Kent and Surrey borders and just N of Ashdown Forest. The churchyard is entered through a lych-gate beneath the overhang of a 16c timber-framed cottage; there is a similar

Shelley's Folly; *see* **Hamsey**

lych-gate at Penshurst in Kent. The church, of local sandstone, is a graceful building standing boldly on a knoll in the centre of the village, its broach shingled spire visible from afar. The earliest part—the N wall—is 13c, and the nave, S aisle and chapel were added and the chancel rebuilt a century later. The tower was added in the 15th century, though the two angle buttresses and the spire look earlier. The piers of the nave arcade are 14c, but the capitals and bases are 100 or more years later. The theory is that there may have been a fire about 1500, which damaged the piers and necessitated repair. This might also account for the pinkish tinge on some of the arch stones, and the absence of a chancel arch. The roofs have been restored, but have their old tie-beams and king-posts. There is a wall tablet in the chapel to Richard Randes (d. 1640), rector of Hartfield, with a Latin epitaph, presumably written by himself, the translation of which reads 'He lived obscure and always shunned the vulgar throng, that is wont to reek of the odours of vine crowned Bacchus. But alas! he lived badly and now imprisoned in the darkness of the tomb, he tea-cheth thee what he late began to learn himself.' A full translation is provided and it is worth reading.

Bolebroke, a mile N, is the relic of a much larger 16c brick manor house, which once belonged to the Dalyngrigges and later to the Sack-villes. All that is left is a charming detached gatehouse with two octa-gonal zinc-covered cupolas, the house itself, which was probably the E wing, and a little brick and timber granary with a flight of stone steps and a four-centred stone archway. The house looks eastward over a long lake bisected by a cause-way; the façade has four gables and mullioned and transomed windows arranged asymmetrically. There are clusters of brick chimney stacks.

Hassocks* [4] Old maps marks Hassocks Gate, presumably a toll-

118

gate on the London–Brighton road. The modern town of Hassocks has grown up round the railway station and has nothing of interest.

Hastings [9] One of the most evocative names in English history and certainly the place of greatest historical importance in East Sussex. William of Normandy was blown off course to a point near Pevensey, and the battle took place at Senlac, seven miles to the N; but Hastings has long been associated with both. The name derives from the tribe Haestingas, and the town was important enough to have had its own mint in 984. William made it the premier Cinque Port and chief town of the Rape, which was governed by the Count of Eu. After his coronation the Conqueror built a stone fortress on the West Hill, and later Robert, Count of Eu, built a collegiate church within the precincts. It had a dean and eight canons; one of its Deans was Thomas à Becket. During the reign of Richard I an Augustinian house was founded, probably by Walter de Scotney; it consisted of a prior and three canons. But owing to the encroachment of the sea the Priory was in grave danger of being swept away. In 1413 Sir John Pelham gave them a site at Warbleton to which Henry IV licensed them to remove; it was known as the New Priory of Hastings. The County Commissioner's certificate of 1536 describes it as having 'Priests 3, Novices 1, Incontinent 4' and the house 'holy in ruyne'. Thomas Harmer, the last Prior, surrendered on a pension of £6. The castle's heyday was in the Norman and Plantagenet reigns; but its temporal power ended in 1216 when King John ordered it to be dismantled. Henry III refortified it, but the storms of the late 13c finished Hastings as a port and the castle ceased to have any military importance. The collegiate church continued until the Dissolution, when it was destroyed. Little of the

Hartfield lychgate

great castle is left; much of the sandstone rock has crumbled away into the sea, and wind erosion has necessitated brick patching to stop further subsidence. Apart from the curtain wall most of the ruins are of the collegiate church, which has several Norman windows, a reconstructed 13c chancel arch and the remains of the central tower. The town—that is the Old Town—lies E of the castle, and was built up the Bourne valley between the East and West Hills, the two sandstone bluffs, which are in fact the end of the Forest Ridge. It was built after the last sacking by the French in 1377, and may have replaced an earlier town now under the sea as

the name Rock-a-Nore, the rock to the N, seems to imply.

The foreshore is known as the Stade, Saxon for landing place. There is no harbour, and since the rise and fall of the tides is the highest on the S coast, the boats have to be hauled up a long way to be beached above the high water line; until 1939 they were wound up by horse-drawn wooden capstans. The nets are dried, and have been since the 17c, in the netshops, a curious and unique huddle of slim towers, weatherboarded and tarred, ranged along the beach. Among them is the Fishermen's Church (1854), now a museum, containing as its centrepiece the

Enterprise, built in 1909, the last of the sailing luggers. Hastings is the only coastal town in Sussex which is still essentially a seafaring place; fishermen are much in evidence, and 'Today's catch' can be bought from the huts among the net shops.

The town consists of two long narrow streets up either side of the valley—High Street and All Saints' Street, each with a raised pavement as the hill slopes up, each with a medieval church, St Clement's at the bottom, All Saints' at the top. Between the two streets is Bourne Road, named after the rivulet which once watered the town, recently widened and ruined. But, sandwiched between the hills, the two long streets have remained im-

mune and are a delightful example of a medieval town, in some ways as good as Rye. All Saints' Street has a large number of 15c and 16c timber-framed houses; off it run various alleys, or twittens, and above it is East Hill House in Tackleway. High Street is a little grander, and although there are one or two timber-framed houses, it is mainly 17c and 18c. At the top of the street are two fine Georgian houses, Torfield House and Old Hastings House. Climbing up the West Hill are The Croft, Croft Road and Hill Road, all with tightly packed houses, a charming medley of timber-framing, 18c-brick and early 19c-plaster with bow fronts and balconies. At the

▷

Hastings
(*top*) Shops on the front (*bottom*) Net Shops on the beach

bottom of High Street was once the Great Seagate; now there is towards the W a fringe of shops and houses of uneven heights, mostly 18c, with tiled roofs and gaily painted walls. On a summer's day the old town of Hastings could easily be an Italian fishing port. Above St Clement's church—a steep climb up West Hill—are St. Clement's caves, a labyrinth made by prehistoric waterways. They are round-arched, smooth and completely dry. On the walls of one is

Pelham Crescent, **Hastings**

a relief carving of a large chalice, which may be about 900 years old. Other reliefs were done during the Second World War, when the caves were used by soldiers—successors to the smugglers who found them useful for contraband in medieval times.

There were originally seven medieval churches; but by 1372 three had been destroyed by the sea or invaders. Two survive, both built after the final sacking of 1377. St Clement's at the foot of High Street and hemmed in by houses, is late 14c and has an embattled tower of chequered stone and flints. The inside is large, light and spacious; seven bay arcades N and S and no chancel arch. The piers where the rood screen once was each have a small decorated niche. A waggon roof runs the whole length, and the nave has two brass chandeliers. The chancel windows have four-centred arches and are 15c. A wall monument in the chancel to John Collier 1760 with cherubs and garlands, and at the W end a panel of benefactors adorned with cherubs and a coat of arms. All Saints' stands high at the old northern entrance to Hastings. It was built in 1436, probably about 45 years after St Clement's. The tower is similar with flint and stone chequerwork; inside is a groined roof with a round hole for the bells, surrounded with carvings of animals and fruit. The nave has arcades with six octagonal piers and a trussed and raftered roof. Above the chancel arch is a 15c Doom, showing Christ seated on a rainbow and wrapped in ermine; on the left an angel with red wings ending in peacock feathers. Low down the souls of the damned are seen somewhat unusually hanging from gallows. There are six hatchments on the nave walls and in the N aisle the Royal Arms of George II. Near All Saints' is the RC church of St Mary Star-of-the-Sea 1882, an impressive and beautiful design by Basil Champneys, surprising in its sim-

plicity. Plain arcades, a rib-vaulted roof and a high Dec clerestory and balcony.

Very early in the 19c Hastings, following in the wake of Brighton, became a seaside resort. Architecturally it lacks the Regency elegancies of Brighton and the *fin de siècle* panache of Eastbourne, being in the main sober mid-Victorian. The sandstone cliffs, ending abruptly in the sea, made eastward expansion impossible; the new town had to be built W of Castle Hill and inland, and the old town was left to mind its own fishing business. The first terrace was Pelham Crescent built in 1824 for the Earl of Chichester, then the owner of the castle. This remarkable crescent involved the blasting away of the southern face of the rock; the balconied houses with shallow bow fronts are ranged on either side of St Mary-in-the-Castle, a replacement of the ruined collegiate church above it. Starkly classical it has a portico with four plain columns beneath a pediment; the inside is semi-circular with the altar against the straight S wall. Contemporary Commandment Boards and late 19c painted panels were recently re-discovered. Light comes from a central window in the ceiling and small rectangular clerestory windows. Beneath the church are catacombs where Pelhams and others are buried. The church is now used by the Pentecostalists and known as the Hastings Temple, very suitably since its design was largely inspired by the Pantheon. Round the corner of Castle Hill and somewhat inland is Wellington Square, also about 1824, a long, sloping rectangle of elegant balconied houses. The rest of the new town, which is on a rather irregular plan owing to the undulating terrain, is mid-Victorian, respectable but unremarkable. The sea front is a single terrace called White Rock with the White Rock Gardens on the hill behind and the Pier, gay and gorgeous, stretching out in

front. The parish church of the new town is Holy Trinity, oddly sited and squashed in between Robertson Street and Trinity Street. A distinguished design by S. S. Teulon built in 1851–9, it lacks the tower he intended for it. The inside is high, wide and handsome—a wealthy church in enriched EE with a Perp rood screen, alabaster pulpit with double staircase and an apsidal chancel with decorated cusped sedilia and oak choir stalls.

St Leonard's [9] stretches westwards and is to Hastings what Hove is to Brighton. The difference is that, although the name derives from a medieval church near the sea, which was ruinous in 1410, it is entirely of 19c origin. James Burton, a builder and father of Decimus Burton, the architect of the screen at Hyde Park Corner, bought land in 1828 stretching along the sea shore for two-thirds of a mile. It was a speculation that paid off. There was a handsome gate on the front dividing St Leonard's from Hastings; this and much else has disappeared, but in Maze Hill and Upper Maze Hill, looking down into St Leonard's Gardens—a deep, romantic ravine, originally a quarry, now full of forest trees and a lily pond—are several survivors of Burton's work. The first is the Clock House, of golden sandstone and looking exactly like a church; after being derelict it is now being repaired as a private house. Further up is North Lodge, the entrance to St Leonard's Gardens, castellated with a four-centred archway. On the sea front the Royal Victoria Hotel—renamed when the Queen as Princess Victoria stayed there—flanked by a heavy colonnade on either side, is the centre of Burton's development, and behind it is the Masonic Hall in heavy Greek revival style, formerly the Assembly Rooms. Continuing westwards the Marina is broken to make way for St Leonard's church, standing a

Cade Street Chapel, **Heathfield**

velopments are a grim example of speculative building.

Heathfield [5] To the motorist travelling along the A265 Heathfield means an especially ugly village, almost a town. It used to be known as Tower Street and sprang up round the railway station on the Polegate to Tunbridge Wells line, now closed. But the real Heathfield lies a mile to the S, a single street with some brick and weatherboarded cottages around the church. Heathfield used to be famous for its Cuckoo Fair, held on April 14 and known as Hefful Fair in Sussex dialect, which suggests that the place was then pronounced Hethfield; according to legend an old woman would let a cuckoo out of her basket to usher in the summer. The church of Hastings sandstone has an EE tower with a broach shingled spire; inside under the bell chamber, presumably put there later, is the date 1445 in Arabic numerals, thought to be the earliest use of these figures in England. In the churchyard are two headstones and a tablet set into the wall with terracotta plaques by Jonathan Harmer, son of a Heathfield stonemason (see Introduction); one is to his son, Sylvan Harmer. The inside is spacious with four-bay Dec arcades on N and S; the quatrefoil clerestory windows make it unusually light. The nave is furnished with box-pews and has its old tiled floor; the roof its tiebeams and plain king-posts. There is an unusual collection box—a solid oak pillar with iron clamps. The S door is 14c and there is a 15c crypt. There are four hatchments and the Royal Arms of George III. The windows were renewed during the restorations and partial rebuilding of 1861 and 1869; in the N aisle is some stained glass (1953) showing the Revd Robert Hunt celebrating Communion in Virginia in 1607 with the figure of a Red Indian in the left light and his squaw kneeling in the right. In

little back up the slope; it looks directly at, and seems to be almost on, the sea. Built of brick in 1963 by Sir Giles and Adrian Gilbert Scott, to replace Burton's church, which was a war casualty, it is an effective and exciting design. Gothic but with semi-elliptical arches outside and in. Also some quirky but original furnishings—a boat pulpit made by Jewish craftsmen on the shores of Galilee and a ship's binnacle for a lectern. The stained glass is all by Patrick Reyntiens. The rest of the Marina seems to be Victorian; but at the extreme end, near Bopeep, is a terrace of three-storey villas, which must be a survival of Burton's plan.

Haywards Heath* [4] is a rather planless modern town, which has grown up round the railway station opened in 1841, the junction for Lewes and Brighton. The weekly cattle market was transferred to the station from Cuckfield in 1868. Haywards was a manor in the parish of Cuckfield and gave its name to the de Hayworthe family, who lived here in the 14c; the former Station Hotel was renamed the Hayworthe a few years ago. Trubweeke, now the name of a modern house, was also a medieval manor and Boltro Road—which might be Latin-American—derives from Bulltrough Farm, which still exists under the boring name of Old House. Some of the more recent de-

Bentley Wood, by Serge Chermayeff; *see* **East Hoathly**

Heathfield Park is the Gibraltar Tower, built in 1711 to the memory of Lord Heathfield, Governor of Gibraltar, 'which fortress he gallantly maintained during four years' (1779–83) investment by the united forces of Spain and France'. Manor House near the church is built of stone, brick and plaster. Other houses are Broomham, 17c and 18c, with an unusually large chimney stack, and curiously named Ballcocks near Vines Cross, of plastered timber-framing and 18c brick. Heathfield ironworks were noted for their production of high quality cannon.

At the hamlet of *Cade Street* a roadside monument states that Jack Cade, the rebel, was killed in 1450 by Alexander Iden, Sheriff of Kent. He did not actually die here,

but was found in a garden, where he received a mortal wound, causing him to die on the way to London. The Independent Chapel (1767) is a square brick box with an oval window on the S front; it is painted white and picked out in black. Inside it has pillared galleries, and both inside and in the churchyard are tablets and headstones with terracotta plaques by Harmer.

Heighton, South [7] Just above Denton in the Ouse valley and like it becoming suburbanised. The church was struck by lightning about 1740; it was not repaired, fell into decay and was condemned for public use in 1780. Manor Farm has an 18c doorway and black mathematical tiles.

Hellingly [8] (pronounced -lye) is a small village with charming tile-hung cottages, some of them Tudor, surrounding the church-yard, which is circular, or rather oval, in shape and rises in places 6–7 ft above the roads around it. It is the only 'ciric', or Celtic burial ground, in Sussex to be preserved intact. Barrows were placed within raised circular mounds so that the dead could rest in a dry place and because a circle, e.g. Stonehenge, was the old pagan symbol of mortality. There can be little doubt that it was used by the Saxons for pagan and later for Christian burial. The cottages on the N side were carefully built and in some cases set at an angle so as to preserve the arc of the churchyard, in which are two headstones decorated with

124

Harmer plaques. The church was originally Transitional-Norman 12c. Two round-headed windows with banded shafts on the N wall of the chancel, and two 13c windows opposite have a decorative course running beneath them. In the S wall of the chancel is a 14c ogee-headed low-side window. The N chapel has an EE arcade behind the altar with rather battered masks at the terminals. There is also a relic of Norman cable moulding set in the wall. The nave arcades are plain EE and the side windows 15c. Both nave and chancel have trussed and raftered roofs with king-posts. At the W end is a modern organ gallery with linenfold panelling. The tower was rebuilt very creditably in 1836. There are two distinguished houses in the parish—Horselunges, a timber-framed 15c manor house, well restored by Walter Godfrey in 1925, just S of the church, and Carter's Corner, a gabled Jacobean mansion lying about 2½ miles to the E. It was the home of the 1st Lord Hailsham, who took his title from the neighbouring town. Hellingly Hospital is the East Sussex County Mental Hospital, and 'gone to Hellingly' has a sad and unmistakable meaning to Sussex people.

Heron's Ghyll [5] on the Crowborough–Uckfield road, consists only of a RC church and the adjoining school-cum-presbytery. The church, EE (1904) by F. A. Walters, is of ashlar and has a N tower with a tiled cap; it looks more C of E than Roman. The pulpit has 10c Dutch carving in the panels.

Herstmonceaux [8] *see* **Hurstmonceux**.

Hickstead [4] *see* **Twineham**.

Highbrook [1] was until 1884 within the parish of West Hoathly. The church is a reminder of the strong antagonisms within the Church of England in the 19c. Two affluent ladies disagreed so violently with the practices at West Hoathly, at that time a bigoted, Protestant, 'black gown' church, that they decided to build a new church at Highbrook, despite the absence of a village. It is a successful and pleasing design in EE style by Carpenter and Ingelow, consisting of a nave, chancel and N aisle with a tower and shingled broach spire—a far more suitable church than Turner's Hill, built 11 years later. The chancel has linenfold panelling on the walls and a reredos with carved gilt figures of Christ and the 12 apostles; the floor is a chequer-board of black and white marble. The E and W windows are by Clayton and Bell.

Hoathly, East [5] (pronounced -lye). The church has a Perp tower with an angle turret; the W door has the Pelham arms in the spandrels and the buckle as label-stops. The nave and chancel were entirely rebuilt in 1856 in a Dec style. The church must be of 12c origin, since there remains a Norman pillar piscina with zigzag decoration on the shaft, which was dug up in the churchyard; beside it is a recess with an ogee arch, presumably for a later piscina. The E wall of the chancel is adorned with highly-coloured mosaics, somewhat pre-Raphaelite. On the outside of the S wall is a tablet to Samuel Atkins, gardener to the Duke of Newcastle, 1742—a slate slab surmounted by an urn and with appropriate swags of flowers and fruit. The Duke lived at Halland Place, which was in the parish. In the tower is a wall monument to John Mittell (1734), with an urn in front of an obelisk. Hardly anything remains of Halland Place, built in 1595 when the Pelhams moved from Laughton. Some of the outer walls survive, smothered in ivy, about 6 ft high; the only complete building is a 17c brick barn, formerly a coach-house, with a hipped roof, mullioned and transomed windows, all now bricked up, and wide, brick pilaster strips.

Seven ancient limes look like the relic of an avenue.

Bentley Wood is a surprising modern house in a secluded position. Designed in 1934 by Serge Chermayeff it so shocked the Rural District Council that they refused permission. But client and architect won the day at a public enquiry. It is mainly of glass, unpainted cedar and weatherboarding, and after 42 years still looks contemporary.

Hoathly, West* [1] (pronounced -lye) has a street of tile-hung and weatherboarded cottages, many of them with Horsham-slabbed roofs. In the centre and opposite the church is the Manor House, originally the dower house to Gravetye, with a handsome stone façade of 1627, mullioned windows and brick chimney stacks. Just S of it is the 15c Priest's House, timber-framed with a topiary yew hedge bounding the garden; it is now used as a museum.

Outside the village are Selsfield House with an early Georgian stone front of five bays, and Gravetye Manor, late Elizabethan with mullioned and transomed windows, four gables with finials and groups of brick chimneys. It was built for Richard Infield, an ironmaster, between 1598 and 1603, but its most famous occupant was William Robinson, the pioneer of modern gardening, who added the N wing and lived here until his death in 1935 at the age of 97 (*see* Introduction). The church stands in the centre of the village and has a 15c tower with a broach shingled spire. Brick paths lead to the doors and the churchyard has a number of sandstone table tombs. The nave and chancel are Norman in origin, but only one small window above the nave arcade survives; the rest is 13 and 14c. The chancel has an E window of three stepped lancets under one arch, and on the splays of the N windows are 13c red leaf patterns. There are 13c triple sedilia and two piscinae. The elaborate and handsome roof was put in

West Hoathly; Manor House

at the restoration in 1870. The S aisle is Dec, but must have been a widening of an existing aisle, since the arcades are clearly EE. The SW single-light window has glass by Kempe. The 13c font is plain and square with a central column and four supporting pillars. In the NW corner of the nave is the movement of the old clock, believed to have been made locally between 1410 and 1422; it struck the hours until 1965 when it was removed from the tower because it could no longer be repaired. Just inside the S door is an oak churchwardens' chest; it is about 10 ft long and was adze-hewn out of a solid trunk about 1150. The oak may easily have sprung from a B.C. acorn.

Hollington [9] is now a northern suburb of St Leonard's. The church, which stands alone about $\frac{3}{4}$ mile to the W, looks 13c in a drawing of 1800; but was so drastically restored and altered in the 19c that it has no interest. The only ancient feature inside is one oak tie-beam in the nave. It is surrounded by woodland, is some way from any habitation and known locally as 'The Church in the Wood'. Charles Lamb, the essayist, and Thomas Hood, the poet, each describe visits to the church in 1823–26.

Hooe [8] is on slightly rising ground above Pevensey Level. The village has vanished and the modern settlement is at Hooe Com-

mon over a mile to the NE. The church stands alone at the end of a winding lane. The only relics of the earlier church are the Norman font of Sussex marble and an ancient muniment chest, hewn out of a whole oak trunk and bound with iron clamps (cf. West Hoathly). The present building is mostly 15c, it has an embattled W tower with a tiled cap and an angle turret. The S porch has large leaves in the spandrels and weatherworn masks as label-stops; inside are stone benches on corbels. The much-needed restoration of 1890 has left the inside too much swept and garnished. The nave has a barrel roof and the modern pulpit an early 18c sounding board with a star in-

126

lay. The N chapel is 13c and has EE lancets. In the upper lights of the E window is some 14c Flemish glass, showing Edward III and Queen Philippa, and SS Peter and John.

Horsted Keynes* [4] (pronounced Canes) is a rather spread-out village with a wide and well-kept green and a station on the Bluebell—formerly Lewes–East Grinstead—line. It derives its name from the Norman family of Cahanges who presumably had property here. The church is on rising ground, and there is a slight dip between it and the village. It stands in a circular churchyard (cf. Hellingly) and has a brick path leading to the 17c S porch. It is cruciform with a graceful shingled broach spire. Externally the details seem all to be 13c, but inside its Norman origin is at once apparent from the plain unmoulded eastern arch of the crossing and the two arches to the N and S; the W arch of the crossing is 14c with foliage corbels. There is also a Norman doorway reset in the N wall when the N aisle was added in 1888. The chancel has 13c lancet windows, the E window being a stepped triplet with glass by Kempe who also did the W window. In a recess in the N wall is a 13c effigy about 3 ft long of a cross-legged knight; near it is a stone slab with a floriated cross in relief. One of the S lancets contains armorial glass roundels; the upper two appear to be medieval. Against the S wall are two white marble monuments—to Mrs Edward Lightmaker (d. 1704) and William Pigott (d. 1722); both are surmounted by coloured armorial shields and have swags and cherubs at the foot. The pulpit, probably late 17c, has richly carved panels inset; these were the work of Mr Wyatt, a parishioner, about 70 years ago and look as if they were copied from a German design. There is an extraordinary handrail of ropes, and balusters with outsize

Hooe

acorns. The nave roof has plain tie-beams and rafters, but no king-posts. Ludwell and Pierpoints are two good timber-framed houses, standing opposite each other at the cross-roads. Treemans, SW of the village, has an agreeable medley of styles, some Tudor brickwork, some timber-framing, a five bay W front 1693 of chequer brick and a wing of ashlar with mullioned windows.

Horsted, Little [5] the church stands beside the East Grinstead–Lewes road. It has a stout Perp tower with an angle turret, unusual in this part of Sussex. The rest is mainly EE, but was much restored by Scott in 1863, who heightened the turret and added a spirelet. Its

earliest and most interesting feature is the arcade (1080) outside the N wall of the chancel, pierced for two windows; it is reminiscent of the Saxon church at Bradford-on-Avon. The nave has two two-light trefoil windows (1270) and there is a similar low-side window in the chancel. A small slab with a raised cross lies almost hidden under an arched alcove, and there is an Easter sepulchre which may be the tomb of the founder or a benefactor of the church. Horsted Place is a large Victorian mansion by Samuel Daukes (1851) with internal decorations by Pugin. There is no village here, only the rectory near the church and a farm or two at Horsted Green $\frac{1}{2}$ mile to the north.

Hurstmonceux [8] is well known on account of its castle, now the Royal Greenwich Observatory. It is also the original home of the trug-making industry. The trug—the word is supposed to have connection with trough—is a garden basket made of thin laths of wood; it is now known and marketed far outside Sussex. The castle was bought for the Observatory in 1946 and is not open to the public. The park has become somewhat urbanised by tarmac roads and signposts, and dotted about among the woods rise vast domes like Brobdingnagian mushrooms. However, they have been tactfully placed and do not impair the romantic beauty of the castle itself, which at least is being used and not being left to rot. Hurstmonceux is one of the earliest important brick buildings; it was built in 1441—about the same time as Eton—by Sir Roger de Fiennes, to whose family it came through a marriage into the de Monceux family. The use of bricks for grand buildings at this time was a new fashion from Flanders and the bricks used may have been made by Flemish workmen who came over specially. It was not built as a fortification, but as a castellated manor house and has never been the scene of any battle or siege. Consequently, though much of the inside became ruinous in the 18c it is perfect and undamaged, and the golden-red walls rising from the moat are a sight of exceptional loveliness. The buildings form a rectangle, almost a square, and the S entrance over the drawbridge is flanked by two 84 ft high towers—the Watch Tower and the Signal-Tower; they contain two tiers of loopholes for crossbow defence. Between the towers is a mutilated badge of the de Fiennes. Sir Roger's son, Richard, married Joan, heiress of Thomas, Lord Dacre, and was in her name declared Lord Dacre in

Hurstmonceux;
Dacre monument

1458. Hurstmonceux remained with the Dacres until 1708, when it was sold. One of its more eccentric chatelaines was Georgiana, daughter of the Bishop of St Asaph and wife of Francis Hare Naylor, with whom she had eloped. She was often seen riding through the park on an ass and attended church accompanied by a white doe. In the 19c it passed through various owners, until it was bought in 1911 by Col Lowther, who partially restored it to its old glory. The restoration was completed in the 1930s by Sir Paul Latham at great expense and in excellent taste; he was the last private owner.

Hurstmonceux Place, just outside the park, is a large brick house (1720), added to by Samuel Wyatt and likewise associated with the Hares; it is now divided into flats. The church stands opposite the castle entrance and is nearly 2 miles from the village centre at Gardner Street. A mounting-block against the wall is provided for horsemen. The earliest part is the tower (1180) which forms the NW corner of the nave and has a shingled broach spire; the N aisle arcade is of the same date. The rest is 13c–14c and built of sandstone, but the Dacre chapel and E wall of the chancel are of brick, one of the earliest examples of church brickwork in Sussex. The aisles are lit by dormer windows put in at the Victorian restoration. Inside, there is much old quarry-tiled flooring, and the nave has a trussed roof with tie-beams and king-posts. The high nave arcades have good capitals, single leaf on the earlier northern piers, early stiff-leaf design on the south. The font (1380) is a square sandstone bowl with a round stem and four octagonal corner shafts. Near it is another slightly older, broken font with trefoil-headed side panels; it was found in a farmyard. At the end of the nave is a small sculpture of a child attributed to Jean Goujon, and in the chancel a touching memorial by the Belgian

Hurstmonceux

sculptor Kessels to Georgina Hare Naylor, the mother of Augustus Hare, author and traveller. On the chancel floor is a canopied brass to Sir William Fiennes (1402) whose son Sir Roger built the castle. The chief interest, however, is the Dacre chapel. Here is the superb tomb erected in 1534 to Thomas, 8th Lord Dacre (1470–1533), and his son Sir Thomas Fiennes who predeceased him. It is built of Caen, Bonchurch and Purbeck marble. Beneath the rich, ornate Gothic canopy lie two figures in Milanese armour carved in Caen stone, their hands in an attitude of prayer, their heads resting on Brocas helms, and their feet on the bull of the Dacres and the alant (wolf-hound) of the Fiennes. Above the arch is a richly carved cornice of shields and helmets. When the tomb was restored, an old suspicion that the figures were not those of Lord Dacre and his son was confirmed, since the tabards are of the Hoo family and have been altered. They may have come from Battle Abbey after its dissolution in 1539, and, as the Dacre finances were low at that time, they may have been bought for a song and altered. In the churchyard are some tombs with terracotta Harmer plaques; two are let into the W wall on the outside.

Hurstpierpoint* [4] known locally as Hurst, is built around a crossroads. The high street has a few Georgian houses, but nothing of great note and is in the main Victorian and later. The medieval church was pulled down in 1843, and a new church designed by Sir Charles Barry built on the same site, as the old sandstone tombs testify. It is a stylish building in 14c manner with a slim stone spire. The nave has five-bay arcades with clustered piers and a clerestory. The E window is by Kempe, and in the S aisle E window are a number of 15–17c medallions collected by Bishop Butler in the 18c. In the chancel

floor are four black marble tomb slabs, two with coats of arms to Sir John Stapley 1676 and Nicholas Monke 1688. In the S chapel, now the vestry, very shabbily placed behind a radiator, is the 13c tomb of a crusader, cross-legged, and against the N wall of the nave is a recumbent 14c knight, much mutilated and enclosed by contemporary iron railings placed far too close. Both these medieval relics need attention and re-siting. Danny, about a mile to the SE, was for 200 years the home of the Campions, whose memorials are in the church. The E front is E-shaped Elizabethan, of red brick with blue brick diapers; the S front is Georgian. Having been for a time a school, Danny is now flats. On Wolstonbury Hill above Hurst are two clumps of trees planted by the Campions and known as Campion's Eyebrows. Hurstpierpoint College, about a mile to the NE, is one of the three Woodard schools in Sussex (see Introduction). It was built in 1851–3, just before Lancing, and designed by R. C. Carpenter. The chapel was built 10 years later by his son, R. H. Carpenter. The material used is knapped flint, in contrast to the brick of Ardingly, and gives the buildings a somewhat harsh appearance.

Icklesham [6] The plain village with a drab string of villas on the Hastings side does no justice to a place which was first mentioned in 772. In 1066 it was a large parish, including the hill on which New Winchelsea was later built, and stretched down to the Rother's mouth; Winchelsea is still in the civil parish of Icklesham. On Hog's Hill to the S is a smock windmill with sails and a fantail; but the glory of Icklesham is its church. The Norman tower in three stages was the N transept of a cruciform church; it is entered through a round-headed doorway with early single scalloped capitals and the

third stage has unusually large bell-openings. The peculiar hexagonal W porch was reconstructed by S. S. Teulon in 1848 from a round porch built in 1785. Inside the church is light, spacious and dignified; the nave has three-bay arcades with round arches and piers and late Norman capitals of leaves and scallops, all about 1175. The rib vaulting of the tower is of the same date. In the early 13c the N chapel was added, with a blank arcade of five arches against the N wall and lancet windows. Work may also have begun on the larger S, or St Nicholas's, chapel. This also has a blank arcade of seven arches (the easternmost being a sedile) which are 13c as is also the restored Geometrical tracery of the windows. This was the manorial chapel and still belongs to the lord of the manor. Stop and look at the fine vista from the nave to the SE. When Teulon removed the old roofs which were rotten, he found traces of a Norman clerestory, which was closed in in the 14c when the roof spanning nave and aisles was built (cf. Cuckfield). On the N wall is a large board with the terms of two medieval charities—the Cheyney Trust of almshouses, burnt and rebuilt about 1850, and the Fray bequest of 1592; the money is still paid out at its face value—hardly the benefactor's intention. In the archives are detailed plans made in 1798 for a possible invasion. Precise livestock records were made; sixteen surrounding parishes were divided into two groups of eight and each parish given exact directions where to move. Captain Lamb of the Yeomanry and Provisional Cavalry in Sussex was to be in charge and his orders gave 'Directions for making bread' including boiling 2 oz of hops for an hour. Luckily it never happened; but Icklesham was ready.

Iden [6] A pleasant open village centred upon a cross-roads. To the N, a little way beyond the Rother,

Icklesham mill

the Kent Ditch divides Kent from Sussex, and the village is more like Kent in character. The church is approached by an ugly concrete path, sadly inferior to the traditional brick. The 15c tower with one Norman window has an angle turret—often found in Kent and sometimes in East Sussex—and in the second stage a small priest's room with a contemporary fireplace. Space and light are the first impressions inside; the Perp windows are nearly all filled with clear glass, the Victorian pews have been reduced in number, those that remain stripped of stain and varnish and the organ moved from the chapel to the W end of the N aisle

in 1958. The N aisle and chapel were built in the 15c at the same time as the tower by Sir William Scott of The Mote, whose arms are over the W door; the S aisle was demolished in the 16c and the arcades filled in. The slab of one of the original stone altars was found in the churchyard and restored as the high altar in 1959. The altar rails are early 18c and the pulpit part of an old three-decker. In the chancel is a brass to Walter Seller, rector of Iden, 1427, vested for mass with his hands in an attitude of prayer (cf. Clayton). The church has been embellished with various gifts, among them a priest's stall with misericord and a rare 14c–15c

crucifix over the pulpit—both from Lady Conway's collection. Also in the N chapel a coloured wooden Virgin and Child 17c Spanish, in the N aisle an early English alabaster saint and by the chancel arch a 17c Flemish statue of St Christopher and the Christ Child. Oxenbridge is a striking 15c thatched farmhouse a little to the N. The timber-framed front is concealed by white plaster; a flagstone path leads to it from the road and the house stands proudly, surrounded by grass and uncluttered by creepers, beds or bushes. Much of the timbering inside remains and the screens passage has the original arched doorway in the back wall.

Iford [7] is a small farming village just above the level of the Ouse marshes, known as the Brooks. Excavations have shown that the Ouse once washed its shores, and a paved Roman causeway was discovered some years ago. Low flint walls surround the fields and cottage gardens. The church, built of rough flints like the cottages, with stones inserted here and there, is 12c and has had little alteration. The Norman tower between nave and chancel has a short shingled spire, and, inside, four arches. The western arch has good chevron mouldings, the eastern arch plain roll moulding; the side arches are unmoulded. The sanctuary is lit, rather dimly owing to the richly coloured Victorian glass, by three deeply splayed round-headed lancets at the E end surmounted by a small circular window or oculus, and a similar lancet on either side. There is a simple round-headed Norman piscina. The nave has Dec windows filled with bad Victorian glass. In the N wall is a three-bay arcade 13c, the relic of a vanished aisle. The roof has tie-beams and king-posts, and rather skied at the W end, is a George III Royal Arms. The 13c font is a circular stone basin, supported by a central column and four round pillars.

Swanborough Manor House has a great hall dating from 1200 with a fine 15c roof; it was probably a grange of Lewes Priory, a few miles away. The rest of the house dates from the 15c and 16c. Swanborough gave its name to a Hundred and a court was held there up to 1860. The late Lady Reading, founder of the WRVS, lived here and sat in the House of Lords as Baroness Swanborough.

Isfield [4] is a long straggling village and used to have a small railway station on the Tunbridge Wells–Lewes line. The church lies a good ½ mile off the road and stands alone and quite near the Ouse. It was originally Transitional; the lower part of the tower and the S window of the nave are of this date. In 1893, the N aisle was added, the chancel arch rebuilt and the tower embattled and given a spire instead of a Sussex cap. The chancel has on the S side two plain sedilia and a piscina with an elaborate Dec canopy. On the N wall under an arched alcove is a tomb, probably an Easter sepulchre, with crosses of beautiful design. But the most important 14c embellishment was the addition on the S side of the Shurley chapel. It has handsome Dec windows and is furnished with oak linenfold panelling and pews; there is a squint to enable the family to see the elevation of the host. The chapel's chief interest, however, is the series of monuments to the Shurleys. One tomb (1527) has lost its brasses, but two others have brasses to Edward Shurley (d. 1558) and his wife, and Thomas Shurley (d. 1579) and his wife. The finest monument is the alabaster altar tomb (1631) with recumbent figures of Sir John Shurley and his two wives and, kneeling below them, his nine children. His first wife was the daughter of Sir Thomas Shirley of Wiston in West Sussex, and his second wife the daughter of George Goring of Danny, Hurstpierpoint, and widow of Sir Henry Bowyer of Cuckfield; the country squires tended to marry mostly within their own county. In the S wall of the nave are some fragments of medieval glass, showing the instruments of the Passion. In 1775 the tombstone of Gundrada, wife of William de Warenne, founder of Lewes Priory, was discovered beneath the floor; it was brought to Isfield from the Priory at the Dissolution. It was returned to Southover church where a chapel has been built over it. Isfield Place, the old home of the Shurleys, can be seen across the fields from the church. It is a mellow, square 17c house of brick; the garden is enclosed by a stone wall with a low tower at each angle.

Jevington [8] lies in a combe, the only break in the Downs E of the Cuckmere valley. The church stands up on the Downs, a little above the village, and has a Saxon tower, in which the original windows, now blocked up, are clearly visible on the N and S faces; the arched headings are of Roman bricks, and the herring-bone and long and short work are prominent. Inside, set into the N wall of the nave, is a Saxon tablet showing Christ thrusting a cross-shaped sword into the serpent's mouth; it was discovered beneath the floor in 1875 and in manner is not unlike the Saxon mural tablets in Chichester Cathedral. The N aisle was added in about 1228 and is lit by four EE lancets; there is an unusual transverse arch across the aisle, which may indicate that it was two chapels divided by a screen. The chancel arch is EE and has a round-headed squint on either side; the squints were originally on a slant, but were misguidedly straightened at the restoration in 1871. The chancel has an E window of three long, ogee, trefoil-headed lancets under a broad, low, internal arch, probably very early 14c; it has rather good 19c glass. On the chancel arch wall over the northern squint is a black marble tablet to 'Nat. Collier M.A. late rector of this church, who died Mar the first 169½.' The ambiguous date reflects the dispute whether the year started on January 1 (New Style) or on March 25 (Old Style). January 1st was legally established as the first day of the year in 1752. The choir has oak stalls made of beams removed from the tower. There is a plain square font c. 1400.

Keymer* [4] (pronounced Kymer) is an ancient place though there is little sign of it today, since it is almost engulfed by subtopian Hassocks. The 12c and 13c church was rebuilt in flint in 1866 in EE style. The only original part is the apsidal chancel, much altered, and a 14c window in the N wall. The low 'flounced' spire in two stages is unique in Sussex and is a reproduction of its medieval predecessor as shown in the drawing by Earp (1802) in the Sharpe Collection.

Ockley Manor, a mile to the N, is a handsome early 18c red-brick house with stone angle dressings and a brick dovecote. Above it is Oldland Mill, 18c, which has been recently restored and is the property of the Sussex Archaeological Trust.

Kingston [7] is sometimes known as Kingston-near-Lewes to distinguish it from two other Kingstons in West Sussex. A suburban outcrop S of Lewes encroaches; but the village street with low flint walls to the cottage gardens remains intact. The churchyard at the end of it is entered by a tapsell gate, and among the graves is one 'bed-post' carved with the name of 'Arthur Hume Simpson, a Sussex Priest' d. 1920. The church, dedicated to St Pancras like Lewes Priory, is built of flints and has a nave and chancel with no aisles. It is entirely 14c though the small W tower with a Sussex cap may be earlier. The chancel arch is so wide as to be almost round-headed; it has no capitals and the chamfers continue to the base. There is an early round font, heavily moulded, on a round base. Kingston Manor is a partly Georgian house, which has several carved fragments from Lewes Priory in the garden.

Laughton [5] (pronounced Lorton) is in flat country with great woods on the N and to the S the solitary marshes of Glynde Level. Its chief interest is its association with the Pelhams, Earls of Chichester, who were lords of the manor from the mid-14c until recent years. It was Sir John Pelham who, in 1356, was granted the badge of the Buckle of the King's swordbelt in honour of his feat of capturing the French King at Poitiers. The tower at

Laughton church and at many others in the neighbourhood has Pelham buckles on the label-stops of the W door. Laughton Place, the original home of the Pelhams before they moved to Halland and after that to Stanmer, is 1½ miles away, alone at the end of a winding lane. It was once a fortified manor house with a moat; but all that survives is a ruinous brick tower (1554), looking forlornly over Glynde levels. It has a rich projecting cornice and shows the Pelham buckle above the windows. The tower of the church, built of sandstone, is 15c but the nave is 13c and has two lancet windows surviving. The chancel is of flint and appears to be 18c Gothick, though there are no records, it has crocketed pinnacles at the E corners, and a blocked priest's door with a high ogee arch and a typical band of quatrefoils. Over the chancel arch is the rood beam on which are two helms—one a Tudor headpiece about 1540, the other a small 'funerary helmet' about 1660, which was used for placing on a knight's coffin together with other insignia. Above the arch are the Royal Arms of George III. The tracery from a Perp screen is set into panelling on either side of the altar. Beneath the chancel is the Pelham vault, containing 31 coffins; it was sealed in 1886 after the burial of the 3rd Earl of Chichester. The nave roof is of single frame construction with tie-beams and king-posts.

Lewes [7] The naturally strategic position of the old county town can at once be seen by climbing to the top of the castle keep, the fortress built by William de Warenne, to whom the Conqueror gave the Rape of Lewes. Southwards it surveys the whole river valley down to Newhaven; northwards it looks towards Mount Harry (not named after the King, but probably derived from an ancient pagan word meaning a place of worship), where in 1264 the forces of Henry III and

Simon de Montfort met in conflict at the Battle of Lewes. The defeat of the King's army resulted in the Mise of Lewes, an agreement which was the foundation of parliamentary government. Lewes was already important in Saxon times; it had two mints and, in the reign of Edward the Confessor, 127 burgesses. But with the Norman conquest its importance became far greater. The danger of French invasion was ever present, and de Warenne's first task was to fortify the town. The castle contained two mottes or mounds—the south western motte, on which the keep is built, the north eastern, the Brack Mount, surveying the river valley. Much of the flintwork in the keep is late 11c or early 12c, but the two projecting octagonal towers were added a century later; they now have charming Gothick windows inserted instead of the narrow loops. Only the gateway remains of the original Norman gatehouse; but in the 14c the magnificent machicolated barbican was built in the moat by the last of the de Warennes. Its drawbridges have long since disappeared, but the grooves for the portcullises are still clearly visible; the S front has excellent knapped flintwork. In 1620 the castle was dismantled and materials sold to the citizens of Lewes; hence the disappearance of all the domestic buildings, which surrounded the Bowling Green. At the entrance to the castle is a small museum, where a collection of neolithic and Bronze Age relics are admirably displayed; these and later collections and photographs give an excellent idea of the historic and prehistoric importance of Lewes.

After building the castle William de Warenne's next task was devotional. He and his wife, Gundrada, decided to make a journey to Rome; but upheavals in France stopped them getting any further than Cluny, where the great abbey impressed them so profoundly that they promised to found a priory at

Lewes, the first Cluniac house in England. The Abbot of Cluny sent Lanzo and three other monks across in 1076, and de Warenne gave them the small church of St Pancras in Southover and enough land to support twelve monks. The Priory was designed on an ambitious scale, worthy of its impressive mother house; the church was nearly 450 ft long, larger than Chichester Cathedral. Its endowments were large and widespread, including tithes of all de Warenne's lands, special rights in the markets and fisheries of Lewes and the church and manor of Castle Acre, Norfolk. Lanzo, the first prior, who reigned for 30 years, was a man of great piety; the Priory was known for its spiritual excellence and the monks respected for their devotion and charity. For a time Lewes Priory was notably prosperous and was in credit when most other Cluniac houses were in debt; its wealth and influence were equalled only by Battle Abbey. But in 1264 King Henry III's army used it as their headquarters before the Battle of Lewes. After the battle its courts and altars were defiled by de Montfort's men; the buildings were damaged and the church burnt. The military occupation and the succession of foreign priors, appointed from Cluny, who sent back money to the mother house, reduced the Priory from affluence to penury, and in 1279 its temporal state was described as desperate. At last in 1480 the Pope issued a bull releasing Lewes from subjection to Cluny; but the monks could still only make their profession to the Abbot of Cluny, which was highly inconvenient owing to the almost perpetual state of war. The proposal to raise Lewes to the status of an abbey found no favour at Cluny; but the Abbot finally agreed to grant the Prior the special privilege of professing monks. One of the later priors, Thomas Nelond, 1417–32, is commemorated by a magnificent brass at Cowfold, West Sussex,

one of the finest in the country. In 1535 the first steps to suppress the Priory were taken after Layton reported to Thomas Cromwell, Henry VIII's minister, 'I found corruption of both sorts and what is worse treason.' On 16 November, 1537 it was surrendered to Cromwell; there were 23 monks and 80 servants. His treatment of the Priory was unusually savage; he even employed an Italian engineer, Portinari, to devise ways of burning the masonry to the ground. What was not destroyed was pillaged by the townsfolk and William Newton used the Caen stones to build Southover Grange in 1572. The scanty remains lay neglected and overgrown and the site was almost forgotten until in 1845 the railway line from Lewes to Brighton cut right through it. The foundations of the monastic buildings were re-discovered and the small leaden coffins of William and Gundrada, now in Southover church, were found buried beneath the chancel of the Priory church. All that remains above the ground are the S wall of the refectory, the walls of the rere-dorter or lavatory and some walls of the infirmary chapel; the strong Norman masonry is still in good condition despite Portinari's efforts to destroy it. There is also a series of undercrofts; but the buildings are at present unsafe and are railed off to prevent entry. To the E of the Priory wall is a high grassy mound, known as The Mount; its origin is conjectural and it is not known to have had any connection with the Priory.

The town as seen from the castle keep presents a close-packed huddle of red-tiled roofs and most of the houses are 18c. Descending from the W the first notable house is Shelley's Hotel, which has an Elizabethan front bearing the date 1577; it was then the Vine Inn—the carved wooden sign is in the museum at Anne of Cleves' House, a name of doubtful authenticity—and still has some contemporary

Lewes: ▷
p136 In the High Street
p137 Keere Street

wall paintings in one of the rooms. In the 18c some fine rooms were added and it became the town house of the Shelley family. The Old Grammar School near it was rebuilt in knapped flint in 1851. Opposite is St Anne's House 1719, a good solid Georgian house with an Ionic porch added about 100 years later. Next comes the site of Westgate and to the left some of the town wall can be seen; but just before on the right is Keere Street, a charming cobbled lane with some pretty cottages plunging steeply down to Southover Grange. Just inside Westgate and behind the Bull Inn, 15c, is Westgate chapel, founded in 1672 by several Lewes clergymen as a protest against the Act of Uniformity; it started by being Calvinistic, but gradually moved towards Unitarianism. Meetings were first in the Elizabethan house of the Gorings, and two hatchments, one to Henry Goring 1583, hang in the present chapel, which was largely rebuilt in 1913. On the N side of the High Street is Castle Place (No. 166) where are four houses by Amon Wilds, the Lewes architect who built much of 19c Brighton; the two in the centre have pilasters decorated with ammonite capitals. The High Street now levels out and becomes somewhat wider. Its most distinguished building is the County Hall built in 1808–12 by John Johnson in Portland stone; adjoining it is an extension also in Portland stone on the site of the former Newcastle House. It has a pediment with a sundial dated 1717. Opposite is the White Hart, a solid Georgian hotel which was once the town house of the Pelhams. Between the two used to stand the Town Hall; the new Town Hall on the left beyond the cross-roads was built in 1893— rather raw red brick, but containing a magnificent Elizabethan

◁ **Warehouse and brewery on the Ouse, Lewes**

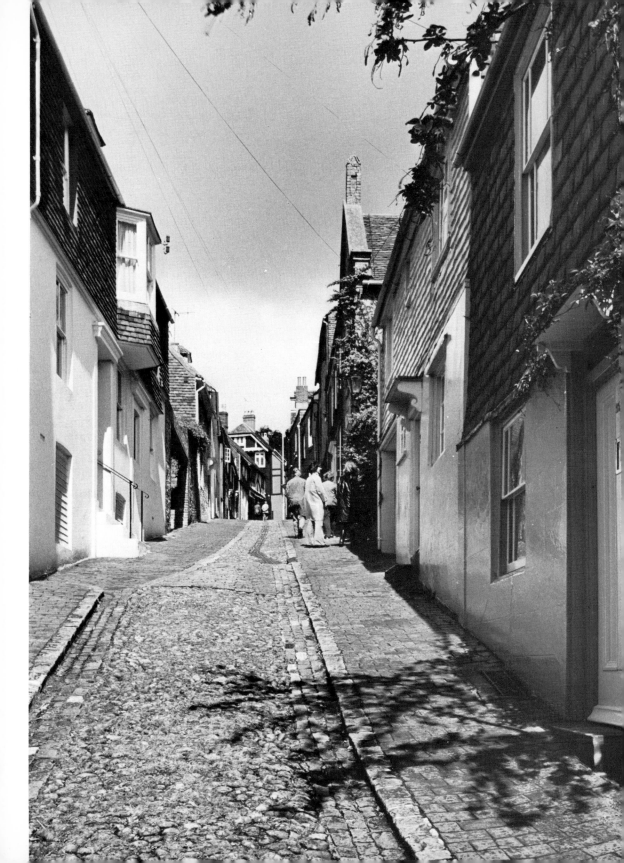

staircase removed from Slaugham Place. Below ground are 14c cellars once used as a prison for the Protestant Martyrs. Round to the left is the brick Market Tower built in 1792 and adorned with the town arms in terracotta by Harmer of Heathfield. In it hangs the old town bell 'Gabriel' cast in 1555, removed from St Nicholas church at the top of School Hill where the splendidly sited War Memorial by the March brothers now stands.

From the crest of the hill before it swoops down to the Ouse can be seen the memorial on Cliffe Hill to the Protestant Martyrs who were burned to death in Queen Mary's reign. The celebrations on 5 November in which a tar barrel is rolled down School Hill, are partly in memory of the Lewes Martyrs as well as of Guy Fawkes. School Hill House and Lewes House are notable among other Georgian houses. The cross-roads at the foot of the hill marks the boundary of the old town wall and is the site of Eastgate. Friars' Walk is named after the Grey Friars whose house lay between Eastgate and the river; nothing except an archway remains. Lewes Bridge, narrow and hump-backed, was built in 1727 by Nicholas Dubois, the architect of Stanmer, and was until 1969, apart from a small bridge at Southease, the only river-crossing between Newhaven and Barcombe. Beyond it the narrow, medieval-feeling Cliffe High Street was perpetually choked with traffic; but Phoenix Causeway to the N, with a new and wider bridge, has brought comparative peace. On the N side are some timber-framed houses with overhanging storeys; the S side is mostly early 19c, built when the street was widened.

The other extramural quarter is *Southover*. At the foot of Keere Street is Southover Grange, built in 1572 by William Newton of Caen stone from the Priory ruins; John Evelyn, the diarist, lived here after his grandmother married Newton as

her second husband. The fine gabled house with mullioned windows has a spacious garden through which the seasonal Winterbourne flows. Southover High Street is mostly 16c to early 19c with a surprisingly urbane interpolation, Priory Crescent 1840, on the S side. Anne of Cleves' House—the queen was granted the manor, but never lived here—is now a Folk Museum. The porch is dated 1599 and the house, like the Grange, was probably built with materials from the Priory.

In medieval times there were 14 churches. Ten within the walls and four without. There are now three within and three without. None of them is outstanding, but all have some curious interest.

St Michael's, the mother church of Lewes, is just below the castle walls and abuts on to the High Street. Its 13c round tower—*see* Southease and Piddinghoe—has a short octagonal shingled spire; it was formerly plastered, but now has an unsightly coating of pebble-dash. After the Restoration the church fell into decline owing to the predominance of Dissenters in Lewes. The three-bay S arcade is 14c; but the N arcade and the arcades of the chancel date from 1748 when they were rebuilt, rather parsimoniously, in wood. The N and S walls were rebuilt at the same time; the S wall has good knapped and squared flintwork. There are two brasses badly placed in the N aisle; one, headless, to a knight, 15c, the other to John Braydford, priest (1457). In the chancel is a monument to Sir Nicholas Pelham and his wife Anne Sackville (1559); the parents kneel at a lectern with their ten children below. This ancestor of the Earls of Chichester led the defence of Seaford against the French; the last two lines of the inscription read 'What time the French sought to have sack'd Seaford, This Pelham did repell them back aboord.'

St John-sub-Castro stands in a

churchyard which was an early, possibly Roman, fortified enclosure. The old church of Saxon origin was a little to the N; the present church was built in 1839 designed by George Cheeseman. The idea of a 'castrum' (fort) seems to have gone to his head, and he decided to give his clumsy and unattractive design a massive castellated tower. The inside has pillared galleries; but someone with 'an eye for colour' has been let loose. Madonna blue galleries might pass; but the barn roof with its interstices coloured orange, yellow and ochre is a visual disaster. On the chancel wall are some urbane 18c and early 19c monuments with a pleasing variety of urns. Outside, set into the N (liturgical E) wall is a late Saxon doorway of large stones with three roll-mouldings; in the E (liturgical S) wall is a round-headed arch with a Latin inscription to Mangnus, a Danish anchorite. It was originally the chancel arch, and was rescued when the chancel fell in 1587. Both doorway and arch have beneath them a 13c stone coffin lid with floriated crosses. In the graveyard is a stone to Mark Sharp 1747, designed by himself, shewing the tools of his trade.

All Saints. Amon Wilds built the long brick nave in 1806; it is somewhat out of scale and seems to shrug its shoulders at the modest 16c tower of rough flints and stone. Less happily in 1883 a Gothic chancel and transepts in dressed flints were added—quite at variance with the classical nave. Inside, Wilds' galleries supported on elegant iron pillars remain. There are two 17c monuments with kneeling figures. One to Robert Massard and his wife (1624)—he was an officer of the jewel house to James I—the other to John Stansfield and his wife (1627); he was grandfather to John Evelyn, the diarist (*see* South Malling). In the tower are two stone figures of children in Georgian dress, moved here from the old

Jireh chapel, Malling Street, **Lewes**

National School. A small George IV Royal Arms.

St Anne's, formerly called St Mary Westout, is on the hill above Westgate and the best church in Lewes. Tower, nave and S transept are Norman. The S arcade of four bays has three plain pointed arches and one round-headed; the round piers have square abaci and capitals decorated with stiff-leaf mouldings—all very good 12c work. The transeptal chapel has a rib-vaulted roof and a round-headed E window. Furnishings include a richly carved pulpit (1620), given by Herbert Springett of Ringmer, 18c. Communion rails and W gallery and plain oak box-pews; also a good brass chandelier. The elaborate nave roof with tie-beams, queen-posts and curved braces is 1538; the chancel rather simpler with king-posts. In the chancel is a 14c table tomb with an ogee-cusped canopy; its brasses are missing.

There are two 17c brasses in the chancel—to Dr Thomas Twine (1613) and Robert Heath (1681)—and a wall tablet to Richard Rideout (1767) in the chapel. Mark Anthony Lower, the Sussex historian, is buried beneath the vestry and commemorated by a window. The font is a Norman bowl with finely executed basket-work; the font at East Dean is similar, although only a fragment of the original survives. Small George IV Royal Arms.

St John the Baptist, Southover. Between church and street is a well-kept row of pollarded limes and oaks. The brick tower with an elegant cupola was built in 1714; in it are set three stones from the Priory, carved with a rose and crown, the de Warenne arms and a mitre with the letters I.A.P.L.—probably John Ashdown, Prior of Lewes. But the church is much older than the tower, having originally been the

hospitium at the Priory gate. It was converted into a church in the 14c when the chapel of St John within the gates became too small and a new hospital was built. The S arcade of four bays has round-headed arches—very much restored—and short round piers. There is no chancel arch, and apparently never was one. The nave roof has tie-beams and king-posts; the windows on the N side are by Kempe. Royal Arms George III. The most important possessions of the church are in a small rather nasty pseudo-Norman chapel built in 1847. These are the two little leaden caskets which contained the bones of William de Warenne and Gundrada. They were discovered in 1845 when the railway line was cut through the Priory church. The bones themselves now lie beneath Gundrada's beautiful tomb slab in black Belgian marble decorated with palmettes; it has a Latin inscription recording her ancestry and virtues. The slab was found in the Shurley chapel at Isfield, where it had been used as part of the tomb to Edward Shurley. No doubt it found its way there after the Dissolution. In the same chapel is a mutilated alabaster effigy of a 13c knight.

St Thomas à Becket, Cliffe. At the junction of Cliffe High Street and Malling Street, the main London–Eastbourne road. Tower and W door are 15c, but the nave arcades are 14c, and the small square chancel may indicate an earlier church. The squint from the S aisle to the chancel ends in an ogee arch. A Dutch painting of the Ascension was given in 1779 by B. van der Gucht, a London art dealer. There are two Royal Arms—a painted arms of George I, and a rare plaster Elizabethan arms of 1598; it has been knowledgeably repainted with the supporters in gold, as they were for the Tudor queens, whereas the kings had them in red.

Lindfield* [4] Despite the suburban encroachment of Haywards Heath on the W and the development of housing estates where large properties have been broken up, Lindfield still has a charming village street with a wide common, a pond usually inhabited by swans and ducks, a number of decent if not outstanding Georgian houses and some timber-framed cottages. It is best approached from the NE up the hill from the Ouse valley. Here the village begins suddenly with a Georgian house—Lindfield House—on the left and beyond it an irregular group of brick and timber-framed Elizabethan buildings, called Old Place, formerly the home of the Challoners in the 16c and 17c. Close by it is the church and opposite some more timber-framed cottages. The church is a handsome cruciform building with a shingled broach spire; the earliest parts are 13c, but it is mainly 14c, Dec, and has a

good flamboyant E window. At the beginning of the 19c it was in a dilapidated and ruinous state; when it was restored, the repairs were carried out, according to Mark Anthony Lower, the Sussex historian, 'without the smallest regard to propriety or respect for antiquity. Some of the most beautiful fragments of 14th century glass I ever saw were removed . . . as were beautiful wood carvings.' A particularly good fresco, of which a drawing exists, was destroyed. However, the architecture of the church was unimpaired, and the arcades and vistas are gracious and well-proportioned. Since then a succession of wealthy parishioners has adorned and beautified the church with generally good taste. The S chapel, known as Masset's chancel after a local family, has in its E window glass designed by Walter Tower of Old Place, a cousin of Charles Eamer Kempe, who also lived there. Above the S porch is a parvise where various relics have been assembled. Among these are an hour-glass, used on the pulpit in post-Reformation days, two clarinets from the old church band and a tussock found in the roof timbers. A tussock, or sod of growing grass, was used by priests for kneeling before carpets or mats were introduced; the word 'hassock' derives from it. Lindfield was granted in 1150 to the College of South Malling (q.v.) and was until 1845 a 'peculiar' of the Archbishop of Canterbury. The head of the College was the Dean; hence the name of Dean's Mill near the Ouse, and Malling Priory, a Georgian house in the High Street.

Litlington [8] is a small village of flint cottages on the left bank of the Cuckmere. For 50 years it has been justly famed for its tea gardens; they still exist and claim to be the oldest tea gardens in Sussex. Anyhow they are entirely delightful and an increasing rarity in an era when such leisurely places seem to be dis-

appearing. The little flint church of nave and chancel is mostly 12c, though the only features of this date are the S door, two blocked-up windows in the nave, visible from the outside only, and two windows in the N wall of the chancel with arches of hard chalk. The chancel also has an Easter sepulchre on the N wall, and 13c sedilia on the S. The porch and small, white weatherboarded belfry were added in the 14c.

Lullington [8] A narrow brick path leads through a copse and up the hill to Lullington church, standing in a grove of trees on the Downs. The claim sometimes made for it that it is the smallest church in the country is invalid, since it is no more than a chancel and the foundations of the nave are clearly visible. It has five windows, one EE lancet and four Dec 14c, all with arches of hard chalk. The only other internal features are a piscina and a square, rude font. The church is built of rough flints and stone, and has a white weatherboarded belfry similar to Litlington. It was originally a chapelry of Alciston and belonged to Battle Abbey; in 1251 it was transferred to St Richard, Bishop of Chichester, and has remained in the Bishop's gift. There seem to be only three cottages in Lullington, and a farmhouse, Lullington Court.

Malling, South [7] Twenty years ago a short lane between flint-walled fields led down off the main road to Malling House, a square Queen Anne house of gray brick with red-brick dressings. Beyond it the lane curled round the garden and eventually discovered the Deanery and the small church. Now it is fringed with council houses, and Malling House, the Police H.Q., is an island among villas. So far the Deanery, a large and handsome 18c red-brick house, and the church are immune; but for how long? South Malling has an

Mark Sharp's tombstone, St. John-sub-Castro, **Lewes**

of Ringmer. There is a wall tablet to Dr Russell, the founder of Brighton's fame and fortune.

Maresfield [5] has a number of tile-hung cottages and a Georgian inn, the Chequers. The village suffers from being at the junction of three main roads, and is never free from traffic. The church was originally Norman and one small window in the nave survives. The nave and battlemented tower are 15c, and the nave roof has king-posts and braces. The chancel and transepts are modern, but some of the old windows have been replaced; the N transept has a well-designed rose window. The pulpit and altar rails are 17c with gold ornamentation. Over the N door is a small plaster Royal Arms of George III. There is an iron tombslab to Robert Brooks (1667).

Mayfield [5] ranks with Burwash and Lindfield in having a street of exceptional charm and interest. Most important is the Archbishop's Palace, now a Roman Catholic girls' school. It was surrendered by Cranmer to Henry VIII in 1545, and later bought by Sir Thomas Gresham, who entertained Queen Elizabeth here in great style in 1571. Later it passed to the Bakers, and in 1740 the great hall was dismantled and fell into ruin, since when it has happily been restored. The 15c gatehouse abutting on to the street has been rather over-restored, but inside, now used as a chapel, is the still magnificent 14c hall. Three huge pointed arches span the 40 ft width and support a timber roof; they spring from elaborate leaf brackets resting on busts or figures. The hall is lit by high two-light windows with transoms. On the E wall is an arched recess with stone diaper work; well-placed in front of it is a Flemish Madonna (1460). At the W are three doorways which led into the kitchen, buttery and pantry. Next

unusual history. The first church here is said to have been built by Caedwalla, King of the West Saxons, in the 7c, probably at Old Malling Farm, a mile N of the present church. In 1158 Archbishop Theodore built a second church and endowed a college for a dean and six canons; three canons were required to spend 40 days a year there. The College was surrendered to Henry VIII in 1545 and later in Queen Mary's reign the church was pulled down and all the materials and contents sold. All that now remains at Old Malling Farm is an 11c garden wall, which

was part of the Archbishop of Canterbury's manor house. In 1624 the Deanery property was bought by John Stansfield, who set about rebuilding the church. It was built in 1628, as a tablet over the porch records, and Mr Stansfield's grandson, John Evelyn the diarist, then a boy of eight, laid one of the foundation stones. The low W tower must be older since it contains a 14c window; the rest of the church, nave and chancel in one, is in the medieval tradition. Here John Harvard, founder of the American university, married Anne Sadler, daughter of the vicar door to the gatehouse is Stone House, 18c, or early 19c, with a Tuscan porch. On the opposite side are first Yeomans, an early 15c hall house, then Walnut Tree House, 15c with close timber studding, and, the centrepiece of Mayfield, Middle House Hotel 1575, also timber-framed with many lozenge-shaped panels, bay windows and an oriel. Further down is the timber-framed Brewhouse. These are the chief houses in Mayfield, but nearly all the other houses are weather-boarded or tile-hung and the general composition of the street is hard to beat. The W side has a raised brick pavement the whole length. The church, which stands high and is clearly visible from the Rotherfield road, is somewhat hidden behind cottages. It is dedicated to St Dunstan who had a forge at Mayfield and is recorded as having built a wooden church in 960. This lasted until the 13c, when the Normans replaced it with a stone church, of which only the tower and the W wall of the N aisle survive; the shingled broach spire was added later. In 1389 the village was swept by a fire; the palace escaped but the church was almost wholly destroyed. The rebuilding did not take place at once, and in the meantime the Archbishop's chapel was probably used as a parish church. The chancel is late 14c, but the rest, including the rib-vaulted porch, was probably built about 1420, and altered again in Henry VII's reign when the nave roof was heightened, a clerestory added and the four-centred nave arcades built. The four and a half bays on each side look very amateurish as if the architect had been careless over his measurements, and the absence of a chancel arch makes the church rather barn-like. The N and S aisles both have 15c oak roofs. The chancel has some 16c stalls and 17c altar rails; the low screen between it and the nave is Perp with pierced quatrefoils. The pulpit is Jacobean, and there are

Mayfield

two elaborate brass candelabra dated 1737 and 1773 with coats of arms of the Bakers, who lived at the Palace from 1617 to 1796. In the floor of the nave are four iron tomb slabs; the best—to Thomas Sands, wine cooper, (1708) has foliage and a coat of arms. There are papers in the church records signed with a X by this Thomas Sands, who, although he owned wine cellars near St Paul's, could not write his name. Another slab to an earlier Thomas Sands has his age 72 written with the 7 backwards. A wall monument to Thomas Aynscombe (1620) shows him and his wife kneeling, with their sons and

daughters. Also two monuments to Michael Baker (1750) and Thomas Baker (1782)—classical, each with a woman and an urn. Royal Arms—Georgian. Harmer lived in the next parish, Heathfield, and there are 11 tombs in the church-yard decorated with his terracotta plaques.

Michelham Priory [8] was a house of Augustinian canons founded in 1229 by Gilbert de Aquila, lord of Pevensey, who gave the Prior of Hastings 80 acres at Michelham. It was never a very wealthy house, nor a very reputable one. In 1283 it was found to be in a highly unsatisfac-

Mountfield

tory state, and fines were imposed for non-residence and other offences. In 1302 Edward I spent a night there on his way from Lewes to Battle. At a visitation in 1441 there was a prior and seven monks, including four canons; the Bishop ordered the addition of four more canons. They were enjoined to keep silence and not to frequent the tavern outside the Priory gate. At the next visitation in 1478 the vestments and church ornaments were in great decay, the whole moral tone extremely low and silence was not being observed. The Priory was dissolved in 1536; its gross value was £191 19s 4d.

Most of the buildings, including the church, have disappeared. But the impressive Perp gatehouse, across a stone bridge over the Cuckmere which feeds the large rectangular moat surrounding the demesne, remains intact and has two rooms over the archway. The outer walls of the church are marked out in stone upon the lawns. The house, which was owned by the Pelhams and then by the Sackvilles from 1603 to 1897, became a farmhouse. It consists of the refectory, including on the N wall the remains of a lavatory, and various Tudor additions. There is a fine crypt belonging to the cel-

larer's buildings and above it a room with a large hooded fireplace, probably the Prior's chamber. The Priory now belongs to the Sussex Archaeological Trust; the house has been skilfully furnished and contains a well-arranged museum. Recently the water mill, which had long been disused and lost all its machinery, has been restored and is now grinding again.

Mountfield [6] The village is uninteresting and the cottages largely modern. Gypsum was discovered here about 100 years ago and British Gypsum Ltd have a large plant surrounded by woods. The church is apart from the village and is very rewarding. Norman and aisleless, it has a buttressed tower and a shingled spire springing from below the apex of the roof, like Arlington. The S porch of heavy oak timbers is 14c. Inside the tower is a primitive staircase made of large square baulks of wood and leading to the belfry. The chancel arch is plain Norman; the squints on either side were probably cut in the 13c, when the chancel was enlarged and the trefoil-headed piscina inserted. The altar rails are 18c. The windows, apart from two roundheaded lancets in the N wall, are 14c. The nave has a waggon roof. The curious font is basically a plain Norman bowl, but has 15c carving of alternate shells and quatrefoils in the panels; the only larger font in Sussex is at North Mundham near Chichester. There are two terracotta Harmer plaques in the churchyard. The first known rector held his house and land from the Echynghams on payment of one rose on St John the Baptist's day for life. Mountfield Court (gardens open to the public) is early 18c with hipped roofs and dormers.

Netherfield [6] A wealden ridge village. The church and school were built in 1859 by S. S. Teulon in memory of Sir Godfrey Webster of Battle Abbey. The church is in

EE style with a tower. The inside furnishings, including a rather wedding-cakey reredos and a stone pulpit with Bible stories carved in relief, are also by Teulon. But it is a successful village church.

Newhaven [7] climbs up the western hill at the mouth of the Ouse. It is an undistinguished little town, and although the street pattern seems medieval, there are hardly any houses earlier than 19c and many a great deal more recent. But it has an air of continental bustle, and the boats and signs such as 'Paquebot' and 'Tenez la gauche' are a reminder that it is a jumping-off place for France. Until some year in the 1560s it was called Meeching and was an unimportant fishing village; but the Ouse suddenly deserted the old port of Seaford and burst through into the sea. Thereafter Meeching became Newhaven, though the old name still survives in several streets. The only building of any antiquity and interest is the church, standing high on the hill, like many other churches dedicated to St Michael, and with a superb view up the valley to Lewes. The early Norman tower with a slightly later shingled spire stands between the nave and the apsidal sanctuary. The bell-openings have twin arches, one with its original baluster. The body of the church was demolished in 1854 and rebuilt by Habershon in uninspired Gothic. The wooden nave arcades and W gallery have recently been painted red and picked out in gold, which certainly enriches and enlivens, though nothing could give them any distinction. The solid, austere beauty of the tower arches and beyond them the dark mystery of the apse, lit only by round-headed lancets, make one mourn the loss of the former nave. The W arch is simple on the W side but has two orders of columns on the E; the E arch is also supported by two orders of columns, echoing those on the western arch. The capitals have slightly decorated scallops.

Newick [4] A large and pleasant village grouped around a green with a Grecian revival pump (1837). Southwards from the green a road leads past School Cottage, formerly Lady Vernon's School, built in 1771—a small two-storey brick building with low wings. Lady Vernon started her school for educating 12 poor girls 'in reading, writing and needlework . . . so as to make them useful servants'. The school continued until 1870, when it became the parish girls' school. Lady Vernon's funds are still available for helping girls towards higher education at any school or university. Further on is the Old Rectory, a Georgian house with a Tuscan porch. The Powells were rectors here from 1818 to 1919. Then the church itself, with a Perp tower, embattled and similar to Hamsey; it has a good W window with Perp tracery, but a Tudor door with a four-centred arch. The S porch has many of its original oak timbers. Like most other Sussex churches, Newick has a Norman origin, and near the porch the wall and one Norman window survive. In the 13c, it was largely rebuilt and remained unaltered until 1836 when the N aisle was added. In 1886–7 it was again enlarged by J. Oldrid Scott, the chancel taken down and removed further to the E, keeping three 14c windows. There is also a piscina, sedilia and a second piscina in the vestry. The rich tiling on the chancel walls, the gesso frieze and the stencilling above are 19c. The reredos by Charles Powell has panels by a pupil of Burne-Jones. The chancel windows have two 14c medallions showing the Agnus Dei and in the choir aisle is a window by Burne-Jones. The pulpit is Jacobean with a sounding board, and in the tower is a pitch pipe, used for the choir until 1860. Below it is a tablet to Lady Vernon (1786).

Newtimber* [4] Newtimber Lane plunges down through beech woods off the Brighton road, and skirts the low flint wall of Newtimber Place. The church, standing in a field and almost hidden by trees, is 13c, but after the addition of a tower in 1839 and a merciless restoration in 1875, when it was coated with stucco, all features of interest have disappeared. There is a Jacobean pulpit and a cartouche under the tower to Thomas and Anne Osborne 1733. By the font is a small piece of moulded oak, a relic of the medieval rood screen. The N transept was formerly a manorial pew, and the church is almost like a family chapel to the Buxtons. Earl Buxton, Governor-General of South Africa who lived at Newtimber Place for 54 years, and his wife, also their two sons and daughter, all of whom died untimely, are all commemorated— undistinguished memorials, but a sad record. Newtimber Place stands in a park and is surrounded by a moat—a modest but charming house, the oldest part being a 16c farmhouse of flint and stone. It was enlarged in the 17c and given an E wing with a front of squared flints with stone quoins, and windows surrounded with brickwork. There is an octagonal flint-faced pigeon-house at the NW corner of the moat with 850 nests. *Saddlescombe* is a hamlet round a green, half-way up the Downs. The ancient farmhouse was once a manor house, is mainly 18c, but has a chimney stack of about 1500, round which is a 17c wing. A chapel is mentioned in the manorial records, and the Knights Templar had a small establishment here in the 12c, which was later passed on to the Knights Hospitaller.

Ninfield [9] The church is somewhat hidden at the end of a lane and only the brick S porch— 1735—is visible through a tunnel of trees, though the churchyard itself is quite open. It has a white weath-

erboarded bell-cote, and the windows in the S wall are 15c. Inside, the restoration of 1885, when the N aisle, similar to that at Catsfield, was added, destroyed much that was of interest. But the large round-headed chancel arch and three lancets at the E end are not bad, and at the same time the Jacobean panelling on either side of the altar and the choir stalls with poppy-heads were brought here from Macclesfield. There is also a Jacobean reading desk and font cover over the small square font. The

opposite and below
Great Dixter, Northiam

nave is generally said to be 13c, though it may be earlier, since records show that a Norman window in the N wall and a narrow, round-headed chancel arch survived into the 19c. Above the chancel arch are the Royal Arms of James I, and at the W end is a 17c minstrel's gallery; the wavy balusters were inserted in 1923. The nave roof is supported by fine moulded king-posts, tie-beams and wallplates. Two farmhouses, Standard Hill (1659) and Lower Standard Hill (1702) are named after the hill where the Conqueror was erroneously thought to have planted his standard before the battle.

Normanhurst [6]

Normanhurst 1975

'How lovely your Ponticums are,
   my dear'
She remarked of the vase in the
   hall.
'But they're nothing but weeds,'
   Lord Brassey would say,
'From the fence by the Park Gate
   wall.

'I planted 'em there when I first
   built the house
'To keep out the public, you
   know,
'But my gardeners say they are
   out of control
'Altogether. My gad, how they
   grow.'

Penhurst

But what would his lordship have
    murmured today
With Normanhurst razed to the
    ground,
Not a brick, not a stone of its
    opulence left
But the ponticums flaunting
    around.

Gone are the marbles and gold
    chandeliers,
Gone the footmen in breeches
    and pumps,
And nothing to show for its
    grandeur survives
But the ponticums growing in
    clumps.

Ladies in diamonds and sable
    and silks,
Nobles and bishops—and kings—
All are a memory, all long dead
But the ponticums—perishing
    things.

A mile E of Catsfield a road to
Battle branches off at Park Gate. It
is flanked by high and unkempt
rhododendron hedges and runs
through the Normanhurst estate.
The grandiose Frenchified mansion
with mansard roofs and angle turrets was built in 1867 for Thomas,
1st Earl Brassey, a steel tycoon; it
was demolished in 1951.

Northiam [6] To the N a dreary
stretch of bungalows, but the village itself is almost entirely white
weatherboarded cottages—one
three-storeyed, standing on the
green below the chained oak, under
which Queen Elizabeth I sat. The
churchyard is entered through an
elegant Georgian iron gateway
with a central lantern holder. The
lower part of the church tower has
two round-headed Norman window arches and is built of dark
brown sandstone; the tower was
heightened in the 15c, given an
angle turret and supported by two
buttresses. A little later the stone
spire, one of three in East Sussex,
was added; it was rebuilt and
heightened by 10 ft in 1860. The
three-bay nave arcades are EE as is
the clerestory; the N aisle has the
Frewen family pew, still used, and
some 15c armorial glass. The
chancel with pseudo-EE lancets
and a flat ribbed and bossed ceiling
was rebuilt in 1837—the gift of
Thomas Frewen Turner—and
designed by Sidney Smirke. He also
added the Frewen mausoleum over
the family vaults, which projects
transeptally; both are heavy and
unattractive. Other more tasteful
Frewen gifts were the panelling,
Communion table and altar rails

148

given by Thankful Frewen in 1638 and the splendid brass chandelier by his descendant in 1727. The pulpit is plain Georgian and the Royal Arms Queen Anne. There are two 16c brasses, to Sir Thomas Beuford, rector, wearing mass vestments, and to Nicholas Tufton, a civilian. Mounted on a modern plinth is an elegant little 18c font bowl, which was found in the churchyard. Northiam has two notable houses—Brickwall and Great Dixter. Brickwall was for nearly 400 years the home of the Frewens, who entertained Queen Elizabeth I here; it is now a school and part is open to the public.

The three-gabled front facing the road is a striking piece of Jacobean timber-framing, built between 1617 (left gable) and 1633 (middle gable). Inside there are some elaborate plaster ceilings and a fine staircase with twisted balusters, all late 17c. The proportions were spoiled when Smirke built the stables in 1832, and again when further additions were made in pseudo-Elizabethan style. Great Dixter is really three houses in one. The original timber-framed hall house of Dixter is late 15c and probably belonged to the Echynghams, whose escutcheon is there. It was bought and skilfully restored by Nathaniel Lloyd in 1910, and consists of the great hall, parlour and, on the first floor, the solar. The hall has a magnificent hammer-beam roof alternating with tie-beams, and the solar a fine carved chimneypiece and king-posts. Mr Lloyd employed and worked with Sir Edwin Lutyens in restoring and adding to the house, which was done with exceptional skill. Lutyens added a tile-hung wing, which, although totally different, is entirely sympathetic. Mr Lloyd then found a derelict yeoman's house at Benenden in Kent and had it transported to Northiam, where it was re-erected as another wing to Dixter. The combination of the two hall houses and Lutyens' wing is delightful, as is the garden designed by Lutyens and Mr Lloyd, who was an authority on the use of yew and box in garden layout. The garden is now maintained by his son, Mr Christopher Lloyd, a well-known gardening writer.

Nutley [4] Main-road village on the edge of Ashdown Forest. The Shelley Arms is a substantial 18c house. The small church is EE (1845) by R. C. Carpenter; the N aisle was added in 1871. The roof is unusually steep and there is a high narrow chancel arch and triple lancets at the E end. Nothing special, but quite agreeable.

Offham [4] *see* **Hamsey**

Ore [9] is a north-eastern suburb of Hastings, standing high behind the town and surveying the Channel. The old church of St Helen, close to Ore Place behind a shrubbery, has long been ruined and is in a state of dire neglect. The tower has a Norman window, the N wall and chancel three Dec windows. Also in the chancel is the canopy of a tomb, which may have contained two small canopied brasses to a civilian and his wife, which were removed to the very ugly new church of St Helen.

Ovingdean [7] is 1½ miles E of Kemp Town. Rows of villas come perilously near, but it still remains a secluded downland hamlet without even a pub. There are flint barns and cottages, a cobbled rectory, rectory cottage—rather smart with white painted quoins and windows—and Ovingdean Grange, a two-storey 18c house and the title of a novel by Harrison Ainsworth. In it he writes lavishly, but not inaccurately, of the church 'Nothing more hushed, more sequestered, more winningly and unobtrusively beautiful can be conceived than this simple village church.' Norman features are the squat W tower with a tiled cap, and, inside, a blocked N door, deep round-headed lancets in the chancel and a plain chancel arch; of course the restorers in 1867 could not resist piercing a round-headed arch on either side, as at Pyecombe. There was a 13c S aisle, but it was destroyed by French pirates in 1377. On a stand in the chancel is the bowl of a small round 12c font. The church was richly adorned by Kempe, who is buried here (1907) and whose coat of arms hangs in the nave. He designed six windows and the frame and canopy of the rood, which contains figures carved at Oberammergau. He also painted the chancel ceiling with an elaborate and beautiful design, which adds colour to the dark mystery of a Norman sanctuary.

Patcham [7] The tentacles of Brighton spread round Patcham, the last village on the London road. The narrow street must have been appallingly congested and malodorous in the days of horse traffic, and quite intolerable with the charabancs of the 1920s. It was rescued in the 1930s by the opening of a bypass, and is now a backwater, quieter probably than for centuries. The church and Court Farm stand on a spur of the Downs above the village. Court Farm, 17c, was once the manor house and used to look rather woebegone; but it has recently become a slicked-up modern residence and is hardly recognisable. Below the garden is a contemporary dovecote, flint-faced with a conical tiled roof, and still containing its potence and 550 nesting-boxes. Opposite, and beside the church, is a 17c barn nearly 250 ft long; the roof has tie-beams and braced arches.

The earliest parts of the church are 12c; its walls are of flint rubble with stone dressings, but have been smothered externally with Roman cement. The 13c tower has lost its battlements and has a modern broach spire. The chancel arch is

149

Pevensey Castle

plain unmoulded Norman and has above it the remains of a painted Doom discovered in 1883. There is a monument in the chancel to Richard Shelley (1594). Patcham Place is a trim 18c house faced with black mathematical tiles, which were chiefly used for small terraced houses facing the sea. It is unusual to find them on a house as large as Patcham Place. The contrast between them and the white painted wooden quoins, the cornice and window surrounds produces a stimulating effect. The house stands near the London road, and has for some years been used as a youth hostel.

Peacehaven [7] Originally called New Anzac-on-Sea, to commemorate the Australia and New Zealand Expeditionary Force, it was built at the end of the First World War, and is laid out on a grid plan a mile long by half a mile deep. However, although it is as unpleasant an example of maritime

suburbia as can be found, at least it is—or was—a brand new place and has not swallowed up an ancient settlement, as more recent building has done at Denton and threatens to do at Bishopstone, unless the watchdogs are out.

Peasmarsh [6] The village is built along the main road from Rye to Northiam; but the church, Peasmarsh Place and the former rectory are away on top of a ridge to the S. The old rectory, now called Peasmarsh House, is 1839 Gothic and Peasmarsh Place was rebuilt a few years ago in neo-Georgian. The church stands beautifully among meadows and well-spaced trees, including an oak of great age. Its Norman origin, about 1070, is at once evident from the S door and the plain chancel arch of reddish ironstone, slightly horse-shoe shaped as a result of pressure from the wall above. About half-way up the pillar on either side is a curious carved stone with a lion-like creature, its

tail returned upon the body; there are two more outside—which cannot have been their original place—one in the chancel S wall, the other at the foot of a buttress, visible but below ground level. The tower and aisles were added about 1170 and the short spire somewhat later. The nave arcades are pointed Transitional and have massive square piers. Again in the late 13c the S aisle was enlarged and the chancel lengthened; a squint was cut in the S side of the chancel arch. The chancel has EE lancets, but the aisle windows are Dec, as is the little niche for a statue carved in one pier of the S arcade. Over the chancel arch is a plaster panel, possibly Elizabethan, with Commandments, Creed and the Lord's Prayer—unfortunately cutting into the stones of the arch. Chancel, nave and S aisle all have 15c collar-beam roofs. The Liddell family, formerly of Peasmarsh Place, produced several well-known people. The Very Revd H. G. Liddell was

Dean of Christ Church, Oxford; his son, Edward, was the joint compiler of Liddell and Scott's Greek Dictionary—known to every classicist—and his daughter, Alice, persuaded his friend The Revd Charles Dodgson (Lewis Carroll) to tell her a story—which became *Alice's Adventures in Wonderland*.

Penhurst [6] church and manor house, known as Church Farm, form a rare and exquisite manorial group, which has remained unchanged for centuries. It stands high overlooking the farms and woodlands of Ashburnham; the approaches to it, according to a 19c report, were so bad in winter that it was almost inaccessible. Barbara Willard writes, 'The ghosts about here are too many to be counted. This is the intensest countryside for miles—turned in upon itself, separate, pinned to the past, silent, undisturbed.' The manor house, standing boldly, is arresting. Built of ashlar in the 17c by William Relph, it is unusually high and has two storeys and a half-basement with a high-pitched roof. A flight of steps up to the porch, transomed and mullioned windows and large chimney stacks with tall, square brick shafts give the house an air of distinction. Just behind it stands the church, built of wealden sandstone between 1340 and 1500. The Perp tower has buttresses at the corners and is crowned with a Sussex cap; on the S side of the nave is a much-decayed timber porch. Inside, apart from the new plaster on the walls, the furnishings have remained intact. The oak box-pews and panelling were made on the Ashburnham estate and were the gift of Lord Ashburnham; during repairs the name of 'J. O. Sinden 1858' was found carved underneath a pew. The pulpit and reader's desk are Jacobean; the pulpit is thought to have come from Long Melford, Suffolk. There is a 15c rood screen and on the N side a squint; close to it is a small font with an elegant

Pevensey Castle

cover given by Mr Lovell of the manor house in 1883. The nave roof has two tie-beams and king-posts; on the king-posts over the chancel arch is a hook, from which the crucifix was probably suspended. The chancel has a barrel roof with moulded ribs and carved bosses and the altar rail has simple turned oak balusters. The E window has some remains of medieval glass containing the arms of the Pelhams, which may indicate that they were paramount lords of the manor; there are Pelham buckles on the W door of Ashburnham church. At the foot of the sanctuary step is an iron grave slab to Peter Gower. A round-headed arch on the N side of the sanctuary leads into a small chapel, added in the 17c as a private pew probably by William Relph. There is mention of an ironworks at Penhurst in 1546.

Pett [9] gives its name to Pett Level, an expanse of marshland between it and Winchelsea. The little medieval church recorded in the Sharpe Collection had nave, chancel and shingled bell-cote. It was pulled down in 1869 to make way for a rather perky Victorian successor on the same site. Relics from the old church are the octagonal font (1753) on a fluted plinth, a marble monument to Cordelia Sayer (1820) with a sickle and sheaf of corn, reputedly by Westmacott, and a Grecian tablet to George Wynch (1836) with two urns and decorations of ivy below and a lily and butterfly above. In the altar table has been set an elegantly carved 17c panel with two cherubs' heads in the centre, possibly from former altar rails. Low down and attached to the chancel arch is a small brass to George Theobald 1641 'a lover of bells … who gave a bell freely to grace the new steple'. Elms Farm and Carter's Farm are both 16c; the latter has stone chimney stacks with crow-stepped sides.

Piddinghoe

Pevensey [8] is now a shrunken village about a mile from the sea with a single street of flint and cobbled houses. Evidence of its former importance is there in the much restored Mint House and the Court House, or Town Hall; Pevensey had its own Mayor and Corporation. But far more impressive are the walls of Roman Anderida, enclosing an area of nearly ten acres. They are 12 ft thick and are built of sandstone rubble with coursed facings of green sandstone and ironstone. After the Conquest the Rape of Pevensey was granted to the Conqueror's half-brother, Robert, Count of Mortain, who built a moated castle within the Roman walls, which were—and are—still in good condition on all sides except the S. The castle has a gatehouse, keep and three angle towers and is a reminder of Pevensey's importance in medieval times. In 1940 when a German invasion seemed imminent, the castle was prepared for defence; the towers were reinforced and roofed with concrete, and pill-boxes disguised as ancient masonry were constructed on top of the keep. Fortunately they were not put to the test. Presumably the Normans built a church at Pevensey, but there is no trace of it today, since the church is entirely 13c. It is built of sea-shore pebbles; stone was used only in the quoins, windows and arches. The first impression inside is the gentle grey-green light diffused by the green sandstone of the nave arcades. On the S there are five bays with piers alternately clustered and octagonal, on the N the arcade is cut short by the tower and there are only three bays. The clerestory windows are between and not, as is more usual, above the arches. The long chancel 55 ft has had a chequered history. In the 17th century a wall was built blocking it off from the nave; it fell into ruin and decay, and became a cattle shed, a coal store and a useful hiding-place for

Playden; screen

contraband. In 1875 the vicar rented it from the lay-rector for 1d a year and carried out an extensive restoration, opening up the whole church and restoring the waggon roof to its original state. The tower was heightened by a stage—very well done in pebbles like the original—and the spire rebuilt. The three lancets at the E end and the twin deeply moulded windows on the S wall are EE. The chancel arch has been much restored, but has stiff-leaf capitals; the nave has a king-posted roof. On the N wall is a gorgeous alabaster tomb to John Wheately (1616); he lies on his side, protected by two lions on the floor, flanked by black columns with figures and topped off with a pediment and cartouche. The relics of Pevensey's mayoral status are shown in a glass case, and above the muniment chest is an offertory box with a long handle used in the days of box-pews. The William and Mary Royal Arms, which formerly hung in the church, is now in the Court House Museum. It is a rare version and is thought to have been used only between February and April 1689.

Piddinghoe [7] (pronounced Pidd'nhoo) is 1¼ miles N of Newhaven and was formerly notorious for its association with smugglers. Whether the curious saying 'Piddinghoe people shoe their magpies' had any reference to smuggling is not known; but the other saying 'where they hang their ponds out to dry' referred to the whiting made of ground chalk, which used to be laid out on shelves to dry. A few cottages and the church cluster round the village green, though it is no longer green, and are happily bypassed by the Lewes–Newhaven road. The church of flint and stone stands on a low bluff rising from the river's edge; a herring-bone brick path leads up to the porch. The round tower—one of the three in the Ouse valley—and the nave are early 12c.

The tower has a short octagonal shingled spire with a sea-trout weather vane, not a dolphin as Kipling thought when he wrote 'where windy Piddinghoe's begilded dolphin veers'; the flint-work was over-restored in 1882 and spoiled by snail pointing. The nave arcades are both 12c—early and round-headed on the N, late and pointed on the S. The chancel, rebuilt in the 13c, has an EE arch with stiff-leaf carving on the capitals. The E window is a triplet of plain lancets with a large round window above. The square 13c font rests on a square base and has four recessed ogee-headed arches on the sides. There is an early 19c barrel organ.

Playden [6] No village here—merely a pleasant residential district at the top of Rye Hill. The sandstone cliff falls abruptly to the marsh below Playden. There is nothing of interest except the church built about 1190, which is beautifully proportioned and has great dignity of design. Of the nave arcades the westernmost arches are pointed 13c, the other three round-headed 12c; these are graceful Transitional arches with unusually tall piers. The tower, between the nave and chancel, rises one stage above the rest of the church and from it springs a slender shingled spire, visible for miles across the marsh. The upper stage of the tower is reached by a heavily built 17c wooden ladder within the tower space. The E and W tower arches are EE and richly moulded. The chancel screen is Perp; another more interesting screen to the N chapel is Dec (1310) and has seven bays with flamboyant tracery. The pulpit and Royal Arms (1787) are both Georgian. In the N aisle is a stone slab (1530) to a Flemish brewer, Cornelis Zockermans; the inscription is in Flemish and two beer barrels are engraved upon it. The clerestory has been closed in and the roof sweeps down with a fine spread of golden-red tiles.

Plumpton [4] The village of Plumpton Green adjoins the railway station and is entirely modern. The small church built in 1893 has an odd octagonal tower, but no particular distinction. Immediately S of the station is Plumpton Racecourse. The old settlement lies nearly two miles to the S just under the Downs; but is hardly a village, since it consists only of the church, Plumpton Place, the former rectory—now called Laines—a post office and an inn. Plumpton church used to stand entirely alone in the fields, its churchyard surrounded by a low wall; but since the building nearby of the East Sussex Agricultural College in farmers' Georgian, an outcrop of cottages, sheds and greenhouses has sprung up. The church is built of flints and has a low shingled spire. The nave walls are 12c, the W tower and chancel 13c, the latter extended before 1854. The chancel arch was rebuilt in 1867 and again in 1932. Before the first rebuilding Nibbs (1851) describes three Norman arches dividing nave from chancel. The restoration of 1867 was drastic and wall paintings discovered under the whitewash were destroyed. A. S. Cooke in *Off the beaten track in Sussex* describes how he was there when the workmen were actually destroying them. He must, however, refer only to those above the chancel arch, because paintings on the N wall were discovered in 1955 by Mr Clive Rouse, and have recently been carefully revealed. Round a small, formerly blocked-up, Norman window is a scroll design; to the E is Christ in Majesty and to the W St Peter with keys. On the S wall are some post-Reformation texts. The church has brick flooring throughout; the nave roof has tie-beams and king-posts, the chancel one tie-beam and queen-posts. At the W end are 18c Commandment Boards. In the churchyard are two bed-post tombs—one painted, apparently to two children, Dorcas and Catherine Tyler,

the other carved, to the Revd John Woodward (d. 1917). Both are in poor condition.

Plumpton Place is a half-timbered E-shaped Tudor house, embowered in trees and surrounded by a moat. The N wing is the earliest part and a stone dated 1568 with the initials I M (John Mascall) may refer to it. His descendant, Leonard Mascall, in Henry VIII's reign, is said to have introduced carp into England. The walls are a mixture of flint and brick, restored at various times; there was some rebuilding in brick in the 18th century and on the N side the original timber-framing is partly filled with brick. In the 19c the house fell into disrepair and was carved up into workman's tenements. But after the First World War it was bought by Mr Edward Hudson, owner of *Country Life*, who with Sir Edwin Lutyens restored and transformed it into the romantic and beautiful house of today. Lutyens designed the two cottages and the Palladian arch, which form the entrance to the bridge over the moat; he also added a large music room on the site of some sheds and included in it an original brick fireplace. An early 17c screen divides the hall. W of Plumpton on the Downs is a plantation in the form of a V, planted to commemorate Queen Victoria's Jubilee.

Polegate [8] is an entirely modern place of no distinction. It is built around a railway junction for Eastbourne, Hastings, Lewes and, formerly, Tunbridge Wells. Otham Court, a farmhouse on Pevensey Level about a mile to the N, is the site of a Premonstratensian Abbey founded in 1180 by Ralph de Dene. But its bleak, unhealthy situation on the undrained marshes, remote enough even today, made life unbearable and the canons protested that they could stand it no longer. They were first offered the church at Hellingly by Rikewarde de

Brade, a benefactor of the abbey; but in 1207 Sir Robert de Turnham began building an abbey at Bayham and Ela de Sackville, the patroness, gave permission for the monks of Otham to settle there. The only recorded Abbot of Otham became the first Abbot of Bayham. Thereafter Otham became a grange, visited periodically by a canon to serve the chapel which in a desecrated state survives. It has a mutilated sedile and piscina, and a blocked-up Dec window, which must have been inserted after the departure of the monks.

Portslade* [7] should not be confused with Portslade-on-Sea, a rather dreary western extension of Brighton and Hove. The old village lies nearly a mile inland and still has relics of its separate identity. The church, like the old parish church of Brighton, stands up on the hill and is also dedicated to St Nicolas, patron saint of sailors for whom it was a landmark. It was originally Transitional-Norman, and the columns and S arcade of the nave are of this date; the N aisle was added in 1860, but the columns and their capitals are a faithful imitation of those on the S. The tower and chancel are early 13c. The chancel has two lancet windows above the altar and is a good example of EE; fortunately all the windows have clear glass. The sedilia are beneath arch hood-moulding terminating in crudely designed mask stops. In 1444 the advowson belonged to the Premonstratensian canons of St Radegund, of Bradsole near Canterbury, (see Bayham Abbey), which indicates that pilgrims to the shrine of St Thomas à Becket used St Nicolas, Portslade as a place of worship, while they stayed at the manor house, which was owned by the monks. Fragmentary remains of the medieval house can be seen in the grounds of the 19c manor house, now a Convent School, just N of the church. The Brackenbury chapel at the W end of the nave was built over the family vault in 1874. A brass plate (1499–1519) was brought here from West Blatchington.

Poynings* [4] The road off the Downs appears for a moment to be heading straight for the tower of Poynings church, which stands on a hillside at the mouth of the Devil's Dyke combe. It was rebuilt by Thomas de Poynings and his brother Richard in 1370 and remains today much as it was then. It has a grandeur comparable with Etchingham, but although built only 10 years later, the style is Perp with very few traces of Dec. The church is of flint rubble with stone dressings, cruciform and aisleless with an embattled, central tower. The S transept, known as the Poynings chapel, is enclosed by a good oak screen with a central double door and four side bays; the upper parts are divided into three lights with elaborately foliated heads. The pulpit and altar rails are 17c; the font is a plain octagonal prism with trefoiled ogee-headed panels round the base.

The small village is less distinguished than its church; Poynings Place, the ancient manor house of the Poynings family, has long since disappeared. But it is an ancient place as the lynchets still visible on the Downs to the E show.

The deep combe known as the Devil's Dyke, or commonly the Dyke, has a long-established legend. The Devil, incensed by the enormous number of churches in the Weald, determined to dig through the Downs and let in the sea. He was, however, disturbed by a devout old woman lighting a candle in her cottage to say her prayers. The Devil fled and the Downs were never breached. Up the side of the Downs can be seen the track of the Dyke Steep Grade Railway, closed in 1908.

Preston [7] was once a small farming village on the Wellesbourne, a chalk stream which flowed into the sea down the Old Steine in Brighton; but it has long ceased to be more than a suburb with a station called Preston Park. A few cottages survive in North and South Streets, but otherwise the only relics are the church and manor house, which stand side by side. The church is 13c and has nave, chancel and tile-capped W tower. The series of wall paintings were so badly damaged by a fire in 1906 that despite restoration they are hardly decipherable. On either side of the chancel arch are St Michael weighing souls and the martyrdom of St Thomas of Canterbury; and on the N wall of the nave are the Last Supper, the Nativity and the Adoration of the Magi. The altar is a stone altar-tomb to Edward Elrington (1515) removed from the N wall; it has quatrefoil panels on the front and both ends, each having a coat of arms. Preston Manor House has fragments of a house built in the 14c and enlarged in the 16c; but the house as seen today is mostly the rebuilding in 1738 by Squire Thomas Western, whose name survives in Western Road, Brighton. The house is now the Thomas-Stanford museum, named after the last private owners, Sir Charles and Lady Thomas-Stanford, who gave it to the Brighton Corporation.

Pyecombe* [4] (pronounced Pyecoombe) A shepherd's village on the Downs. The church, smithy and a few cottages are a good ½ mile from Pyecombe Street, where the people fled and built a new village in 1603 after a visitation of the plague. The 12c and 13c church had some horrible treatment in the 19c when the outer walls were covered in rough-cast. Fortunately this has recently (1973) been removed, and the flint and stone texture of the original walls once again revealed. The inside treatment was also tasteless and severe; a pseudo-Norman E window was inserted and two round-headed arches made on either side of the original Norman chancel arch. On the S wall of the chancel is an unusual piscina (1300) with two bowls under an ogee arch; there are some 13c tiles on the floor. Over the chancel arch are the Royal Arms of George III. But the chief interest in this church is the late 12c lead font, one of three in Sussex, the other two being at Edburton and Parham both in West Sussex. The Pyecombe font has an elaborate pattern of scroll work. The churchyard is entered by a tapsell gate, which turns on a central pivot. The smithy at Pyecombe was famous throughout Downland for its shepherds' crooks. The forge today has become an ironwork craft centre; but crooks are still being made for shepherds, tourists and the occasional bishop.

Ringmer [7] A large village in flat country with a wide green and cottages set well back from the road. The church is mainly 14c with later additions. The only relics of an earlier church are the 13c bases of the nave arcades and some stones in the S wall carved with Norman ornaments. The original tower was burnt down in the 16c and its replacement was again burnt about 1800; discouraged by these visitations, the parishioners built a wooden turret, which remained until 1884, when the present tower was built, a gift of William Christie of Glyndebourne. It is a succesful and harmonious design by Ewan Christian (*see* Hamsey: *Offham*) and has one Perp window inserted in it. The outside walls of the church are an interesting medley of flints, brick, sandstone and Isle of Wight greenstone; the roofs are partly Horsham slabs and partly tiles. Inside, the nave arcades are 14c, but the piers and four-centred arches of the two chapels are late 15c. There is a number of monuments, some with interesting associations. In the nave is a black marble slab to the Revd Henry Snooke, whose wife

was Gilbert White's aunt; White wrote some of his letters from Ringmer vicarage and made the acquaintance of Timothy, the Snookes' tortoise, upon which he based his study. In the S chapel are a canopied monument to Herbert Springett (1620) with kneeling figures, a tablet to Sir William Springett (1643) whose daughter, Gulielma, married William Penn and a marble monument to Ensign Grunden (1793) by Westmacott with a figure of Fortitude. A painted board records the bequest in 1831 from Mrs Henrietta Hay of Glyndebourne of £2,000 'for the comfortable maintenance of 13 poor residents of Ringmer or Glynde'. There is a small George III Royal Arms.

The N chapel has a Jacobean plaster ceiling with decorated beams. In it are a 17c monument to Francis and Elizabeth Jefferay (*see* Chiddingly) with kneeling figures, and a tablet to the Revd John Sadler (d. 1640), whose daughter married John Harvard, founder of the American university. Both chapels have their old quarry-tiled floors. In the sanctuary are two black marble tomb slabs to Lady Campion (1669) and Mrs Elizabeth Wynne (1672) with armorial bearings. On either side of the chancel arch are two hatchments with the arms of Hay of Glyndebourne.

Broyle Place, a mile or so E towards Laughton, is on the site of a palace of the Archbishops of Canterbury who stayed there on their journey from Canterbury to South Malling college. The present house is a brick Tudor building with mullioned windows and is all that remains of the far larger house of the Springetts, squires of Ringmer. After they left, it became a farmhouse until it was restored with great care in 1955–7. Wellingham House, in the hamlet of *Upper Wellingham* (accent on -ham like Beddingham) is thought to be on the site of a religious house connected with

South Malling college and there is a village tradition that a church existed there. In 1871 a lead coffin was unearthed and the surrounding soil was found to be full of fragmented bones. The present house is late Georgian with a Tuscan porch and was built by John Rickman, a brewer; the Rickmans were a well-known Quaker family and John Rickman gave up brewing on conscientious grounds. The records of the Society of Friends in Lewes have many references to the Rickmans, who worshipped regularly at the Meeting House in Friar's Walk and whose graves are in the garden there, the former Quaker burial ground. The pavilions at the side of Wellingham House were added in 1961; in the garden is an exceptionally fine cedar, a gazebo and a shell grotto. Among the farm buildings is a barn with a trussed and raftered roof, which must have been part of an older house. The additions to and restoration of the house are an example of sensitive and informed conservation; it is open to the public at times in aid of charitable causes.

Glyndebourne became world famous, after the opening of the opera house in 1934, designed for John Christie by Edmond Warre. But there has been a house here for 700 years, successively the home of the Morleys and the Hays from whom it came by marriage to the Christies. The parish boundary between Ringmer and Glynde runs beside it; but the owners of Glyndebourne have always been more closely associated with Ringmer. The house was originally built of chalk and faced with brick; in the W wing is some timber-framing, and there are also some mullioned windows and Tudor panelling. But what appears today is mostly Victorian Tudor, built for William Christie in 1876 to designs by Ewan Christian, who afterwards built the church tower. Although an imitation of past styles, Ewan Christian's work here and elsewhere is extremely sincere and quite without ostentation.

Ripe [8] is a small, undisturbed village, well away from the main road. It is referred to variously in Domesday Book as Ripe or Echentone. The second name survives in Eckington Manor, opposite the church, a chequer-brick, early 18c house with a hipped roof, dormers and arched chimney stacks; also in Eckington Lodge at the other end of the village—an older house, early 17c, with mullioned windows. Ripe church is approached up a brick path and is built of knapped flints and sandstone. It has a battlemented Pelham tower, 15c, with the buckle on the W door labelstops and shields in the spandrels. Inside, the most immediately striking feature is the five-light E window with elaborate Dec tracery and many fragments of green and yellow 14c glass. On the S side of the chancel is a 14c sedile, with room for two, and beside it a large trefoil-headed piscina. The nave roof has tie-beams with long thin king-posts (see Chalvington). There is a George III Royal Arms. Ripe is, and has always been, a farming village, and some of the recorded legacies are interesting. John Topyn (1493) left a cow, value 8s, to sustain the images of St John and St Dominic, and Thomas Jeffery (1527), who founded the Lady Chapel, left 'two of my best kyne' for two tapers, one to burn before Our Lady of Pity, and the other before St Peter. He added 'when it shall happen the said two kyne to wax olde and dekaye, then I will that the churchwardeynes shall sell the said Kyne and with the money to bye other two kyne.' What more could any churchwarden want?

Robertsbridge [6] The name is a corruption of Rotherbridge. The Rother enters from the NW, bifuicates and divides the village in two. Robertsbridge was quite a substantial place in the iron industry days,

but it has never been a parish nor had a church of its own, the parish church being at Salehurst. There is a number of timber-framed houses, many dating back to the 14c. Near the bridge in Northbridge Street is an L-shaped house (1500), now divided into tenements; the chimney stack and the floor inserted in the W wing are 1600. On the E of the main street Rose Bank, half-timbered, is of 14c origin, again with a chimney stack and first floor added in the late 16c. The Seven Stars Inn, now two shops, and part of the Robertsbridge Stores are also 14c, with similar later additions; St Catherine's Chapel, now a guest house, is a century later. Besides these houses there is a number of 17c and 18c houses. This all points to a prosperous place; no doubt the citizens provided lay help for the monks at the abbey, and received the benefits of medicine, culture and spiritual guidance. The steel industry started in Robertsbridge at the end of the 16c.

The Cistercian Abbey of Robertsbridge was founded in 1176 by Alured de St Martin, who married Alice, widow of John Count of Eu. Local benefactors who added gifts of land were the de Echynghams and the Dalyngrigges of Bodiam. Henry III visited the abbey twice, and on the second occasion in 1264, on his way to the disastrous Battle of Lewes, he extorted large sums of money from the monks. Unlike the Augustinians at Michelham, the abbey seems to have had a good reputation. The Cistercians were a fairly strict order, and pious monks of Canterbury chose to leave the Benedictine order for the stricter Cistercians. Robertsbridge was not a rich abbey; it escaped the first suppression and survived until 1538, when Thomas Taylor, abbot, and eight brethren surrendered it.

The only relics are incorporated in Abbey Farm. The farmhouse was probably the abbot's house; it is a three-storey rectangular building

of stone rubble with ashlar dressings, but now has a 17c wing on the S and a kitchen wing on the E side. The lowest storey has three vaulted double bays; the ribs of the vaulting form rather flat two-centred arches and spring from two circular columns down the centre line of the vault. The first floor has two late 13c doorways and part of a large window, all now blocked up. Much of the original roof remains, including three out of the four principal trusses and two octagonal kingposts with four-way braces to the main collars. At the SE of the house are fragmentary remains of the Frater. E of the Frater is a building which may have been the Warming House; it was converted into an oast-house, but is now ruinous.

Rodmell [7] is a small sheep-farming village, like others in the Ouse valley, and lies half-way between Lewes and Newhaven. The village street of flint cottages leads off the main road eastwards and down to the Brooks. At the end of it is the church, built of flint and stone in the 12c with a tower and short pyramidal spire similar to Iford. A herring-bone brick path leads up to the porch, and there is a fine view from the churchyard across the Ouse, marred only by a hideous cement factory. The most striking feature inside is the round-headed chancel arch with elaborate mouldings of billet, lozenge and zigzag; it is, however, pseudo-Norman and replaces a pointed arch, though the original mouldings have been faithfully copied. In the gable above are two circular windows and a lancet. The chancel has a Perp E window and a Norman window in the N wall; in the floor is a black marble slab (1716) to John Montague with armorial bearings. Between the chancel and the S chapel is part of a 14c screen. There used to be a square squint on the S side of the arch; this has now been filled in, but the chevroned basalt pillar, which supported it in the centre, is

Huggett's Furnace Farm, **Rotherfield**

preserved near the font. The nave roof has four plain tie-beams and queen-posts; the chancel one tie-beam, slightly bowed. There is evidence that the mouldings of the chancel arch and the basalt pillar of the former squint were made from materials taken from Lewes Priory after its destruction in 1537. The S arcade has two late Norman arches; the central pillar is unusual in having a square capital with elaborate stiff-leaf decoration. The 13c font has flat blank arches on the sides and rests on five columns. There is a George III Royal Arms. Rodmell Place stood S of the church, but has completely disappeared except for some cellars. The street has some cottages with square oak window bars instead of mullions; this type of window was used in cottages before glass was

available for humbler use. Northease Manor House, just N of the village, has been modernised and slicked up, but was an ancient chapelry of Rodmell. There are two large aisled barns of the 17c. Leonard and Virginia Woolf lived at Rodmell for many years.

Rotherfield [5] A hill-top village just E of Ashdown Forest; the Rother rises within the parish. The street, on two sides of the centrally placed church, has many cottages of brick—tile-hung and weatherboarded. Nothing of great distinction, but compositely charming. The church's dedication to St Denys derives from a visit by Bertwald, Duke of the South Saxons, when a sick man, in 785 to the Abbey of St Denys in Paris. He returned healed and built a church

to St Denys and a priory, to which the Abbey may have sent over 13 monks, the minimum number to establish a new foundation. Nothing of it remains, and its site is uncertain, though it is thought to have been just S of the church. The present church is very much later. It is built of sandstone and ironstone, and has a battlemented early 15c tower with an angle turret and shingled spire. The porch has groin vaulting converging on a boss and stone seating on either side; above it is a chamber—too small to have been a priest's chamber and more probably used as a store. The inside is a delight, and, although restored in 1873 and 1893, escaped massacre. The nave has a waggon roof and is furnished with box-pews, rising slightly at the W end so that those at the back can see the

altar just as well as those in the front. On each side are three-bay EE arcades and above the high chancel arch are 14c wall paintings of the Doom, Christ and angels and St Michael weighing souls. The N aisle has a painting of doubting Thomas and the Nevill chapel some simple 13c masonry patterns. This chapel on the NE, which is the vestry and mainly blocked up by the organ, is the oldest part of the church; the windows are 13c, but the walls and arch leading to the aisle are 12c. There is some 14c glass in the lancet window, and the roof is embossed with grotesque heads and the badges of the Nevills. There is a Perp screen between the chapel and the chancel, which is 12c–13c and has simple EE sedilia, piscina and lancets. The five-light E window, however, is Perp and has glass by William Morris with

Rye Town Hall

figures by Burne-Jones; the Victorian alabaster reredos spikes up into this beautiful window and should be removed. The Jacobean oak pulpit with sounding board is especially grand and striking—and no wonder, since it was made by Francis Gunby of Leeds in 1632 for the Archbishop's chapel at Bishopthorpe; it was discarded by Archbishop MacLagan, who wished his chapel fittings to be classical, and bought by Mrs Goodwyn, wife of the rector, in about 1890. The octagonal font cover (cf. Ticehurst) is dated 1533 on one of the panels and is of French workmanship; the door bears the Nevill coat of arms. The font itself is of local ironstone, a late Norman bowl, discovered by Canon Goodwyn lying in a field. By the N door is an iron grave slab with two crosses, but no date or inscription—possibly 14c. The Royal Arms is George I (1723).

Rottingdean [7] has some ugliness along the Brighton–Newhaven road, but the long High Street, which runs northward from it still has a rather jolly seafaring feel, and there are many flint-and-brick walls and cottages. North End House was the home of Burne-Jones; Kipling and Stanley Baldwin, both of them his nephews, often stayed there. The church is built up the side of a hill and overlooks a very pretty green with a pond, in the centre of which is a little island where some ducks have a maisonette. The nave is of Norman origin, shown in part of one N window, and there is a central tower with the usual tiled cap; the rest is EE. Being built on a hill the centre aisle slopes steeply upwards to the E end, three steps up to the tower space and another three up to the sanctuary. There is of course a good deal of glass by Burne-Jones, the best being the Tree of Jesse and Jacob's Ladder in the tower lancets. The whole of the S aisle and the chancel lancets were rebuilt by Gilbert Scott in 1856.

Rye [6 and Inset] the eastern bastion on the Sussex coast, became attached to Hastings, the premier

Rye

Cinque Port, in the reign of Henry II. All through the Middle Ages it was involved in raids and wars with the French, and was three times sacked and burnt, the last time in 1448. But although the French attacked and menaced it, the sea did not; unlike Old Winchelsea, which was submerged, Rye was built on a low hill, high enough to be immune from the sea's inroads. Of course the sea deserted it as it did New Winchelsea; but being on the Rother it remained a port as well as a substantial market town and borough. It still returns a Member to Parliament. And there it stands, a perfect small hill town with the church at its apex. From every quarter Rye is a delight, but especially when approached from the E across the marsh. The streets of tightly packed houses are clearly built on a medieval plan, and they range from the 15c to the 19c. Most visitors to Rye enter through the Land Gate, a massive 14c entrance with two round towers on either side of the archway: of the Strand Gate at the bottom of the Mint nothing but a few stones remains. The street rises quickly and then turns right-handed into the High Street, which runs the whole length of Rye, becoming narrower at the western end where it is called The Mint, and falls gently to the Strand and the warehouses on the River Tillingham. Below the High Street and running parallel outside the walls, of which there are scanty remains, is Cinque Ports Street. Between the two streets is a steep cobbled lane in which is the 'Monastery', actually a 14c chapel of the House of the Austin Friars. Apart from one or two regrettable modern stores the High Street is full of charming buildings. Most distinguished is the Old Grammar School, 17c brick with distinctly Dutch influence in the gables and pilasters. Opposite, the George Hotel (1719) is a comfortable, solid country hotel with an Assembly Room (1818) adjoining. The Mid-

land Bank has fluted pilasters and a frieze, and the Apothecary's Shop on the corner of East Street has a curved Georgian shop front with glazing bars. Up the hill off the High Street are East Street and Lion Street, at the top of which can be seen the church and the Town Hall. East and Lion Streets are linked at the top by Market Street, which is slightly wider, but not a square. In it is the Old Flushing Inn, a 15c timber-framed house with 13c cellars. On the ground floor is a wall painting (1536) with vigorously drawn leaf scrolls and animals. Almost next to it is the Town Hall (1743) by Andrews Jelfe, typically Georgian, brick with stone dressings and crowned by a parapet and cupola. Turn up towards the church and then right into Church Square, which is not a square so much as a close. Off it runs West Street in which is Rye's most famous house, Lamb House, for long the home of Henry James and later of E. F. Benson. Built of chequer brick, it has four bays, a panelled parapet and pilaster strips. It used to have a garden room at the end of the wall—destroyed in the Second World War—and there Miss Mapp in E. F. Benson's novel would observe the comings and goings of artistic ladies, retired colonels and other Rye characters. West Street also contains Tower House, early 18c, and several timber-framed houses. Then round to Mermaid Street, a steep, cobbled lane, containing the Mermaid Inn, 15c with a 13c cellar, like the Flushing; the back is later, 16c, and the doorway Georgian. Below the Mermaid is the Old Hospital dated 1576 on one of the gables; the three-light windows are late 17c and the doorways with flat hoods are Georgian. At the bottom is the Borough Arms, white and weatherboarded. Further round again is Watchbell Street, where are several timber-framed 15c houses and the former Independent Chapel, early 19c brick. At the east-

ern side of Church Square are the Water House, formerly a public cistern, a brick 18c building with a dome, and the Ypres Tower. This was built as the castle of Rye by William of Ypres in Stephen's reign; it was used as a prison for 400 years until the 19c. It has four round towers and used to have a tiled cap; this was shaken down in air raids and not replaced. As you turn back, observe the flying buttresses at the E end of the church; then come round again to Lion Street and enter. But first notice the handsome clock with its ebullient 18c frame and quarter boys. The clock itself was made at Winchelsea in 1561 and the great 18 ft pendulum swings to and fro in the N transept. The first church was Norman and both transepts are principally 12c, the N transept having a Norman doorway and the S various fragments of dog-tooth moulding. There is some blank arcading on the W walls, and the round-headed arches from transepts to aisles prove that the Norman church had aisles. The present nave arcades of five bays are EE and vary in form and size—some piers being round and some octagonal. Above the arcades is an ambulatory and a clerestory rebuilt in 1882. Also 13c are the two chapels N and S of the chancel. No further alterations were made until the 15c, when the arches and piers of the crossing were heightened and rebuilt. Above it was raised the battlemented tower, given its tiled cap in 1702. An unusual addition was the two-storied annexe W of the S transept; the upper was probably a priest's room and the lower a sacristy. Each floor has a large circular window. The screens between transepts and chapels are plain Perp. Note the pulpit with 16c linenfold panels and the fine two-tier chandelier dated 1759. There is no medieval glass; but the S aisle has two windows by Kempe. There are many memorial tablets—none of special note; one

162

Terracotta Urns by Harmer, **Salehurst**

to Catherine Owens (1797) by Flaxman—very ordinary—and another to John Woollett (1819) by J. Bacon. Royal Arms Queen Anne—one of the best in the country.

Rye Harbour [Inset] is an odd little place with a salty appeal, out on the marsh and shingle near the Rother's mouth. It consists of several factories and sheds, two pubs, a dilapidated Martello tower and a scatter of fishermen's and lifeboatmen's cottages. The small church designed by S. S. Teulon in 1848 is very suitable; it is a single room with an apsidal E end, tre-

foiled lancet windows and a small tower and spirelet on the N side. Camber Castle can be reached on foot from the road to Rye Harbour.

St Leonards [9] *see* **Hastings**

Salehurst [6] A very small village ½ mile from Robertsbridge, for which Salehurst is, and always has been, the parish church. Long and large, it was built of Hastings sandstone between 1250 and 1360; it is rather stylish and may have been the work of the monks at Robertsbridge Abbey, close by. The embattled tower has four shields on the W face with the arms of Peck-

ham, Echyngham and Culpeper, and a round-headed 13c W door with roll and fillet mouldings. On the S is a timber porch; but, unusually, the main entrance is by the tower. Inside, the nave has two arcades of six bays with octagonal columns. The clerestory windows were re-modelled at the restoration in 1861 and the roof completely renewed. In the chancel is an oil painting (1649) of the Revd John Lord, vicar 1639–81, and in the chapel behind the organ a tomb with a crocketed canopy. Two windows—in the N and S aisles—have in their upper lights some 14c drawings of birds; they are much

Sedlescombe

damaged but one is certainly a pea-cock and another seems to be a falcon. The 12c round font has a chain of salamanders crawling round the base of the shaft. At the W end are four hatchments, and on the floor six iron tomb slabs of the 17c and early 18c. Among the graves are two table tombs with Harmer terracotta plaques—a winged cherub's head—at each end, and three headstones with the usual basket of fruit. Great Wigsell, to the NE, is a manor house built of coursed ashlar in 1625 by Henry English. The N front has three bays and a central three-storied gabled porch. Inside is a contemporary staircase in six flights.

Seaford [8] (accent on ford) As an ancient 'limb' of Hastings, chief of the Cinque Ports, Seaford was an important place. It ought to be as attractive and interesting as Rye; but unfortunately it is not. Apart

from the church hardly anything of the old town remains and it seems to have grown up in a higgledy-piggledy fashion without the guidance or control of a great landowner, like Bexhill and Eastbourne, or good architects as Brighton had in Wilds and Busby, not to mention Nash and Barry. When the Ouse deserted it for Newhaven in the 16c, the place obviously decayed. The town is not actually on the sea, and for many years there was an ugly dip of waste land between it and the sea front, which was the old bed of the Ouse. This is now rather hard to see, as some of it has been filled up and built over; but for a long time the rather stark row of hotels and boarding-houses along the front was separated from the town itself. The town has superb coastline views, the white bluff of Seaford Head to the E, the cliffs beyond Newhaven to the W. The good air has made it an especially

favoured place for preparatory schools; there must be at least a dozen. The church is large and obviously early in origin; there is a blocked Norman arch and clerestory on the S side of the tower and traces of herring-bone masonry in the N wall of the nave. The walls are an interesting mixture of cobbles, sandstone, flints and sarsens (*see* East Blatchington). The tower is in four stages, the third stage in a chequerboard pattern of sandstone and flints. Alterations were made in the 13c, and the nave has EE arcades and clerestory. The capitals have stiff-leaf decoration, except for one on the S side, which has various grotesque figures illustrating the Crucifixion, Baptism of Christ, Souls in Hell, Daniel in the lion's den and the slaughter of the Innocents. On a pillar in the nave is an early, possibly Saxon, sculpture of St Michael and the Dragon, found in 1778; it is com-

Sheffield Park

parable in style to the sculptures from Selsey in Chichester Cathedral. The E end and transepts were designed by John Billing in 1861–2.

Sedlescombe [6] slopes gently southwards, its tile-hung cottages on either side of a green with a pillared well-house (1900). The Manor House, now called Manor Cottages, is timber-framed, early 17c, and has gables, pendants and a decorated barge-board. The church, N of the village, has a Perp W tower, battlemented and buttressed with an angle turret. The inside has suffered from heavy-handed restoration in 1866, and nearly all the stonework is new. There is a 16c font cover and four Jacobean oak pew backs. The nave has Perp arcades with octagonal piers, all except one heavily restored. The roof has four tie-beams and king-posts, and there is a small George III Royal Arms. Two fragments of armorial glass in the N aisle and three windows by Kempe in the chancel. There was a Sackville connection here, shown by the helm in the S aisle and the stone cartouche to Thomas Sackville (1692) in the vestry. Also in the S aisle are a hatchment and memorials to the Sharpe and Brabazon families of Oaklands; Hercules Brabazon, the painter, was a close friend of Gertrude Jekyll. Oaklands has now become the Pestalozzi village, a sociological experiment where children of all nations are brought up together.

Selmeston [8] lies just N of the Lewes–Eastbourne road. The small flint-built church is prettily situated on a bank above the lane in a circular churchyard surrounded with hart's tongue ferns. It was largely rebuilt by Ewan Christian in 1867, and the Dec and Perp windows are copies of the originals. The small S aisle is separated from the nave by an early 15c timber arcade of three bays, supported by two octagonal wooden pillars. Although considerably restored, this wooden arcade is unique in Sussex. The nave has a trussed and raftered roof. In the N wall of the chancel is a monument, which was formerly an Easter sepulchre. The old marble altar slab with consecration crosses is still in use.

Sheffield Park [4] is known to the public today mostly for its railway station. When the single line from Lewes to East Grinstead was closed in 1960, a group of railway enthusiasts bought the station and the

Sheffield Park Station

track from Sheffield Park to Horsted Keynes, christened it the Bluebell Line and established it as a novelty where tourists can take a short trip on that now obsolete means of transport, a steam train. The station, built in 1882, still has an air of Victorian importance, and on the 'up' side is a collection of iron signs, including one for 'Volvolutum—the world's finest soap'. To a

lesser, but more discerning, public it is known for the park itself and for its magnificent gardens, laid out for John Baker Holroyd, 1st Earl of Sheffield, between 1769 and 1794. It is within the parish of Fletching and is mentioned in Domesday Book as Sifelle, later Shifeld and then Sheffield. The manor was originally owned by Simon de Montfort, whose army camped on Fletching Common before the Battle of Lewes. In 1299 it passed to the Lords De La Warr until the 15c when it was seized by Henry VI. The De La Warrs acquired it again in the 18c, and sold it to John Baker Holroyd in 1769. The core of the house is Tudor, but it was greatly enlarged and Gothicised by Wyatt in 1775 for the 1st Lord Sheffield. It was Wyatt's first major essay in Gothick. After surviving a period as a country club the house is now again privately owned and is open to the public. The rooms are being sensitively restored and furnished, and the elegance of Wyatt's decoration,

long obscured by Victorian dinginess, is once more apparent. The view from the balcony down the lakes shows the superb skill of Brown's landscaping and Arthur Soames's imaginative planting. Edward Gibbon, after finishing *The Decline and Fall of the Roman Empire* in Lausanne, returned in 1793 to live with his friend Lord Sheffield; Gibbon died the following year and was buried in the Sheffield Mausoleum in Fletching church. The gardens were laid out by 'Capability' Brown and Repton for the 1st Earl and improved later for the 3rd Earl, who made the two lakes linking the gardens and the house

with the two older lakes below. But the planting of trees and shrubs, which add such great distinction, was done by Mr Arthur Soames, who bought the estate in 1910. Azaleas and rhododendrons, in which he specialised, flaunt their splendour in May, and in October groups of scarlet and golden maples planted against silver birches and conifers, and beneath them quilts of blue gentians, give heraldic glory to the dying year. The gardens now belong to the National Trust and are open from April to mid-November. There was once an iron foundry at Sheffield mill and another just N of the station. In the

The ruins of Nymans, Handcross (*see* **Slaugham**)

Detail in the gardens, Nymans ▷

1790s the Upper Ouse Navigation Trustees under Lord Sheffield's chairmanship were formed to make the upper reaches navigable; the last commercial barge went up the river in 1862. The Sheffield Arms at Sheffield Green is a handsome late 18c house, probably built when the turnpike road from Godstone to Lewes was opened.

Slaugham* [4] (pronounced Slaffam) is so secluded as to be a surprise. Standing on a hillock in woodland country, the cottages are grouped prettily round a green and some have Horsham-slabbed roofs. On one side is the church, built of ironstone with a low tower crowned by a Sussex cap. Its Norman origin is proved by a blocked doorway in the N wall, and by the late 12c font, on one side of which is a rude emblem of a fish, the Early Christian symbol. Apart from the 14c E window, it is mostly EE, but was much restored in 1858–60. The chancel is richly adorned with an alabaster reredos and on the E walls on either side are figures of St Mary and St Richard of Chichester, designed in 1921 by Walter Tower, a cousin of Kempe, the stained-glass artist. The pulpit is thought to be Italian and was given in 1890; beside it is an oak panel which was part of the old pulpit in use until then. In the chancel is an Easter tomb (1547) containing brasses to Richard Covert and his three wives, each with a scroll to their lips. In the Covert chapel is another brass (1503) to John Covert and a fine Renaissance monument by Flynton (1579) to Richard Covert and his family; it has 17 kneeling figures over each of which is an initial. In the wall behind the organ is a Romano-British jar. A little to the S of the church are the fragmentary ruins of Slaugham Place, the Jacobean home of the Coverts.

Handcross was until recently a bustling village on the London–Brighton road; but it has now been bypassed. It has an old, but much modernised, inn. Nymans, an E-shaped 'Elizabethan' house in sandstone, was built for Lt. Colonel Leonard Messel in 1925–30 and designed by Sir Walter Tapper. It was burnt just after the war, and, except for a wing, is now a hollow-eyed, romantic ruin, looking rather like an 18c folly. Messel was a well-known horticulturist, and Nymans Gardens, in which Robinson and Miss Jekyll had a hand, now belong to the National Trust; they are well worth a visit, especially in July, when the huge white towers of Eucryphia Nymansensis make a spectacular show.

Southease [7] is a miniature village on an eastern slope below the Lewes–Newhaven road. The church, built of flint and rubble and standing on a small green is largely pre-Conquest; it has a 12c round tower, one of the three in the Ouse valley, capped by a small conical spire. There is a Norman window just W of the entrance porch, and a pair of wide, blocked arches on either side of the chancel, which originally opened into short aisles; no trace of these remains except a piscina on the outside of the N wall The original chancel, which projected a few yards further, was rebuilt in the early 14c with the present E window. The simple interior has a curious wooden chancel arch with timber-framing above, and the walls adorned with somewhat vestigial 13c paintings, restored in 1934. On the N wall are scenes from the life of Christ and on the W wall a Majesty. The furnishings include an Elizabethan altar table, Jacobean altar rails, a few pews of about the same date and a pulpit made from the oak of a three-decker. There is a George III Royal Arms, and Commandment Boards on either side of the altar. The nave and chancel roofs have tie-beams and rafters of very rough and irregular contruction; there is quarry-tiled flooring throughout. At the W end is an organ built about 1790 by Allen of Soho with a mahogany case and gilt pipes; it was formerly in St Anne's, Lewes and then at Offham. There are few small organs of this date and type in existence; others are at St Margaret's, Westminster, York Minster and Buckingham Palace. One of the bells is about 1280 and is the third oldest in Sussex. Among the parish records is an entry in 1604 of a widower who married again; the rector, an evident cynic, observed in minute Latin 'A shipwrecked sailor seeks a second shipwreck.'

Stanmer [7] The village and church are in a large park on the southern slope of the Downs between Brighton and Lewes. Stanmer Park was until the Second World War the home of the Pelhams, Earls of Chichester, an ancient Sussex family, whose crest, the Pelham buckle, is found on many East Sussex buildings (*see* Introduction *and* Laughton). The house was built in 1724 for Henry and Thomas Pelham, and is the only known complete English work of Nicholas Dubois. Externally it is plain, but the internal plasterwork is distinguished. Like the village it suffered much damage during the war, when the estate was a battle school, but it has been well restored by the Brighton Corporation. It is now part of Sussex University, the upper rooms being used as flats (*see* Introduction). Stanmer is unusual in that, when the Pelhams enclosed their park, they did not remove the village, but included it and the church within their demesne. The church, close to the village pond, was rebuilt in 1838, an elegant replica of its 13c predecessor, with an embattled tower and a slim spire. The outside is of knapped flints with stone dressings, the inside pleasing in proportion and detail with EE lancet windows. In the chancel is an oval black plaque to Elizabeth Scrase (1732), on the floor a black tomb slab to Edward

Michelbourn (1700) with a brass roundel containing his arms. In the nave is a small marble monument to Sir John Pelham (d. 1580) and his son (d. 1584) brought from Holy Trinity, Minories, London. On the W gallery is a small carved George III Royal Arms.

Staplefield* [4] was formerly a hamlet of Cuckfield, but became a village on its own when the EE church by Benjamin Ferrey was built in 1847. None of the houses scattered round the large green seems any older except the Jolly Tanners inn. The church has a three-tier stone bell-cote and lancet windows with glass by Kempe; the E window is a stepped triplet. Also by Kempe about 1870 is a frieze of pre-Raphaelitish paintings showing figures against trees, high up on either side of the chancel. At the W end in two glass cases are documents giving the history of the church, gifts and expenses since the day it was built.

Streat [4] The name suggests that this small compact village on a sandy ridge a mile N of the Downs was on a Roman road, though there are no other indications of this in the neighbourhood. The 12c and 13c church of flint and sandstone was heavily restored in the 19c. The Norman N and S doors mentioned by Hussey in 1852 have disappeared. There are two inscribed cast-iron slabs on the floor; the smaller—1731—is to Sarah Saunders, daughter of Thomas Saunders of Wadhurst, where there are 30 iron tomb slabs in the church. So these two were probably made at Wadhurst, since Streat is well outside the iron smelting country. On the N wall are two elegant marble monuments to William Dobell (1752) and Mary Dobell (1764); they are of various marbles and adorned with garlands of fruit and flowers with urns at the top and cherubs at the foot. Over the chancel arch is a Charles II Royal Arms.

Streat Place is a Jacobean house built soon after 1607. The handsome E-shaped E front is slightly asymmetrical because of an extra gabled bay to the N wing. The back of the house is very much more modest and looks like a farmhouse. It may be the remains of an earlier 16c house as are some of the outbuildings. On the railway embankment N of Streat grow masses of Elecampane (*Inula Helenium*) much used by medieval herbalists as a cure. If you suffer from bronchial or digestive troubles, an aromatic infusion made from the crushed roots may do you a power of good.

Tarring Neville [7] A very small farming hamlet on the E side of the Ouse valley. The name must indicate an ancient connection with the Nevill family, and Rodmell on the opposite side of the valley has an inn formerly called The Abergavenny Arms. The church is approached by a rough grass path flanked by six pollarded elms. It has a tower with a Sussex cap, unfortunately tiled instead of shingled, and the flint walls were smothered in roughcast at the restoration in 1892. The 13c chancel has a triple lancet E window, and on the floor is a black marble tomb slab to Mr Diones Geere of Rottingdean and his wife (1743). The chancel arch is simple EE, and the S aisle, under one roof with the nave, has a two-bay arcade with double chamfered arches and round piers. The octagonal font, 14c was built into the S wall at the restoration; but according to Hussey it was formerly built into the N wall.

Telscombe [7] A westward lane off the Lewes–Newhaven road winds for two miles over the Downs and ends at the little shepherds' village of Telscombe, snugly sheltered in its combe and remote from the hand of the developer. It consists of a handful of cottages, a modest manor house and the church. It

owes its perfection to the late Ambrose Gorham, squire of Telscombe for many years, who watched over its preservation with great diligence and bequeathed it, subject to strict trusts regarding building, to the Brighton Corporation. The flint-built church has a Norman nave and chancel and a tower with a Sussex cap. The N aisle and chapel each have a two-bay arcade with round unmoulded arches and elaborate capitals; the tower arch is likewise unmoulded but is pointed. The old lectern—now disused—and reading desk have pieces of medieval carving in them. The 13c square font has flat pointed arches and ogee-headed recessed arches in the base. There is a carved Carolean Royal Arms. There are no houses of special importance, but the general picture is one of singular charm.

Three Bridges* [1] is a railway junction. The new town that has grown up around it joins Crawley New Town on the W and threatens Worth on the E. It has nothing to commend it, except trains.

Ticehurst [6] standing on a high ridge, has a little square mostly of weatherboarded cottages; just to the S beyond the village stores, which has a shelter supported on elegant early Victorian iron pillars, is the church. The tower has an embattled stair turret with gargoyles and a short shingled spire, hardly more than a cap. The porch has a Dec niche above the arch, occupied by a modern statuette of the Virgin and Child, and a parvise chamber above it. The ribbed vaulting converges on a central boss with arms of the de Echynghams (*see* Etchingham). The chamber has a low domed roof with beams thought to have come from a wrecked ship; it was formerly used as a prison. The nave has four-bay 14c arcades on each side with octagonal piers and a high 15c arch to the tower. The roof is modern, but

◁ Details of a stained glass Doom, **Ticehurst**

Udimore

has its original tie-beams and king-posts. At the restoration in 1856 the Perp E window was inserted and the large Dec clerestory windows; the tracery is said to have been copied from drawings of the originals, but the flowing designs in large circles seem somewhat clumsy and out of proportion with the nave arcades. In the S chapel is an iron tomb slab let into the floor with arms of the May family; the N chapel, known as the Courthope chapel after the family who have owned Whiligh for 460 years, has a wall monument to George Courthope (1714); a cartouche without figures on the chancel floor is a small brass to John Wybarne and his two wives; the knight's armour

is of a style nearly a century earlier than his death, though his wives' dresses are contemporary. Did his executors find the brass of another man, remove the escutcheon and put the new brasses to the two wives on either side? In the N window of the sanctuary is some 15c glass removed from the E window in 1879; it is unusual in having undamaged figures—Salome with her sons, SS John and James, the Virgin and Child and St Christopher. There is also a Doom picture and the arms of the de Echynghams. Other fragments of medieval glass are in the N aisle. The font has a distinguished 16c cover with eight panels, four of which open on hinges; each is carved inside and

outside with intricate geometrical patterns. Whiligh, the home of the Courthopes, is about 2 miles NW—a 16c gabled house, somewhat altered in 1836. The timbers for the roof of Westminster Hall came from the Whiligh estate in the 14c; when the roof was repaired in the 1930s, oak was once again provided from Whiligh.

Tidebrook [5] is hidden away among lanes between Mayfield and Wadhurst. The church by Rushforth (1856), its E end almost abutting on to the road, is EE and of sandstone. The inside is very successful; windows are all simple lancets, a triple and two singles at the W end, five stepped lancets above the altar. The nave has two twin lancets on the N, singles on the S, and a roof with braces and collar-beams. In the chancel are three large and very high sedilia. The most notable feature is the excellent stonework of the windows, and the unplastered splays, which give an impression of great depth.

Turner's Hill* [1] stands high on the wealden ridge with wide views of the North and South Downs. E of the cross-roads is a group of five paired houses built in 1921 by Lord Cowdray for his estate employees and designed by Sir Aston Webb. Timber-framed above, sandstone below and with Tudor brick chimneys, they are entirely pseudo, but all the same handsome, confident and well-spaced—gracious living for game-keepers. The church by Lacy Ridge 1895–97 is Dec and of sandstone; the tower and porches were added in 1923 by Sir Aston Webb. It is a somewhat heavy and unsuccessful effort, and too grand a church for a small village. The reredos is said to have come from St Mildred's Poultry in the City of London, which was demolished in 1872. It may be a composite piece, the caryatids coming from one source and the main relief from another. The E window and side windows in the chancel are all by Kempe.

Twineham* [4] E. V. Lucas writing in 1904 says of Twineham that 'situated on a byroad between two lines of railway, it has preserved its bloom'. 70 years later this is still true, and one of the terrible railways—neither of which was very near—from Horsham to Shoreham is now closed. Twineham is a scattered place of farms and cottages, and a charming and very rustic church. It was built of brick in the late 16c—a time when Gothic church architecture had virtually ceased. Landowners no longer lived in fortified castles, and architects were more in demand for private

houses than for churches. Twineham and East Guldeford are the only Tudor churches in East Sussex; it has a depressed four-centred chancel arch and a Jacobean pulpit and pew. The tower has a modest shingled spire and the churchyard some fine oak trees. While not a building of any great distinction or noteworthy features, it has a great deal of simple country charm.

Hickstead, a hamlet within the parish on the Brighton road, was until a few years ago unknown. Now it makes headline news, because of the International Jumping Competition which has been established there. Hickstead Place, which adjoins the jumping arena, is a small but distinctive Jacobean manor house, though part of it dates from the 15c. It is a low, mellow two-storeyed house of brick with Horsham-slabbed roofs; magnolias and creepers clothe the walls. In the garden is a curious building known as the 'Castle', the purpose of which is not known. It is a brick-built tower of two storeys with crow-stepped gables. Hickstead was connected with the Knights Hospitallers as part of their manor of Saddlescombe (*see* Newtimber).

Uckfield [5] is a large village on a southern slope with a fine view of the Downs. The upper part of the high street has some Georgian houses notably Hooke Hall with a coved porch, the Maiden's Head Hotel with bow-fronted windows and Church House, next to the church. The lower part of the street is Victorian and neo-Georgian. The church, apart from the 15c tower, which was heightened and given a new spire, was rebuilt in 1839. Externally it is agreeable enough, but the inside is an undistinguished mixture of styles. The chancel arch is 'Early English' while the aisles have four-centred, 'Tudor' arches and 'Georgian' galleries. There are various monuments from the old church, but none of any special interest or dis-

tinction; also a brass (1610). There are various outcrops of Hastings sandstone in the neighbourhood similar to those near Tunbridge Wells.

Udimore [6] is a rather sparse village on a ridge with fine views towards Winchelsea and Fairlight. Its church is off the road and close to the farmyard of Court Lodge, where Edwards I and III stayed when it belonged to the Echynghams. It shares with other places a legend of supernatural removal; the chosen site was supposedly down in the marsh, but the stones were removed nightly and a voice heard, saying, 'O'er the mere'. Believe it, if you like; but the *OED of Place Names* prefers 'Boundary of the wood'. The only traces of the Norman church are a small blocked window and two blocked doorways. It was largely rebuilt in the 13c, and an aisle added, which has now disappeared though the arches are clearly visible. The short W tower with a squat, tiled cap is EE; so also is the chancel with three well-spaced stepped lancets in the E wall and lancets at the sides. Nave and chancel have plain tie-beams, but no king-posts. The Royal Arms is George III 1772 and at the W are two recently restored belfry boards. Fragments of medieval glass are in a S window. The odd little pudding-basin font on a pedestal represents an 18c forgery. By an ancient edict, fonts might not be made of wood; but the parsimonious churchwardens had a wooden bowl carefully painted to look like stone on the outside and like lead within—to give the impression that they were conforming to church laws.

Wadhurst [2] is a pretty village on a ridge with a long street of tile-hung cottages, an early Georgian vicarage and Hill House, tile-hung with a Doric porch. The church stands a little back up a side street; the churchyard is intersected with

dark-coloured brick paths and has a large number of sandstone tombs with decorated headstones. The tower is Norman in origin—one twin bell-opening and a small round-headed window on the N survive—and has a graceful shingled spire. The 15c porch is two-storeyed and has ribbed vaulting; it contains various tablets to the Luck family, one of them with a Harmer plaque. There are two more Harmer plaques in the N transept and the sanctuary. The Norman walls of the nave were pulled down when the 13c aisles were added; each has an arcade of four EE arches and piers alternately round and octagonal. The church is wide and well-proportioned, and is well lit by the clerestory windows. The nave roof has tie-beams and king-posts; the S aisle roof is dated 1592. Wadhurst must have had an important iron foundry. On the floor of the church are 30 very handsome iron tomb slabs 1617–1790; those in the chancel have shields and initials in relief. No other church has as many iron tombs. Also in the chancel are some black marble tomb slabs with the usual armorial roundels at the head, a small alabaster tablet to Mary Dunmoll (1651) with a kneeling figure and a large tablet by William Palmer to John Barham (1730) with armorial bearings on top, Corinthian columns and cherubs on either side and draperies in the centre. At the W end is a modern screen (1957) by Duncan Wilson of glass and wrought iron—somewhat fanciful but successful. At the entrance to the churchyard is Churchgate House, timber-framed and tile-hung with a Georgian door. At the hamlet of *Pell Green* is the Rehoboth Chapel 1824, an attractive little weatherboarded building with three round-headed windows. Wadhurst Station, a little to the N, is worth looking at as an interesting example of mid-Victorian station architecture.

Waldron [5] The church is mostly EE and has a Pelham tower; the angle turret, the Perp W door, as well as the E window replacing three lancets, the jambs of two of which can be seen on the outside, were all added in the 15c. The nave is unusually wide; there is a wooden chancel arch, presumably inserted at the restoration in 1862, but there is no sign of any previous arch, possibly owing to the exceptional width. The 13c N aisle is also remarkably wide. At the W end of the N aisle, lying on its side, is a very large round stone font, which may be Saxon and was discovered in the fields in the 19c. There is an urbane, classical wall monument to Capt John Fuller (1722) in grey and white marble; it has a sarcophagus resting on clawed feet and a white marble urn on either side. The Fullers were ironfounders. In the churchyard are two tombs with Harmer's terracotta work—one a table tomb with numerous small rosettes inserted, the other a more usual plaque with an urn. The Spiked Rampion (*Phyteuma spicatum*) is, according to Bentham and Hooker's *British Flora*, found only about Waldron.

Warbleton [5] A brick path leads up to this distinguished church, on the wealden ridge with a southward view and standing partly within a Roman earthwork. Opposite is a range of modernised brick cottages, formerly the workhouse, and next to them an inn, the Warbill-in-tun, a rather laboured joke; this is all, and the main village is at Rushlake Green, two miles away. In the churchyard wall is a stone erected in 1888, which reads 'Close by in the meadow beyond stood the abode of Richard Woodman, farmer and iron master, Burnt at Lewes, 22 June 1552'; he was a Protestant martyr. There is a tombstone to John Fox (1815) with a terracotta inset by Harmer. The church has a Perp tower, which was used as a place of refuge during the

Marian persecutions; outside on the S wall of the chancel is an arched recess. The chancel is EE and has two lancets; the other windows were altered in the 15c, when the N aisle was added, divided from the nave by a four-bay arcade. In the aisle is a large rectangular squire's pew dated 1722, supported on two pillars and approached by a staircase; above it are two small hatchments. There is some medieval glass in the N aisle window, one fragment with an armorial shield; there are a few small fragments also in the E window of the chapel. The W window is by Kempe (1882). On the floor of the chancel is a large brass (1436) to Dean Prestwick of St Mary's College, Hastings, under an ogee canopy with Latin inscriptions. Behind the organ, unworthily placed, is a handsome wall monument by Rysbrack to Sir John Lade (d. 1740); in the centre is a bust of Sir John in Roman draperies flanked by two Corinthian columns and surmounted by floral swags. Two miles E at *Rushlake Green* are the scanty remains of Warbleton Priory, a small house of a prior and three canons, which transferred here from Hastings in 1413 owing to the inroads of the sea; Sir John Pelham gave them the site. The remains of the chapel are built into the stable of a farmhouse.

Wartling [8] is a small and pretty village, built on a hillside just above Pevensey Level; it has several tiled and weatherboarded cottages with massive brick chimney stacks, 16c. The church has a small, weatherboarded shingled spire springing from the roof. The chancel seems to be 13c, but the windows are now obscured by a number of rather dull 18c tablets to the Curteis family. The two-bay arcades on the N and S of the nave are 15c. The church is furnished with 19c boxpews and over the chancel arch are the Royal Arms of George II. Under the tower are two Harmer

Wilmington church and Priory

plaques removed from the church-yard; these are believed to be the only cast-iron examples of Harmer's work—which was usually in terracotta—and were probably made at Ashburnham, which was the only forge still working in Harmer's time (1762–1849).

Westfield [6] is an unremarkable village in a rather dull tract S of Brede; but it has a good church. A brick path between an avenue of clipped Irish yews leads to a porch with an oak door dated 1542 in iron figures hung on a pair of wrought-iron strap hinges. Another date, 1624, is on a buttress to the tower; this obviously does not apply to the tower itself, which is 14c, though

according to early records the lower part may be pre-Conquest. In it are some stone stairs leading to a chamber, which overlooked the nave. The nave walls are Norman, and there is a Norman chancel arch with carved capitals; as often happened, e.g. Mountfield, when the chancel was extended about 1251, a squint was cut on each side of the arch. In the early 19c the E wall of the sanctuary was rebuilt; the three stepped lancets, similar to Udi-more, but less well-spaced, were inserted. Later the chancel roof and tie-beams were painted—rather well—and much more recently in 1957 the small and elegant little organ, perched up on a fluted support, was built. The N aisle was

added in 1861, and, although the round-headed windows are not very good, the pseudo-Norman arcade is quite harmonious; on the N wall are the 18c Commandment Boards. The pulpit is Jacobean and has an 18c sounding board with a star inlay. At the W end is a modern Royal Arms. The church has quarry-tiled floors.

Westham [8] (accent on -ham) is beneath the shadow of Roman Pevensey. The street has two timber-framed houses; otherwise it is of little account. But the majestic battlemented Perp tower of the church dominates. The church was built soon after the Normans landed and may have been part of

Wilmington Priory

the Hospital of St Cross; originally cruciform, it had an apsidal chancel and apsidal transepts, traces of which remain. The walls have an interesting texture of flints, sandstone and seashore pebbles. In the S wall of the nave are three original Norman windows, small and deeply splayed. In the 14c the N wall and transept were pulled down and an aisle added with an arcade of octagonal piers. There are 15c screens to the chancel and S transept; but the rood screen is squashed by a heavy modern rood-

179

loft, more in the Devon tradition. In the upper lights of the E window are complete figures of Christ and the 12 apostles in 15c glass. In the Lady Chapel is the pre-Reformation stone altar; it was used as a gravestone in 1602, two of the crosses being cut off, and became part of the paving of the church. The nave roof has king-posts over the font, but queen-posts the rest of the way; the beams are said to be ships' timbers. Nave and chancel are paved with herring-bone brick-work, and the S transept has square quarry-tiles.

Westmeston [4] stands at the foot of the Downs, and is no more than a cluster of houses and the flint and sandstone church. The nave is 12c and the N door is Norman; but additions were made in the 13c and 15c. The roof has some Horsham slabs on the S side and the W end has a shingled 14c bell-cote with a pyramidal cap. Inside there is a 17c pulpit; but the drastic restoration of 1862, when all the windows were re-modelled and mural paintings destroyed, like those at Plumpton, has robbed it of interest. The W window is by Kempe, the E window a somewhat glaring effort by Capronnier 1873. Westmeston Place is a two-storeyed gabled house, early 16c with later additions.

Whatlington [6] A small, ridge village with weatherboarded cottages and a white-painted Methodist chapel, now turned into an antique shop. The church is away down a lane and hidden by trees. It must have been in a pretty bad state in 1862, when it was subjected to a most ruthless restoration. The western bell turret was taken down and a horrid little tower and spire built on the N side. Inside medieval glass was removed, wall paintings destroyed and a 1643 pulpit and squire's pew thrown out. Very little of interest is left. What features there are are EE—lancets in nave and chancel, a low-side window

and sedilia recess; the square bowl font is the same date. The carved pulpit was exhibited at the Great Exhibition in 1851. The old rectory, just below the church, is a pretty little timber-framed and tiled house.

Willingdon [8] is too near East-bourne to be safe, and has been largely suburbanised. But there are still some nice flint and cobbled cottages with flint-walled gardens. Willingdon and its endowments were granted to Wilmington Priory, a cell of the Abbey of Grestain, and the vicar was appointed by the abbey until the dissolution of Wilmington in 1414. The church has an EE tower at the NW corner with a short shingled spire; the nave, rebuilt in the 14c, is rather oddly set at an angle to it and the roof line of the earlier nave is visible on the tower. A N aisle with finely moulded arches was added, possibly the work of the monks at Wilmington. The nave has a roof of beautifully warped tie-beams and king-posts, and the 14c font is of green Eastbourne sandstone. There are a lot of monuments to the Parkers of Ratton, a now vanished manor house. In the sanctuary are two gay cartouches with swags and cherubs and a small alabaster kneeling figure of Sir John Parker (1617). In the Ratton chapel are more—a small kneeling figure of Mrs Elinar Parker (1598) and an impressive table tomb to Sir Nicholas (1619) where he lies in alabaster with his children kneeling around him. Sir George (1726) has a white marble monument with arms and an urn, and there is another in the nave to Sir Thomas (1663); it does not look at all 17c and could well be by the same hand as Sir George. The Parkers petered out in 1750 and were succeeded by the Thomas family. Freeman Thomas became Marquess of Willingdon and was one of the last Viceroys of India; his banner hangs in the chapel.

Opposite the church is the Hoo, a large, attractive, rambling house in Lutyens vernacular style (1902). The brick wall on to the street has two oval oculi and inside is a small courtyard. There are several gables of differing heights—one tile-hung, another weatherboarded—and long oriel windows at the corners with small panes and many glazing bars.

Wilmington [8] is well known for the Long Man, a giant figure of uncertain age cut out in the turf on the side of the Downs; he stands with a staff in each hand, but unlike the Cerne Giant in Dorset he is sexless. (*See* Introduction.) In the Middle Ages, however, it was probably better known for its priory, a small alien house established in about 1243. It belonged to the Abbey of Grestain in Normandy to which Robert, Count of Mortain, Lord of the Rape of Pevensey, made considerable benefactions, including many manors and lands in the Rape. Wilmington as an alien house was suspect and was frequently seized during the French wars. In 1380 it was seized by Richard II and the Prior of Michelham was given custody of it. It was suppressed in 1414 in common with all the other alien houses. The ruins have been built into a farmhouse; there is a 15c gateway with two towers, a room with a vaulted ceiling and a cellar. It now belongs to the Sussex Archaeological Trust and there is an agricultural museum. A print of 1790 shows the priory buildings pretty well intact and the church was obviously part of them. Such a small community did not need a chapel on its own; so a church was built for the use of the monks and the villagers, the priests using the chancel and the laity the nave. The walls of the chancel, the round-headed window casings of Caen stone and the stone ledges used as seats by the monks are all 12c. In the N wall is a strange little stone figure, formerly on the

Winchelsea church

outside wall, which may be a primitive Madonna or an angel. The N chapel, now filled by the organ, was built in the 13c; it has an unusual window known as the Bee and Butterfly window. The central figure of St Peter may be Flemish, but the bees and butterflies around it, all, except one, identifiably English, look like transfers. The nave has a 14c roof with tie-beams and king-posts. The chancel arch was heightened and rebuilt in 1883, but the rood beam is still in position; at the same time the S aisle was built to replace a small transept which connected the church with the priory. It is divided from the nave by two EE arches supported by a pillar of

hard chalk. There is a Jacobean pulpit with a sounding board and a small Victorian Royal Arms. In the churchyard is an enormous yew, which may be older than the church; its girth is 23 ft. The long village street runs northwards from the priory; many of its charming and well-kept cottages no longer house farm workers, but have been bought by retired professional or business people. But in outward appearances Wilmington still looks what it was for 900 years—a downland farming village.

Winchelsea [6] Linked in history and rather self-consciously described today as Antient Towns,

Winchelsea and Rye are very different—Rye a busy and bustling market town, Winchelsea a wistful and nostalgic village. Three medieval gates—one away down a lane—and the relic of a great church are all the buildings that remain to show its former importance. Its history is fierce and warlike. At the Conquest Old Winchelsea lay 2 or more miles to the SE; it had been given by Edward the Confessor to the monks of Fécamp, a gift that was renewed by Henry III and like Rye it was attached to Hastings, the premier Cinque Port, and became a leading member. But it had two implacable enemies—the French, who constantly raided and sacked it, and, even worse, the sea, which finally destroyed and submerged it at the end of the 13c. The people fled and built themselves a new town on a sea-washed promontory to the NW; much of the land was taken from the parish of Icklesham, to which a large part of Winchelsea still belongs. New Winchelsea was built by Edward I, as Warden of the Cinque Ports, on a grid plan and divided into 39 squares or quarters; relics of this plan are still evident on the N side, where the streets all intersect at right angles, and the church occupies one of the squares in the centre. On the seaward side the Strand Gate was built, and the proud bastion as it stands today may be the gate through which Edward I rode back unharmed

after his horse had leapt over the wall and down the precipitous hillside. In Henry V's reign a smaller gate, the Land or Pipewell Gate, was built on the landward side, and later still a third, the New Gate, now half a mile to the S and alone in a leafy lane; its four-centred arch must be Tudor, though it may replace an earlier gate. But New Winchelsea was no more immune from attack than its predecessor. Three times it was sacked by the French in 1359, 1380 and 1449. In 1350 it saw the defeat of the Spanish fleet by Edward III, and in 1377 the men of Winchelsea, led by the Abbot of Battle, repulsed the French force which had sacked Rye. But this was Winchelsea's last moment of glory; the sea, which had drowned the old town nearly

200 years before, now began to recede, and after 1450 Winchelsea ceased to be a port. The plan for New Winchelsea was never completed, and though there was a Mayor and Corporation until recently, the town hall and market place were never built. Beneath the houses are over 30 vaults, intended as stores for Gascon wine. The place had evidently greatly diminished by the 18c; both Defoe and, 70 years later, John Wesley, described it as the skeleton of a city. However there is nothing decayed about Winchelsea today and there are many attractive houses. Greyfriars, to the S, is early 19c, and has in its garden the ruin of the 14c Franciscan church. Only the chancel survives, with the chancel arch and a polygonal apse; other pieces of wall are very fragmentary. Mariteau House is a five-bay 18c house with a pediment, and the New Inn, opposite the corner of the churchyard, is also 18c with a medieval rib-vaulted cellar.

But the glory of Winchelsea is its church—fragment though it is. There were originally three churches—St Giles, St Leonard and St Thomas; of the first two no traces, and of St Thomas only the chancel and ruinous transepts remain. There was a central tower and probably a nave; it is uncertain whether the nave was ever completed, but there is some evidence that the central arch was filled in after the collapse of the tower and destruction of the nave. The church was built in the early 14c, when the Dec style was in full flower; in proportion it is grand, in detail elaborate. It is some of the finest Dec work in Sussex, and shows that the burghers of Winchelsea had plenty of money to employ skilled architects and carvers and to import Caen stone from Normandy. The windows all have intricate flamboyant tracery with cusps; the E windows have five lights, the side windows of the chapels three. They all are filled with stained glass by

Winchelsea mill

Strachan, the gift of Lord Blanesburgh in 1931 in memory of his brothers and nephews. They may be criticised as over-romantic; but they fill the church with glorious colour and add to its splendour. In the N window of the sanctuary is some medieval glass formerly in the E window and thrown out when the Perp tracery was replaced by pseudo-Dec in 1850. The chancel is divided from the chapels by three-bay arcades with tall clustered piers; the smaller shafts are of Sussex marble. Both chancel and S chapel have sedilia and piscina with elaborate crocketed canopies and cusped arches. The monuments are famous. In the N chapel are three recumbent figures of a warrior, a lady and a young man in polished Sussex marble, believed to have been transferred from Old Winchelsea. They have richly carved canopies with ogee arches and large, stylised trefoil leaves in the centre. In the S chapel, once the Alard chantry, are the two Alard tombs of outstandingly beautiful workmanship. The recumbent stone figures lie beneath carved and crocketed canopies, similar to but somewhat higher than those in the N chapel. The eastern effigy is believed to be of Gervase Alard, Admiral of the Western Fleet under Edward I; he wears complete armour, mailed from head to foot, a lion couchant at his feet. The recessed triple canopy is filled in with diaper work, and the central gablet springs from heads of Edward I and Queen Margaret. The western tomb is similar, but a little later. The effigy is supposed to be of Stephen Alard, Admiral of the Cinque Ports and the Western Fleet, and founder of the Alard chantry. Here the gablet springs from heads of Edward II and Queen Isabella. Below the tomb of Gervase Alard is a slab with a floriated cross inscribed in old French with the name of Reginald Alard (d. 1454). Behind the altar in the S chapel is a Jacobean monument

to Margarita Godfrey, wife of Thomas Godfrey, 'an eminent man and Jurat of this town'; it has alabaster ribbon work. The organ was built in 1931 and, like the windows, given by Lord Blanesburgh; on it hangs a crudely painted Georgian Royal Arms.

Withyham [2] (accent on -ham) has long been the home of the Sackvilles (see Introduction) and its church has interest on that account. It stands on a high bank above the road and has a charming westward view over a lake with Hartfield's spire piercing the distant woods. The medieval church was struck by lightning in 1663 and rebuilt between then and 1672. It is therefore almost exactly the same date as Ashburnham, likewise a family church, but, unlike it, has lost its contemporary furnishings. As a building it is ungainly and lopsided by reason of the Sackville chapel, and the S aisle, added in 1841, with dormer windows and a roof rather clumsily supported on struts, was not an embellishment. The Sackville chapel, enclosed by contemporary iron railings, which would look better painted glossy black than dull maroon, has a painted coffered roof and is hung with banners and hatchments. It contains four white marble monuments, one 17c and three early 19c, which harmonise into a group because of the sentimental realism they have in common. The grandest is in the centre—a memorial to Thomas Sackville, who died aged 13 in 1677, a baroque design by Caius Cibber, showing the boy reclining on a mat and holding a skull, while his parents kneel on either side gazing sadly at him. Around the table tomb is a frieze of children, some holding skulls to signify death in infancy. The other monuments are to the 3rd Duke of Dorset by Nollekens (1802) with three cherubs hanging a garland over the urn and a portrait; to the 4th Duke by Flax-

man (1815)—a Greek woman sits by an urn beneath a portrait medallion; and to the 3rd Duchess by Chantrey (1825)—two girls by an urn. A later monument to George John, Earl De La Warr by Tyler (1869) has a kneeling girl holding a wreath over the waves. The most recent is a slate plaque by Reynolds Stone (1962) to V. Sackville-West, poet, author and gardener, the wife of Sir Harold Nicolson of Sissinghurst Castle, Kent. On the S buttress of the chancel is an iron slab (1610) to William Alfrey. Over the chancel arch is a Doom painted by the Revd Earl De La Warr, rector in the 1850s. In the Lady Chapel are Italian paintings bought for the chapel at Buckhurst—a 14c altar piece and four 15c pictures with scenes from the Passion, probably by a pupil of one of the Italian masters. Of Old Buckhurst, the original home of the Sackvilles, little remains; the Tudor gatehouse was joined on to an oast-house in 1911 and the whole house extended eastwards. Before its final destruction in 1690 a new house was built on the site of an old hunting lodge. It was enlarged by the 1st Duke (1687–1765), considerably rebuilt by Repton in 1830, Victorianised in 1884 and given a Lutyens wing in 1900. In recent times these accretions have been removed and Buckhurst Park is now much as the 1st and 2nd Dukes knew it.

Beside the church is the large rectory, Georgian in appearance with a charming veranda added in 1809; but parts of it may date from the 15c. Penns-in-the-Rocks is mainly Georgian, but is again basically earlier; originally called Rocks Farm, it belonged to the Springetts of Ringmer and when Gulielma Springett married William Penn, she brought it as part of her dowry. There is hardly any village at Withyham, only the Dorset Arms, an attractive Georgian weatherboarded house, and, near it, Duckings, a 16c timber-framed house

Sackville monument, **Withyham**

Worth church

near a hammer pond. It is recorded in 1509 as an ironmaster's house and no doubt the railings in the Sackville chapel were cast here. *Blackham* is a scattered hamlet to the N. The small church 1902 by L. W. Ridge stands high. It is built of rough hewn sandstone, simple EE with a wide chancel arch and a five-lancet E window. At the W end is a little bell turret, octagonal and of stone.

Withyham St John [2] An out-lying part of Withyham very nearly in Crowborough. The small church in a forest grove was built by the De La Warrs in 1839; the design by W. L. Blaker is an almost exact copy of Newman's church at Littlemore near Oxford. The apsidal chancel

was added by Lady De La Warr in 1870 and in 1871 St John's became a separate parish. The stone altar, highly unusual at that time, is another indication that the De La Warrs had Tractarian sympathies. The floor is black and white chequerboard marble and at the W end is an elegant gallery with very slender pillars. The lancet windows have glass by Kempe, who also designed the coloured reredos, carved at Oberammergau (*see* Ovingdean).

Wivelsfield [4] Still a farming village clustered round the church, ¼ mile off the main Haywards Heath road and separated from it by open fields as yet mercifully undeveloped. The church's earliest

feature—the yew tree near the lych-gate is probably even older—is the Norman N doorway *c.* 1070, similar to one at Bolney, which was carefully rebuilt when the N aisle was added in 1869. The core of the church is 13c, but the S chapel, with a curiously high-pitched roof, was added in the 14c as a chantry, and the tower at the SW corner about 1500; on either side of the belfry window are carvings of an owl and a musician. Inside, the S aisle has a modest EE arcade of two arches, rather crudely worked; the E wall of the chantry chapel is lit by a single lancet and below it is an arch for the altar, which was painted with a black and white lozenge pattern, visible until recently. Restorations and additions have been wisely directed and tactfully carried out. In 1869 the chancel was extended slightly, in 1925 oak seating with linenfold bench ends was given, and in 1937 Sir Ninian Comper, working with his son Sebastian, was asked to rearrange the choir and sanctuary. He ousted the Victorian choir stalls, designed a simple and slightly larger altar with well-proportioned cross and candlesticks, supplied new Jacobean-style altar rails and re-laid the floors to their proper levels. Lastly in 1954 the organ was moved from the S chapel to the W end. The result of all these changes is one of harmony and dignity, and a church that has been cared for with intelligence and taste. The Jacobean pulpit is a remodelled three-decker; the original sounding board now forms the base.

Great Ote Hall, 1 mile SW, is a 15c manor house and a good example of the materials used in this part of Sussex. The house has stone foundations, walls of timber and plaster, gables with carved pendants at the apices, a roof of Horsham stone and groups of handsome red-brick chimneys. Over the windows on the E side are the initials of Thomas and Mary Godman (1600). The house belonged to the Godmans from 1540 to 1718, when it passed to the Shirleys of Wiston in West Sussex; thereafter it had various owners, but was recently bought back by the Godman Trust. It was for a time the home of Selina, Countess of Huntingdon, friend of George Whitefield, the Methodist preacher. She founded the branch known as Lady Huntingdon's Connection and built the Ote Hall Chapel in 1778 at the junction of the Chailey and Ditchling roads. There is also not far from it a small brick Baptist chapel (1780)—perhaps put up as a rival to Lady Huntingdon's. It is highly unusual to find three places of worship in so small a place. At Wivelsfield Green were the world-famous Allwood's Carnation Nurseries, founded by three brothers who came to Sussex from Lincolnshire at the turn of the century. A cultivar of the Sweet William raised in the 1930s is named the Sweet Wivelsfield. The nurseries are now at Hassocks.

Wivelsfield Station on the main line is a ridiculous misnomer, since it is neither in the parish, nor anywhere near Wivelsfield.

Worth [1] has no village and the suburban villas of Three Bridges creep dangerously near. But the church stands secluded and alone, its only neighbours the old rectory and a charming tile-hung cottage roofed with mossy Horsham slabs, close by the lych-gate. A short lime avenue leads up to the church, which at first sight looks somewhat modern owing to a thorough but not disastrous restoration in 1871 by Salvin, who built the tower and spire. Before that the N transept had a hipped roof, from which rose a low timber bell-tower with a broach spire—a far more attractive arrangement than Salvin's replacement. The apse also, which was supported by buttresses and had a debased Gothic E window, was taken down and re-erected with a string-course and pilaster strips, in careful imitation of those on the nave walls, and round-headed lancet windows. Apart from the tower, the church is entirely pre-Conquest and is the finest example of a Saxon cruciform church with its ground plan entirely unaltered. The Saxons did not in fact build true cruciforms; the transepts are really side chapels, the N being not quite opposite the S. The superb chancel arch 22 ft high by 14 ft wide is of plain squared stones and rests on semicircular responds; it is the finest and largest Saxon chancel arch in England and, although austerely simple, is not in the least crude. The transeptal arches are likewise plain and massive, and seem even more so than the chancel arch because of the square responds and capitals of large square stones. Each transept has an altar recess, that on the N with a pointed arch and a small lancet window, while the S transept has a large early round arch, partly filled, and a pointed arch below. In the nave are two original arches of the N and S doorways, very high and massive and typical of late Saxon work. The N door is blocked up, but the S door has a 14c door half the height inserted within it. The nave also has three Saxon windows of twin-arched lights, separated by a baluster. The box-pews have gone, but there are other furnishings— elaborate carved and panelled altar rails of foreign workmanship and probably 17c supposedly from an Oxford college; an elaborately carved pulpit 1577 with an inscription in Low German; two 17c brass chandeliers, and a W gallery provided by Anthony Lynton, rector, who died in 1610. The organ was moved from the chancel to the gallery a few years ago—a great visual advantage. There are some traces of flower and foliage painting on the S wall and a piece of 14c glass with the de Warenne arms in the N transept. There are many monuments, including a number of 17c black marble floor slabs with arms and inscriptions and three Flaxmanesque wall tablets in the S transept, 1834–7, signed P. Rouw. Worth has poetical connections; there are monuments to Anne and Roger Bysshe and another to John Shelley, and Crabbet Park belonged to Wilfred Scawen Blunt, whose daughter, Lady Wentworth, was directly descended through her mother from Lord Byron. Like her parents, Lady Wentworth was an Arabophil and kept at Crabbet her famous Arab stud. There seem to be no records showing why Worth had such an unusually splendid Saxon church, and curiously the place is not mentioned in Domesday Book; possibly the survey was incomplete owing to the dense forest.

Index

Abergavenny, Marquess of, *see* Nevill family
Adam, Robert *see* Brighton
Ashdown House *see* Forest Row

Ballcocks *see* Heathfield
Barry, Sir Charles *see* Brighton, Hove
Barry, E. M. *see* Bolney
Batemans *see* Burwash
Bell, Bishop George *see* Berwick
Bell, Vanessa *see* Berwick
Belle Tout *see* Beachy Head
Bentley Wood *see* p. 34, East Hoathly
Billing, John *see* Seaford
Birley, Sir Oswald *see* West Dean
Birling Gap *see* East Dean
Blomfield, Sir A. *see* Coleman's Hatch
Blunt, Wilfrid Scawen *see* Worth
Bodley, G. F. *see* Brighton, Cuckfield, Danehill.
Bolebroke *see* Hartfield
Borde Hill *see* Cuckfield
Brabazon, Hercules *see* Sedlescombe
Brambletye *see* Forest Row
Brangwyn, Frank *see* Ditchling
Brighton College *see* p. 44
Brock, E. F. Loftus *see* Hammerwood
Broomham *see* Guestling, Heathfield
Brown, 'Capability' *see* Ashburnham, Sheffield Park
Browne, Sir Anthony *see* Battle
Broyle Place *see* Ringmer
Buckhurst *see* p. 34, Withyham
Burne-Jones, Sir E. *see* Brighton, Newick, Rotherfield, Rottingdean
Burrell family *see* Cuckfield
Burton, Decimus *see* Flimwell
Burton, James *see* St Leonards
Busby, John *see* Brighton
Bushnell, John *see* Ashburnham
Butterfield *see* Battle

Caburn, Mount *see* Beddingham
Cade, Jack *see* p. 24, Heathfield
Caedwalla *see* Buxted, South Malling
Caen Stone *see* Dicker, Ditchling, Lewes, Wilmington
Campbell, Colen *see* Eastbourne
Capronnier *see* Offham, Westmeston
Carpenter, R. C. *see* Brighton, Catsfield, Highbrook, Hurstpierpoint, Nutley
Carroll, Lewis *see* Peasmarsh
Carter's Corner *see* p. 29, Hellingly
Cavendish family *see* Eastbourne
Champneys, Basil *see* Hastings

Chantrey *see* Withyham
Charles I *see* Ashburnham
Charles II *see* Brighton
Charleston *see* West Dean
Chermayeff *see* p. 34, Bexhill, East Hoathly
Chichester, Earl of *see* Pelham family
Christian, Ewan *see* Hamsey, Ringmer, Selmeston
Christie family *see* Ringmer
Cibber, Caius *see* Withyham
Cinque Ports *see* p. 21, Hastings, Rye, Winchelsea
Circular churchyards *see* Alfriston, Hellingly, Horsted Keynes, Selmeston
Cleves, Anne of *see* Ditchling, Lewes
Clutton, Henry *see* p. 34, Battle
Coates, Wells *see* Hove
Comper, Sir Ninian *see* Chailey, Danehill, Wivelsfield
Compton Place *see* Eastbourne
Coombe Place *see* Hamsey
Courthope family *see* Ticehurst
Crabbet Park *see* Worth
Culpeper *see* Ardingly

Dalyngrigge family *see* Bodiam, Fletching, Hartfield
Danny *see* p. 29, Hurstpierpoint
Daukes, Samuel *see* Little Horsted
De La Warr, Earl *see* Sackville family
Devil's Dyke *see* Poynings
Devonshire, Duke of *see* Cavendish family
De Warenne, William *see* p. 22, Isfield, Lewes
Dew Ponds *see* p. 14
Dixter, Great *see* p. 49, Northiam
Dorset, Dukes of *see* Sackville family
Dubois, Nicholas *see* Lewes, Stanmer

Epstein, Jacob *see* West Dean
Evelyn, John *see* Lewes, South Malling
Exceat *see* Cuckmere Haven

Ferrey, Benjamin *see* Staplefield
Fiennes family *see* Hurstmonceux
Flaxman *see* Cuckfield, Withyham
Frewen family *see* Northiam
Fuller, 'Mad Jack' *see* Bodiam, Brightling

Gage family *see* p. 34, West Firle, Framfield

Glen Andred *see* p. 34, New Groombridge
Gibbon, Edward *see* Fletching, Sheffield Park
Grant, Duncan *see* Berwick
Gravetye *see* p. 45, West Hoathly
Great Ote Hall *see* p. 29, Wivelsfield

Hammond's Place *see* Clayton
Halland Place *see* East Hoathly
Haremere Hall *see* Etchingham
Hare, Augustus *see* Hurstmonceux
Harmer, Jonathan *see* pp. 42, 44, Brightling, Burwash, Catsfield, Chiddingly, Framfield, Glynde, East Grinstead, Hailsham, Heathfield, Hellingly, Hurstmonceux, Lewes, Mayfield, Mountfield, Salehurst, Wadhurst, Waldron, Warbleton, Wartling
Hawkins, Rhode *see* Fairwarp
Henry VIII *see* Camber
Holland, Henry *see* Brighton
Hoo, The *see* Willingdon
Horselunges *see* p. 29, Hellingly
Horsham slabs *see* pp. 29, 42
Hospitaller, Knights *see* Newtimber, Twineham
Hudson, Edward *see* Plumpton
Huntingdon, Selina, Countess of *see* Wivelsfield
Hye House *see* Crowhurst

Iron industry *see* p. 24
Iron tomb slabs *see* Burwash, Maresfield, Mayfield, Rotherfield, Streat, Wadhurst

James, Henry *see* Rye
Jefferay family *see* Chiddingly, Ringmer
Jekyll, Gertrude *see* p. 49, Sedlescombe, Slaugham

Kemp, Thomas *see* Brighton
Kempe, Charles Eamer *see* Alfriston, Barcombe, Brighton, Cuckfield, Danehill, Denton, Glynde, New Groombridge, West Hoathly, Horsted Keynes, Offham, Ovingdean, Rye, Sedlescombe, Staplefield, Turner's Hill, Warbleton, Westmeston, Withyham St John
Kennington, Eric *see* Hammerwood

Kidbrooke Park *see* Eridge, Forest Row
Kipling, Rudyard *see* Burwash, Piddinghoe, Rottingdean
Kitchingham Farm *see* Etchingham

Latrobe, Benjamin *see* Forest Row, Hammerwood
Long Man *see* p. 21, Wilmington
Lutyens, Sir Edwin *see* p. 49, Northiam, Plumpton, Willingdon

Mathematical tiles *see* pp. 29, 31, Beckley, Brighton, South Heighton, Patcham
Mendelsohn *see* p. 34, Bexhill
Montier, John *see* Frant
Morris, William *see* Brighton, Rotherfield
Moseley, William *see* Hadlow Down

Nash, John *see* Brighton
Nash, Paul *see* Camber
Nevill family *see* Cuckfield, Ditchling, Eridge, Fletching, Forest Row, East Grinstead, Rotherfield
Nollekens *see* Catsfield, Withyham
Northease *see* Rodmell
Nymans *see* Slaugham

Oaklands *see* Sedlescombe
Ockenden Manor *see* Cuckfield
Ockley Manor *see* Keymer
Organs, Barrel *see* Bexhill, Brightling, Piddinghoe
Otham *see* Bayham Abbey, Polegate
Oxenbridge *see* Brede, Iden

Parker family *see* Willingdon
Pearson, J. L. *see* Hove
Peke's House *see* Chiddingly
Pelham family *see* p. 34, Hastings, East Hoathly, Laughton, Lewes, Stanmer
Pell Green *see* Wadhurst
Penn, William *see* Ringmer, Withyham

Penns-in-the-Rocks *see* Withyham
Pestalozzi village *see* Sedlescombe
Phillips, Henry *see* Brighton
Piltdown *see* p. 17, Fletching
Porden, William *see* Brighton
Priest's houses, medieval *see* Alfriston, Denton, West Dean, West Hoathly
Prynne, G. Fellowes *see* Hadlow Down

Rapes *see* pp. 21, 22
Reid Dick, Sir William *see* Fairwarp
Repton *see* Bayham Abbey, Brighton, Sheffield Park
Reyntiens, Patrick *see* St. Leonards
Ridge, E. Lacy *see* Turner's Hill, Withyham
Robinson, Sir Thomas *see* Glynde
Robinson, William *see* pp. 45, 49, West Hoathly
Roedean *see* p. 45
Rossetti, D. G. *see* Brighton
Round towers *see* p. 42, Lewes, Southease, Piddinghoe
Rouw, Henry *see* Brightling
Rouw, P. *see* Worth
Rushforth *see* Tidebrook
Rushlake Green *see* Warbleton
Russell, Dr. Richard *see* pp. 12, 24, 29, Brighton, Lewes, South Malling
Rysbrack *see* Warbleton

Sackville College *see* East Grinstead
Sackville family *see* p. 34, Bexhill, East Grinstead, Michelham Priory, Sedlescombe, Withyham
Saddlescombe *see* Newtimber
Scott, Sir Gilbert *see* Rottingdean
Scott, Sir Giles Gilbert *see* St. Leonards
Scott, J. Oldrid *see* Chailey, Newick
Seacocks Heath *see* Etchingham
Sergison family *see* Cuckfield
Shaw, Norman *see* New Groombridge, Hammerwood
Shelley's Folly *see* Hamsey
Sheridan, Clare *see* Brede, West Dean

Shiffner family *see* Hamsey
Shingles, oak *see* p. 42
Shoyswell Old Manor *see* Etchingham
Shurley family *see* Isfield
Smirke *see* Brightling, Northiam
Socknersh *see* Brightling
Sorrell, Alan *see* Bexhill
Spence, Sir Basil *see* p. 45
Springett family *see* Lewes, Ringmer, Withyham
Standard Hill *see* Ninfield
Stone, Reynolds *see* Withyham
Stone spires *see* p. 42, Chiddingly, Dallington, Northiam
Stonehill House *see* Chiddingly
Stoolball *see* p. 49
Sussex University *see* p. 45, Stanmer

Teulon, S. S. *see* Hastings, Icklesham, Netherfield, Rye Harbour
Tower, Walter *see* Alfriston, Lindfield, Slaugham
Travers, Martin *see* Bexhill
Treemans *see* Horsted Keynes
Trevor, Bishop *see* Glynde

Wakehurst *see* p. 29, Ardingly
Walpole, Horace *see* Bexhill
Webb, Sir Aston *see* p. 34, Turner's Hill
Wellingham House *see* Ringmer
Wentworth, Lady *see* Worth
Whiligh *see* Ticehurst
Whistler, Rex *see* Brighton
White, Gilbert *see* Ringmer
Wigsell, Great *see* Salehurst
Wilds, Amon *see* Brighton, Lewes
Woodard schools *see* p. 44, Ardingly, Hurstpierpoint
Woolf, Leonard and Virginia *see* Rodmell
Wyatt, James *see* East Grinstead, Sheffield Park
Wykehurst *see* p. 34, Bolney